Ethics in the 21st Century

Other readers featured in the "Longman Topics" series include:

A LONGMAN TOPICS Reader

Ethics in the 21st Century

MARY ALICE TRENT
Oral Roberts University

PEARSON
Longman

New York   San Francisco   Boston
London   Toronto   Sydney   Tokyo   Singapore   Madrid
Mexico City   Munich   Paris   Cape Town   Hong Kong   Montreal

Acquistitions Editor: Brandon Hight
Senior Marketing Manager: Wendy Albert
Senior Supplements Editor: Donna Campion
Managing Editor: Bob Ginsberg
Production Manager: Joseph Vella
Project Coordination, Text Design, and Electronic Page Makeup:
    Sunflower Publishing Services, Inc.
Cover Design Manager: Wendy Ann Fredericks
Cover Photo: © Jeffrey M. Spielman/Image Bank/Getty Images, Inc.
Photo Researcher: Photosearch, Inc.
Manufacturing Manager: Mary Fischer
Manufacturing Buyer: Roy L. Pickering, Jr.

For permission to use copyrighted material, grateful acknowledg-
ment is made to the copyright holders on pp. 225–226, which are
hereby made part of this copyright page.

Library of Congress Cataloging-in-Publication Data

Ethics in the 21st century/[edited by] Mary Alice Trent.
    p. cm.—(Longman topics)
    ISBN 0-321-24333-1
    1. Ethics. I. Trent, Mary Alice. II. Series.

BJ1012.E8947 2005
170—dc22   2004057427

Please visit our website at http://www.ablongman.com

ISBN 0-321-24333-1

*I dedicate this book to the following family
members for their love and prayers:*

*Carl Williams
Nathan J. Trent, Sr.
Mary Yvonne Cole Trent
Georgia A. Robson Trent
Nathan J. Trent, Jr.
Edna G. Crockett
Inez Johnson Clark
Lucille A. Robson
Betty L. Francis
Cecelia M. Vital
E. Marie V. Simon
Desarae M. Wells
Celeste Aubry
Jahmilah Sekhmet*

*I also dedicate this book to all of my students, who have
been my inspiration for over seventeen years of teaching.*

*Finally, I dedicate this book to Koko
"Canine" Williams, the sweetest dog in the world.*

CONTENTS

How important are integrity, responsibility, reliability, punctuality, and morality in the courtroom, boardroom, classroom, operating room, and newsroom? Would you want anyone associated with the above professions, or any profession, serving you without a trustworthy character? Would you want to work for a supervisor who was lacking in professional ethics? Do Americans in the twenty-first century need to take a crash course in ethics? Think for a moment about the increasing number of corporate scandals, debates over cloning humans, the threat of another shooting pervading school halls, media's soap-opera coverage of exploiting human lives, rising medical malpractice suits, legal bribes in and out of the courtroom, and on and on. Is it possible to have excellence in the private and/or public arena without a code of ethics? Well, if we ask people who have been victims of any of the scenarios above, they will probably answer with an a firm "No." So what do you think? Is it possible to be effective and efficient on the job with questionable professional ethics?

How do we begin to address these questions, and others like them? Most, if not all, employers would concur that they seek to hire employees who are punctual, dependable, accountable, efficient, knowledgeable, skillful, cooperative, and pleasant. (Conversely, I would also venture to say that employees desire to work for an employer who exhibits these same professional attributes.) On a personal level, many people choose mates and friends who are ethical and trustworthy. These qualities are hallmarks of character, for one's character fuels the motivation and the discipline needed not only to attain the skills and knowledge for a particular task but also to perform the task efficiently, effectively, ethically, and punctually.

I wrote this book to begin an honest, open discussion about ethics so that readers can reexamine their epistemological views on a plethora of issues involving ethics. The topics in the readings from chapters 1 through 6 will challenge you to look at specific ethical situations that professionals in particular and people in general grapple with in the twenty-first century.

In each of the five chapters that follow, I present four professional essays, along with one student essay, that deal with ethics in the respective discipline covered in that chapter. Chapter 6 offers five professional essays on the topic of plagiarism and computer crimes. At the end of each essay are questions for discussion and questions for writing; then at the end of each chapter are questions for making connections within the chapter. At the end of the last chapter, there are questions for making connections across the chapters and questions for application with respect to each profession.

The essays in Chapter 1 address issues of ethics related to the classroom environment. The topics begin with William J. Byron's speech on the role of the academy of higher learning to graduate students with not only strong academic discipline but also a solid character. Like Byron, Jeanne Moe and her colleagues emphasize the importance of teaching to build character, and they show how archaeology can be used as a tool to achieve this end. In one of the more controversial topics presented in the chapter, Martin E. Marty and Jonathan Moore take on the religion-versus-education debate. John Merrifield deals with the debate over the equitable use of vouchers, and Sarah Hutchins focuses on the issue of teaching values.

The essays in Chapter 2 address issues of ethics related to the world of journalism and media. Howard A. Myrick in his article defends the role of objectivity in journalism. In contrast, Caryl Rivers contends that journalists are "storytellers, not scientists." Therefore, journalists can hardly escape a degree of subjectivity in their reporting. In his article Matthew Robinson exposes the influence that media polls have on politicians and the voting public alike. Benjamin Radford addresses changes in the quality of the media over the past few decades, while Brendan Smith calls for higher ethical standards in the media.

Chapter 3 deals with ethics in law. Richard Zitrin and Carol M. Langford report on the issue of misrepresentation of clients by their trial lawyers in order to play on the sympathy of the jury. In a similar way, Walter Olson criticizes attorneys who, while handling settlements against big tobacco companies, take advantage of their clients by overcharging them. In addition, Karen Judson discusses cyberethics and the law, and Cynthia A. Stark revisits ethics, the law, and gun control. Christopher Alexis tackles the subject of the lack of equity in the criminal justice system.

Chapter 4 focuses on ethical concerns in the business world. The topics in this chapter deal with business scandals, as in Bruce Frohnen and Leo Clarke's essay. They examine the increased number of corporate scandals and argue that the heart of the matter requires a change in ethical and moral beliefs, not merely laws. Offering his own advice, John R. Boatright suggests a number of strategies for doing business abroad while maintaining ethical standards. Like Boatright, Blair Masching recommends three keys to marketing success. Matthew Grimm addresses adverse marketing to children and the negative impact it has on them, while Jeffery Seglin looks at ethics and business bankruptcy laws.

Chapter 5, on medicine, focuses on issues of cloning, euthanasia, and so forth. Dan W. Brock in his article takes a microscopic look at the pros and cons of cloning and discusses the "legitimate moral concerns about the use and effects of human cloning." Another controversial issue plaguing the medical community currently is stem cell research, and Margaret R. McLean contributes to the debate. Euthanasia takes center stage in Peter Singer's essay. His study of the topic takes into account religious, moral, medical, and legal views. The chapter also includes Sheryl Gay Stolberg and Jeff Gerth's essay on ethics and Internet health fraud and Toni Sanchez's consideration of medicine, faith, and ethics.

Part of Chapter 6 is devoted to plagiarism, but this is not the typical study of plagiarism as seen in most college handbooks. Instead, the chapter engages readers in multiple discussions on various aspects of plagiarism, a problem that all American universities and colleges must address. In fact, Sara Rimer documents the finding that academic cheating, particularly on the Internet, is on the rise in American colleges and universities. Verne G. Kopytoff goes further into the problem by offering Web sites that expose cheaters. To remedy the problem to a degree, Ann Lathrop and Kathleen Foss advocate a college curriculum that includes a course, or courses, in ethics/character education. Chapter 6 also addresses other computer crimes, such as viruses and worms, Karen Judson's focus; and hacking, which John Knittel examines.

Whether or not you believe that Americans in general need to take an accelerated course in ethics, you can conclude after reading this book that the 21st century has its challenges—some of which, of course, we inherited from the previous century. As individuals in a democratic society, most of us want to achieve the American dream. But does it matter how we attain success? Is it possible to be effective and efficient on the job, or in our personal lives, with questionable ethics? Do you think that music and film entertainers of popular culture and the media industry have a greater influence on societal morals than the average American? On a personal note, to what degree do your actions, based on your own system of ethics, influence the environment around you? Consider these questions, and others, as you read this book.

ACKNOWLEDGEMENTS

I am grateful to the following professors for their reviews: Elsa Rogers, International College, Florida; Diane Langlois, Louisiana State University; and Virginia Davis, Tulsa Community College, Oklahoma. I also thank Mark Roberts, Margaret Sehorn, and Peggy Null of Oral Roberts University, Oklahoma, for their encouragement. I thank Lindy Spore, Sherri Worth, and Dana Demet, my interns, for their input. I thank the Creator for giving me the vision and professional insight to do this project.

MARY ALICE TRENT

Ethics and Education

True nobility is exempt from fear:
More can I bear than you dare execute.

William Shakespeare, *Henry VI*

The essays in Chapter 1 address issues of ethics related to the classroom environment. These essays will engage you in discussions on ethics and character education, school choice and vouchers, and religion and educational policies. The goal here is to encourage college students to think about these topics and come to wholesome conclusions, guided by their inner compass.

William J. Byron argues in his speech that colleges and universities must do an even more effective job at developing not only the minds or intellects of students but also their characters. He looks at past decades, when curfews and dress codes were more the norm, and juxtaposes these customs against the current decade, when more and more institutions of higher learning are implementing honor codes. In this article Byron alludes to the work of David Fromkin, who examines eight stages in the universal history of civilization. Byron's sentiment is that we can learn much by comparing where we have come from to where we are now.

In their article, Jeanne M. Moe and her colleagues suggest that instructors can use archaeology to teach ethics, qualities of good character, and noble citizenry. The authors contend that archaeologists deal with a number of ethical issues. When remains of past cultures are found, for instance, archaeologists must determine who needs to be contacted, what information can be released to the public, and how much of the data can be used for research purposes. Moe and her colleagues document the findings

1

of Project Archaeology in Utah, which involved teachers who participated in three institutes on archaeology, ethics, character, and citizenship.

Martin E. Marty and Jonathan Moore in their article examine the heated topic of religion in public schools. The issue of the separation of church and state further fuels the debate for schools, parents, and lawmakers. Marty and Moore also mention another polarized aspect of the issue: Whose religious views would be taught—"fundamentalist [or] liberal in Protestantism, Orthodox [or] Reform in Judaism, conservative [or] liberal in Catholicism"?

John Merrifield explores the ethical pros and cons of school choice and the use of vouchers. Merrifield contends that in the end, vouchers "move only a relatively few children, mostly among existing schools; leave the broken system intact and sanctify its key elements; and mislead observers as to the nature of the real K–12 problem—a low-performing system, not isolated low-performing schools."

While Merrifield takes on the ethics of vouchers, Sarah Hutchins's essay advocates teaching good ethical conduct in schools. An elementary education major, Hutchins deals with some of the challenges that educators must face, such as school-age homeless children and post- 9/11 trauma. Given these present realities, educators have a moral responsibility to help students develop strategies for coping in the real world, as well as succeeding academically in the classroom.

The chapter ends with questions that allow students to make connections among the essays and to ultimately make real-life applications.

The Streets of Life
WILLIAM J. BYRON

In the many commencement addresses I've delivered over the years, I tell the elders—the faculty, administrators, parents and families of the graduates—that they are welcome to "eavesdrop" as I speak directly to the students. Commencements occur, of course, at the end of the academic year. But this is the beginning of the academic year and I've decided to speak directly tonight to the faculty and administrators and invite you students to "eavesdrop," to listen in, as I offer a few beginning-of-the-year thoughts for the consideration of those who oversee and promote quality in the Lees-McCrae collegiate program.

You faculty members and academic administrators provide a challenging academic environment for the development of the extraordinary human potential entrusted to your care. You deserve a lot of credit and a great vote of thanks for what you do in preparing the young for satisfying and productive futures.

It was John Gardner, former secretary of Health, Education, and Welfare and founder of Common Cause, who remarked decades ago in a commencement address at Cornell that historians would look back to the troubled decade of the 1960s and note that higher education in the United States was caught during those years in a "savage crossfire between unloving critics and uncritical lovers." The unloving critics, Gardner explained, wanted to destroy the institutions with no thought of what would replace them; the uncritical lovers wanted to protect the institutions from any change at all, even though the protective embrace would, in fact, smother them. Higher education seems to have made it through that critical period in reasonably good shape. None the less, lots of work remains to be done today if historians of the future are not to look back on the opening decade of this new century in North American higher education and find evidence of neglect on the part of those whose professional responsibility it is to encourage the cultivation of character during the collegiate years through the development of intellect.

This is not to suggest that character is not now being developed or that there is an absence of rigor in your intellectual programs. It is simply to say that one doesn't have to be ill to get better. By that I mean there is always room for improvement in your programs. None of you wants to leave to the student-life professionals—your colleagues on the other side of the academic street, so to speak—full responsibility for attending to a broad and familiar spectrum of campus behavioral issues ranging from civility to sobriety. You have something important to contribute in this regard by providing challenging intellectual programs, by offering your own personal example of integrity and intellectual curiosity, and by voicing persuasively your high academic expectations for all your students. You and your colleagues in student life should be working together on this issue of character development.

If the *New York Times* is to be believed (March 3, 1999), "Three decades after American college students defiantly threw off the vestiges of curfews, dress codes and dormitory house mothers, a revolution is under way in undergraduate life that may

5

be quieter but no less significant." Under a headline that reads, "In a Revolution of New Rules for Students, Colleges Are Turning Full Circle," the report states that "What is evolving is a tamer campus and an updated and subtler version of 'in loco parentis,' the concept that educators are stand-in parents. College administrators are struggling with the two questions that are emerging as central: Are undergraduates really adults? And should they be seen as the college's customers or more as its products?"

As the parent of any adolescent knows, it is difficult to say exactly where trust ends and neglect begins; so to avoid neglect, parents typically tend to yield on trust and tighten up on control. Let me encourage you tonight—regardless of whether you accept an "in loco parentis" role, and regardless of whether or not students expect such a role of you—never to give up on trusting the young. Just rest your trust on a principled approach to your responsibilities, a principled approach that respects the dignity of every student and sees each student as occupying his or her own unique stage of human development. They will disappoint you occasionally, but don't sell them short. Your students are not yet full adults, so view them as works in progress. Please do not regard them as purchasers of academic services entitled to full consumer satisfaction on their own terms. Set high standards in mutually agreed upon terms of trade.

David Fromkin, professor of international relations, history, and law at Boston University, published in 1999 an ambitious book titled *The Way of the World* (Knopf). The book's subtitle is a measure of the ambitious scope of the project: "From the Dawn of Civilizations to the Eve of the Twenty-First Century." The author's synthetic skills enable him to cover, with clarity and style, millions of years in the relatively short span of 222 pages of text. This is a book short in length, but not on insight.

The Way of the World was well received by the *New York Times* (January 17, 1999), whose reviewer, William R. Everdell, stimulated, with the following summary, my desire to read the book.

Fromkin distinguishes eight stages in universal history, most of them hinging on events historians of many stripes can agree on as the most significant in the history of humankind: the emergence of the hominid line, apes with brains, in prehistoric Africa ("Becoming Human"); the discovery of agriculture and the creation of the first cities settlements whose residents were not all farmers ("Inventing Civilization"); the sudden rise of universalizing religious and moral systems all over civilized Eurasia in the sixth century B.C. ("Developing a Conscience"); the birth of the idea of world civilization with the empires of ancient Eurasia ("Seeking a Lasting Peace"); the rise of rationalism and empirical science ("Achieving Rationality") the irreversible encounter, after the 15th century, between human societies in Eurasia and Africa and those in the Americas ("Uniting the Planet"); the industrial modernization that began in the 18th century ("Releasing Nature's Energies"); and finally the steady movement toward democratic government centered in the 19th century and the unsteady movement toward decolonization and world law in the 20th ("Ruling Ourselves").

The first four of those chapter headings look to the past: "Becoming Human," "Inventing Civilization," "Developing a Conscience," and "Seeking a Lasting Peace." The next four look to the present: "Achieving Rationality," "Uniting the Planet," "Releasing Nature's Energies," and "Ruling Ourselves." All eight of those headings strike me as useful pegs upon which to hang some reflections on the condition of student academic life in contemporary American higher education. They can be considered as eight windows through which one can observe student academic life. I recognize, of course, that genuine education takes place on both sides of the campus street; I'm just focusing tonight on the side that is dominated by classroom buildings, libraries, and laboratories.

Consider the relevance to the academic part of the campus culture of all that is involved in "becoming human," "inventing civilization," "developing a conscience," "seeking peace," "achieving rationality," "uniting the planet," "releasing nature's energies," and "ruling ourselves." They have supreme relevance to the strictly academic side of the house.

Fromkin's book has a third part, one that looks to the future. The four chapter headings in the third part of his book are [as follows]: "Anticipating What Comes Next," "Holding People Together," "Taking Nature's Place," and "Entering Yet Another American Century." Those themes provide me with a few more windows through which I'll invite you to look at the students you serve with an eye to the future that is likely to be theirs. Let's now begin at the beginning.

10

BECOMING HUMAN

Remind yourself when you look at your incoming freshmen that they are only four years out of the eighth grade! You can handle them. Most really want to be there with you. Just about all are well prepared and ready, but no one of them is yet fully an adult.

When they arrive on your campus, first-time college students are, of course, already human beings, despite some early evidence to the contrary in August and September of freshman year. They are, however, still becoming human. They are on campus precisely because they (or their parents) decided that they do indeed have human potential that is ripe for further development. That development will take place on the intellectual front under the guidance and encouragement of professors; there will also be development on the social, interpersonal, spiritual, and psychological fronts under the guidance of student life professionals who are your colleagues in the formation enterprise.

15   What is the environment that you should be providing to facilitate this growth? Class schedules and class size can shape or impede that growth. You know that quite well. Yet, AVPs and deans, with the complicity of department chairs, may arrange these things more for the convenience of faculty than the best academic interest of students. In some corners of higher education today, that is exactly the way faculty members want it. But those faculty and academic administrators who want the best for students may have to fight facilities administrators, budget officers, and top management for the time and space needed to allow the students to grow. Aesthetics, too, are important. So is population density in classrooms, labs, and libraries. The academy's architecture, on both sides of the campus street, can be a friend or foe of student academic development.

On campuses all across this country we need more of whatever it is in a building that fosters the "Becoming Human" side of student life.

They are not apes; they are in the process of becoming fully human. They can and will respond to your creative persuasion and encouragement to attend to their longer-term interests.

INVENTING CIVILIZATION

The discovery of agriculture and the establishment of town-like settlements where not all residents were farmers was a consequence of the end of the Ice Age ten or fifteen thousand years ago. Hunting and gathering gave way to farming and more permanent dwellings. Wheels, carts, and plows enhanced productivity. Not everyone was needed to produce the food; some were freed for arts, and crafts, and trade. Although some few of today's college students still think food is grown in the basements of supermarkets, all are sufficiently familiar with ancient history to know that the discovery of agriculture led the way to the creation of the first cities. They also acknowledge that some others produce and prepare their food, and they recognize dependency, if not gratitude, toward others for providing the basics necessary for undistracted life in pursuit of academic goals. They pursue those goals in campus communities, some much like towns or small cities.

The Greek word for city, "polis," provides an etymological clue to subsequent developments that relate to words like polite (behavior expected of those now clustered into closer quarters); policy (guidelines necessary for orderly group activity); police (those who enforce the rules); politicians (those who devote most of their energies to policy formation, legislation, and pursuit of group objectives).

20

Academic vice presidents, deans and faculty are, if you will, the civil servants responsible for the smooth functioning of the academic side of the campus "polis." It is their vision, example, and encouragement that cultivate polite academic behavior. It is their wisdom that produces and applies intelligent policies to guide academic development. Academic officers police student achievement with grading systems, honor systems, and the various rewards and punishments designed to encourage intellectual growth. They, together with faculty, are, year after year, from privileged positions of influence, "inventing civilization."

DEVELOPING A CONSCIENCE

With the rise of civilization came religion and philosophy, and with them came the development of moral conscience. Classroom lectures, great books, and moral arguments in appropriate academic fora will engage students in the formation of conscience, in the discovery of right and wrong in human behavior as displayed in history, in literature, and in themselves. On the other side of the campus street, they will have abundant opportunity to practice their moral principles or, in some sad cases, to discover their deficits in this regard. Relativism is no solution. As it is often said, if you stand for nothing, you'll fall for anything. The academic program helps the young discover that which is really worth standing for.

Campus cultures are defined by dominant values. Those values can be materialistic—they can focus on greed, power, and lust for pleasure, possessions, power and prestige. They can be respectful or disdainful of human dignity. Faculty and deans, as facilitators of growth in all that it takes to become fully human, have to be concerned that they are not implementing or overseeing a value-vacant curriculum.

Will there be differences of conviction as to what is right and wrong in specific circumstances? Of course there will be. The point to establish, however, is that moral arguments, not prejudice or passion, are expected to underlie those personally held positions. Personal integrity requires that one live his or her life truthfully, true to the deepest values and convictions that are freely held by the responsible person who is in the process of becoming ever more human through the process of human moral choice. That process is taking place in the classrooms of this campus.

SEEKING A LASTING PEACE

25　In world history, empires emerged and those in one empire had to learn to live in peace with others. In addition to kingdoms or empires, there were city-states and republics, all far removed from ancient tribes; all these had their leaders; they also had their external friends and foes. At this point in the advance of civilization, say, a half-century or so before the Christian era, it became noticeable that loyalty kept things together within, and hostility (not just suspicion) focused on the outsiders.

Campuses have their empires, as we all know (I salute all monarchs present tonight!); they also have their versions of city-states and republics with shifting leadership but fairly constant loyalties.

Factions can emerge and fights can erupt almost anywhere at any time on college and university campuses. When these are unavoidable, civility has to rule. Academic administrators, AVPs, deans, and chairs are the ones who have to make sure that happens. Wherever human nature is present, there is a potential for difference and even dispute. This is no reason for despair, because it is only out of difference that union can be achieved.

ACHIEVING RATIONALITY

When the minds of men and women—sometimes in pairs, often in groups—are engaged with one another, locked, if you will, in reasoned argument, civility reigns and civilized society prospers. Rationality is indeed an achievement. Responsibility for cultivating the development of a rational mind during the collegiate experience rests primarily with faculty. The cultivation happens formally and regularly in classrooms and libraries.

One way of measuring the challenge you all face in fostering the life of the mind in classroom settings is to consider the out-of-class, out-of-library hours your students spend on campus. Estimate, if you will, the monetary value of the audio-video electronic equipment they have in their rooms (along with tapes, discs, and other entertainment software) against the monetary value of printed matter on their dorm room shelves. The ratio might be about 200:1; it is anyone's guess. Well, you might say, that is hardly surprising; they have well-stocked libraries and resource centers on campus, and they are in the dorms to relax and rest as well as study. True enough. But what about the art of conversation? What about discussion and debate—reasoned argument—on important issues? What about opportunities for the developing youngster to talk to others about his or her childhood, family customs, religious traditions, moral convictions?

Creative programming is needed in dormitories and student unions. Cooperation from the academic side with student-life professionals in developing that programming should be encouraged.

30

The President of Penn State University set a great example for all academic leaders a couple of years ago when, as I understand it, he simply decided to have bundles of good newspapers delivered to residence halls each morning for free distribution to students. Give them something good to read and just trust that the newspaper habit will eventually form. Without creating a budgetary burden, this creative gesture serves to encourage both the life of the mind and the art of conversation. It helps, in other words, to move closer to the goal of achieving rationality.

UNITING THE PLANET

After the 15th century (easy for Americans to remember because of the famous year 1492), discovery, trade, colonization, and conquest led to a virtual European takeover of the rest of the world. Now, centuries later, students from widely dispersed national and ethnic points of origin sit together in your classrooms. Do they share that space in peace and progress? Do they grow in knowledge of the roots of others and in an appreciation of their own roots? Can they pursue this avenue of inquiry through the curriculum? All should, of course, have some exposure to intercultural enrichment out of class, through campus celebrations of ethnicity in food, art, and festival. But if nothing along these lines happens in class, so much the loss for them, so much the continuing academic leadership challenge for you.

RELEASING NATURE'S ENERGIES

All of you have a chance of enlisting student participation in conversations about the impact of the various industrial, scientific, and technological revolutions that produced both the advancement and affluence that today's college students tend to take for granted. No discipline or course of studies should be excluded from these conversations; creative interdisciplinary cooperation can help make this kind of dialogue happen.

Philosophy and religious studies can raise the ethical and moral questions that have to be part of this humanizing conversation. Without the conversation, this generation of students will go sleepwalking into an unknown future. As a molecular biologist from the National Institutes of Health remarked recently, we are today, relative to the future of medicine, where Wilbur and Orville Wright were in 1903 relative to the future of air and space travel.

35   Back in 1945, nature's energies were certainly released. We need to be talking more about the potential for good and ill that this release implies. Who calls the meeting, so to speak, who sets up the conversation, if not faculty members and their academic leaders?

RULING OURSELVES

In the 19th century, the movement toward democratic government gained momentum. Gone were the earlier days of rule by kings and priests; broken was the link between inheritance and political power. No longer tenable was the premise that individuals existed for the state. Americans came to recognize in principle and in law universal rights for the individual.

American higher education well may be the best hope we have for success in using our freedoms well, exercising our rights responsibly, and ruling ourselves intelligently. But, again, it does not all happen in the classroom. As we all know, many students get their first real taste of the political process in those campus campaigns we all sponsor for election to positions in student government. These are wonderful laboratories for the examination and development of all the ingredients needed in a good campaign. Political rhetoric, polling, advertising, issue selection and analysis, campaign finance, getting out the vote—all this and more happens on virtually every college campus in America every year. Chances are, it will be done well and responsibly if academic leaders work closely with the student-life professionals who manage the process.

Although it is pretty much out of fashion now, intramural and intercollegiate debating may stand a good chance of a comeback in the new, "tamer," and more compliant climate some observers see emerging on our campuses. A famous Washington lawyer remarked to me a few years ago that he had "cross-examined 1000 witnesses before ever going to law school; they called it high school and college debating!" And he went on to recall, at age 59, the lasting impact debating and those who coached him in it had on his life.

I've walked you over an eight-stage development path from "becoming human" to "ruling ourselves." At each stage, I've suggested that you as academics have not only an opportunity but a unique responsibility to foster the growth of the human potential entrusted to your care. It is a question of how to help young people become more fully human through the undergraduate experience.

David Fromkin's book in Part Three offers four additional 40 windows through which you can look out over the heads of your current students to the uncertain future that awaits them. They are: "Anticipating What Comes Next," "Holding People Together," "Taking Nature's Place," and "Entering Yet Another American Century." Use any range finder you like; size up the future for yourselves. I want simply to say to you as you struggle to prepare for the challenges of this new academic year in this new American Century, that things are not and never will be as bad as some would have you believe. Let me sign off with these words from historian Gertrude Himmelfarb:

> For almost every favorable statistic, [a] conservative can cite an unfavorable one. He can even go beyond the statistics to point to the sorry state of the culture: the loss of parental authority and of discipline in the schools, the violence and vulgarity of television, the obscenity and sadism of rap music, the exhibitionism and narcissism of talk shows, the pornography and sexual perversions on the Internet, the binge-drinking and "hooking up" on college campuses. Two memorable phrases capture the cultural mood: Daniel Patrick Moynihan's "defining deviancy down," which normalizes and legitimizes what was once abnormal and illegitimate- and Roger Shattuck's "morality of the cool," which makes sin and evil seem "cool" and thus acceptable. ["The Panglosses of the Right Are Wrong," *Wall Street Journal*, February 4, 1999.]

You have the challenge (and the professional responsibility) of setting academic standards. In the end you will find yourselves "defining integrity up." Working through the curriculum, you can help them to overcome a morality that may be at times "uncool," but always courageous. You can help them grow in the direction that the easy life is not the happy life and that the life that is lived well is the life lived generously in service to others. If there is no evidence of this now on your side of the campus street, it isn't going to be there on the streets of life, where their developing human potential will eventually unfold.

Well, thanks for listening, my faculty and administrator friends, and thanks to all you wonderful students being attentive "eavesdroppers" tonight. May you all have another great academic year here at Lees-McCrae. Since this is your centennial year, I wish you all another great century!

Questions for Discussion

1. Whom is William Byron addressing in his speech?
2. What is the subject of his speech?
3. What are the eight stages in the universal history of man, taken from David Fromkin's book?
4. With what final thought does Byron conclude his speech?

Questions for Writing

1. "In the end you [administrators and professors] will find yourselves 'defining integrity up.' Working through the curriculum, you can help them [students] to overcome a morality that may be at times 'uncool,' but always courageous." What does Williams Bryon mean by this statement? Analyze these words in an essay.
2. Byron contends, "American higher education well may be the best hope we have for success in using our freedoms well, exercising our rights responsibly, and ruling ourselves intelligently. But, again, it does not all happen in the classroom." Is Byron's assumption accurate or not? Write an informative essay in response to this assumption.

Archaeology, Ethics, and Character
Using Our Cultural Heritage to Teach Citizenship
JEANNE M. MOE, CAROLEE COLEMAN, KRISTIE FINK, AND KIRSTI KREJS

What do you think of when you hear the word "archaeology"—ancient tombs filled with fabulous treasures, teams of scientists meticulously excavating bones in the hot desert sun, or, perhaps, shelves groaning with artifacts in the basement of a museum?

If ethics and character did not come to your mind, you are certainly not alone. Most people do not associate ethics with archaeology, but the average archaeologist makes ethical decisions on a regular basis (Lynott and Wylie 1995). For example, an archaeologist studies the remains of past cultures; hence he or she must be careful of the feelings and needs of living descendants of those cultures. Who should be notified when human remains are encountered? What information should be published? Similarly, archaeologists often have to decide whether to use information derived from illegally obtained collections for research purposes. Will using illegal collections encourage additional looting and theft of archaeological resources? Museums wrestle with the ethical issues surrounding some of the illegally collected artifacts that have been donated by repentant looters. The precise origin of those artifacts is often unknown, and if there is any possibility that an artifact came from a grave, it cannot ethically be used in an exhibit. For that reason, many fabulous pieces stay in a museum's basement and are never seen by the public. Federal and state laws govern how artifacts, sites, and the resulting information are handled, but within those laws, each archaeologist must use his or her own ethical barometer to make good decisions.

Ethical dilemmas inherent in archaeology make it a good vehicle for teaching ethics and character in the classroom (Moe 2000). The interdisciplinary nature of the field makes it possible to weave ethics and character throughout the curriculum, using archaeology as a theme. Recognizing the potential of archaeology to teach ethics in a meaningful and engaging way, Utah Project Archaeology, the Utah State Office of Education, and the Utah Museum of Natural History formed the Ethics and Archaeology Partnership to explore ways to use archaeology to teach ethics and character. In this article, we explain how we used archaeology to teach ethics, character, and citizenship in a series of professional development opportunities for Utah educators in grades K–12.

ARCHAEOLOGY AS AN EDUCATIONAL TOOL

Archaeologists learn about people who lived in the past from the objects they made, used, and left behind. In the United States, archaeologists study the history of indigenous peoples (Native Americans, Alaska Natives, and Native Hawaiians) to a large degree, but they also study the history of Euro-American settlers,

African slaves, Chinese immigrants, and many other groups. African slaves, for example, left very little in the way of written documents describing their lives because the circumstances of their enslavement did not allow it. Recent archaeological excavations in slave quarters have provided a glimpse into how slaves spent their day-to-day lives, giving them a voice they never had before (e.g., Kane and Keeton 1993). Indigenous peoples have rich oral traditions that preserved their traditions and their history and way of life. Archaeologists often work with Native Americans to confirm and expand the native stories of the past (e.g., Hena and Anschuetz 2000). At the same time, oral traditions can greatly enhance archaeological interpretations (e.g., Swidler et al. 1997).

5   Archaeology is a highly interdisciplinary field. Its main goal is to construct culture histories, but it uses many scientific methods in the process. Archaeologists want to learn how people lived: what they ate, what they wore, how they made their houses, and how they organized their societies. Mathematics is essential for analyzing and interpreting raw scientific data. Reporting data and communicating with other professionals and the lay public are essential parts of an archaeologist's work. Although archaeologists use science and mathematics regularly, they also use oral tradition, ethnographic accounts, and historic documents to interpret artifacts and sites, thus tying the discipline to social studies and the humanities.

Early in our planning, we recognized that personal character was at the heart of many archaeological issues and the solutions to problems. Character development is an age-old mission of education, along with academic development (Lickona 1991). Character education helps students to understand, care about, and act on core ethical and citizenship values (C.E.P. n.d.). Character education reintegrates values into the school program in a very intentional and comprehensive way. The goal is to create schools that are microcosms of the democratic nation that we want to be. It includes thinking about how ethical values undergird relationships and about how those should be woven into the school environment, extracurricular programs, policies and procedures, teaching strategies, and the curriculum itself.

TEACHER INSTITUTES

The Ethics and Archaeology Partnership planned and conducted three teacher institutes in Utah: one in July 2000 that was supported by a Utah State Historical Society grant and two in the summer of 2001 that were supported by a generous grant from the Utah Humanities Council. The project was a statewide effort, with support coming from the Utah Division of Indian Affairs, the U.S. Bureau of Land Management, Utah Division of State History, the Utah State Historical Society, the U.S. Department of Defense (Hill Air Force Base), and the Utah Office of Museum Services.

We held workshops at Utah Museum of Natural History in Salt Lake City and the Edge of the Cedars State Park in Blanding, both of which house extensive archaeological collections. At the workshops, we explored the possibility of inculcating the values of respect and responsibility through social studies, science, stewardship, and cultural diversity. Archaeology and character education provided the threads to tie all the elements together.

We based the workshop instruction on *Intrigue of the Past: Investigating Archaeology* (Smith et al. 1997), which was the Utah Project Archaeology's basic teacher activity guide. *Intrigue of the Past* gives teachers grounding in the fundamental concepts of archaeology, including scientific inquiry. The guide expands on the basic concepts with lessons modeling the analysis and interpretation of data. The final section covers the laws that protect archaeological resources and examines several issues in archaeology: stewardship of resources, solving ethical dilemmas, respecting the feelings of Native Americans and others about archaeological resources, and taking personal responsibility to protect the past.

At additional sessions, we explored the relationship between   10
science and ethics in general and archaeology and ethics in particular. Participants read "Repatriation: A Clash of World Views" (Bray 1995), describing the Native American Graves Protection and Repatriation Act (NAGPRA), which provides for the return of human remains and grave goods to culturally affiliated descendants. They prepared questions for a panel of Native American educators who gave their views on archaeology and its place in the classroom at each workshop. Because the Utah social studies core curriculum includes archaeology in the sixth grade, we scheduled a special session to examine ways to use archaeological ethics to teach social studies units. On short field trips through the museum collections, we provided opportunities to discuss the ethical dilemmas that collection managers face. We wove the concepts and principles of character education throughout the instruction.

During the workshop, we emphasized a problem-solving approach. Participants worked in groups to solve problems about archaeological resource protection, teaching the ethics of science in the classroom, and integrating ethics across the curriculum using archaeology. The instructors emphasized the need to hear all voices in the deliberations.

WHAT DID WE LEARN?

Ethics and Character

As we wove ethics and character education throughout the workshop, we came to understand that respect and responsibility undergird our civic ground rules in all aspects of our civic lives, including science and archaeology. The class members explored how core ethical values form the foundation on which to build a good nation. We looked at those values as the basis for protecting our shared archaeological heritage and for finding common ground in diverse perspectives. We also reflected on the importance of developing a moral compass to guide ourselves to better ethical judgments. We thought about the importance of protecting our shared cultural heritage and ultimately, for respecting the worth and dignity of all humans and valuing everyone's contributions to the human continuum. Workshop participants discovered that ethics can and should be infused throughout the curriculum. One participant said, "As a result of this workshop, I recognize the need to integrate ethics into all subject areas."

Cultural Diversity and Cultural Understanding

Our Native American panelists offered rare glimpses into their cultural and personal perspectives on archaeology and education. The workshop participants were enthralled with the panelists' presentations and appreciated hearing their perspectives first-hand. We used the discussion period to explore cultural differences and similarities. Although cultural differences are very real, we all thought that we found some common ground, which is the basis for cultural understanding.

Shirlee Weight, Utah State Office of Education Equity coordinator, helped with initial project planning and served on the panel of Native Americans who shared their perspectives on archaeology and education. She commented,

> We need to get beyond mere tolerance. In fact, tolerance is almost a negative thing. "Okay, I'll tolerate you, but that's all." We need to get to some real cultural understanding. We need more

awareness at the heart level and these three workshops were a step in the right direction.

Social Studies

As we explored the laws that protect archaeological resources and the ethical issues that archaeologists face routinely, we discovered that archaeology is a microcosm of a democratic society. Archaeologists must interpret, enforce, and comply with several laws that protect archaeological sites and determine how the sites can be used. Native Americans, Alaska Natives, and Native Hawaiians have profound connections, both legal and emotional, to the remains of their ancestors and the places where they lived. Archaeologists must ensure that the rights and interests of indigenous people are honored and protected. For all these professional activities, ethics and good character are essential.

The primary role of social studies is to help students develop a core of basic knowledge and understanding of our shared civic framework, values, principles, and ideals so that they will better understand their function as responsible citizens. In a pluralistic society such as ours, democracy is particularly challenging. Archaeology provides a focal point for examining cultural differences, finding common ground, and making decisions that best serve the needs and values of all citizens.

Democracy in a pluralistic society is not only challenging but also constantly changing to include the voices of all citizens. In the past, archaeologists and museum professionals conducting research and managing collections had not adequately considered the interests of Native Americans (Thomas 2000). Since the passage of NAGPRA, archaeologists and museum professionals are being forced to be more attentive and responsive to tribal concerns. The more inclusive process is beginning to change how archaeologists approach research and museum issues. At the workshop, participants explored how archaeology has evolved, especially regarding the ethics of research and collection, to better protect our national heritage resources for everyone.

Science

Science is fraught with ethical issues. Ethicist J. Bronowski (1965) put it this way: "Science is not a mechanism but a human progress, and not a set of findings but the search for them. Those who think that science is ethically neutral confuse the findings of science, which are [ethically neutral], with the activity of science, which is not." At the workshops, we explored the role of ethics in science in general and in archaeology in particular.

Because archaeological research ultimately involves human subjects no matter how long ago they may have lived, ethical considerations are inescapable. Our discussions revolved primarily around burials, research on human remains, and repatriation of human remains and grave goods to living descendants. Although we found some differences in values related to research and repatriation of burials, we also found common ground for dialogue. Apart from the difficult issues inherent in researching human subjects, we found that archaeologists are regularly faced with ethical decisions concerned with the conduct of research in general, the rights to intellectual property, and the professional responsibilities for protecting heritage resources.

Museum Collection Ethics

20   The participants explored the delicate balance between research, repatriation, and long-term maintenance and display of culturally sensitive artifacts. Over the last century, the role of museums in archaeology has changed dramatically. In the past, museums tended to collect artifacts with little regard for site preservation, the ethical issues surrounding disturbance of burials, or the feelings of Native American descendants. As times have changed, museums have become acutely aware of these long-overlooked ethical issues and have begun to repatriate human remains and certain artifacts to tribes. Similarly, museums have altered their collections policies to ensure site stewardship and long-term preservation.

As a part of educational institutions, museum curators have a duty to help educate the public about archaeology and the ethical issues surrounding museum collections so that people will understand where mistakes were made in the past and how the museum professionals are working to correct them. Workshop participants began to understand and appreciate the difficult and complex role that museum professionals face in managing their collections and exhibits.

CONCLUSIONS

We used archaeology as a microcosm of life in a democratic society; ethics and good character are essential both for the practice of archaeology and for the formation of good citizens. The three institutes allowed the participants and instructors to explore archaeology, ethics, character, and citizenship and to learn how to weave those topics into the curriculum.

Most of the participants reported that they planned to integrate ethics throughout their curriculum as a result of what they learned in the workshops. When asked how he would change his teaching as a result of the workshop, one participant answered, "As a new teacher, this workshop has provided me with ideas and useful techniques to engage my students in learning ethics and character development while learning Utah history." Another participant said that she would stress "more and more the importance of respect for all people and their beliefs." A third spoke of changing "how I treat students, how I construct curriculum, how I assist teachers as a consulting educator." Some said that they were glad to find out that ethics and character were not a "no-no" but actually an integral part of all public education and the Utah state core curriculum. Many reported that they would now be much more comfortable including ethics and character in their classrooms and even making it an integral part of their curriculum.

We identified many universal core values, such as respect and responsibility; examined cultural differences in values that do exist; and searched for the common ground that provides a basis for civic dialogue about difficult issues. We found the work very demanding but essential for the practice of archaeology in modern times. Moreover, it was very similar to other issues that the nation faces, such as the ethics of medical research or the use of public resources to educate the children of undocumented aliens.

We explored the role of archaeology in a pluralistic society.   25
Robert Kelly (1998) who currently serves as president of the Society for American Archaeology, the nation's largest professional organization for archaeologists, has said, "[A]rchaeology's purpose today is to play a role in ending racism." In the classroom, archaeology provides neutral ground for a discussion of cultural differences at a deep level so that a teacher can get beyond mere tolerance and promote cultural understanding. As students learn to understand others, they learn to understand themselves. With understanding comes motivation to be more respectful, more responsible, and more ethical toward others. Achieving those goals is our nation's most important goal and greatest challenge.

THE FUTURE

Over the next few years, we hope to continue offering the Archaeology, Ethics, and Character Workshops in Utah. In addition, the National Project Archaeology program that currently serves thirteen states will soon include many more. As we update our educational materials and expand to broader audiences, we will address ethics education and character development more explicitly and include an even stronger citizenship component.

References

Bray, T. L. 1995 Repatriation: A clash of worldviews. *AnthroNotes* 17, nos. 1–2: 1–8. Washington, D.C.: Smithsonian Institution.

Bronowski, J. 1965. *Science and human values,* revised edition. New York: Harper & Row.

Character Education Partnership (CEP). n.d. *Character education: Questions and answers.* Washington, D.C.: Character Education Partnership.

Hena, L., and F. K. Anschuetz. 2000. Living on the edge: Combining traditional pueblo knowledge, permaculture, and archaeology. *Cultural Resource Management (CRM)* 23(9):37–41. Washington, D.C.: National Park Service, Cultural Resources.

Kane, S., and R. Keeton. 1993. *Beneath these waters: Archaeological and historical studies of 11,500 years along the Savannah River.* Atlanta, Ga.: Interagency Archaeological Services Division, National Park Service, Southeast Region.

Kelly, R. 1998. Native Americans and archaeology: A vital partnership. *SAA Bulletin* 16(4):24–26. Washington, D.C.: Society for American Archaeology.

Lickona, T. 1991. *Educating for character. How our schools can teach respect and responsibility.* New York: Bantam Books.

Lynott, M., and A. Wylie. 1995. *Ethics in American archaeology: Challenges for the 1990s.* Washington, D.C.: Society for American Archaeology.

Moe, J. M. 2000. Archaeology and values: Respect and responsibility for our heritage. In *The archaeology education handbook: Sharing the past with kids,* edited by K. Smardz and S. J. Smith. Walnut Creek, Calif.: Altamira Press.

Smith, S. J., J. M. Moe, K. A. Letts, and D. M. Paterson. 1997. *Intrigue of the past: Investigating archaeology,* 2nd ed. Salt Lake City, Ut.: Bureau of Land Management, Utah State Office.

Swidler, N., K. E. Dongoske, R. Anyon, and A. S. Downer. 1997. *Native Americans and archaeologists: Stepping stones to common ground.* Walnut Creek, Calif: Altamira Press.

Thomas, D. H. 2000. *Skull wars: Kennewick man, archaeology, and the battle for Native American identity.* New York: Basic Books.

Questions for Discussion

1. Why do Jeanne M. Moe et al. argue that "ethical dilemmas inherent in archaeology make it a good vehicle for teaching ethics and character"?
2. In 2002, Ethics and Archaeology Partnership in Utah conducted three teacher institutes that encouraged teachers to explore ways to integrate "ethics across the curriculum using archaeology." What did the participants learn about teaching ethics and cultural understanding?
3. What did teachers learn about teaching ethics in social studies and science?
4. How can archaeology be used to teach ethics and good citizenship?

Questions for Writing

1. Jeanne M. Moe and her colleagues concluded, "We identified many universal core values, such as respect and responsibility; examined cultural differences in values that do exist; and searched for the common ground that provides a basis for civic dialogue about difficult issues." How important are respect and responsibility for all members of a classroom or community? Write an informative essay addressing this topic.
2. What do Moe and her colleagues mean by the following statement? "As students learn to understand others, they learn to understand themselves." Do you agree or disagree? Analyze this topic in detail in an essay.

Religion and Education
The Pitfalls of Engaging a Complex Issue
MARTIN E. MARTY AND JONATHAN MOORE

ILLEGITIMATE FEARS: ESTABLISHMENT, RELATIVISM, AND INDIFFERENCE

Bringing religion into the public school curriculum is not without dangers, and we would do well to be aware of them. Some parents may fear that their children, introduced to various religious faiths, may soon slide into a debilitating relativism where all spiritual options are equal.

Others will resent the introduction of religion because they would like to control which rites and ceremonies, which classroom topics, should be included or excluded. Some parents may want only one religion, their own, presented to their children as a legitimate worldview. After all, public schools may end up teaching about certain subjects that some parents find objectionable, which may weaken a faith's hold on young minds. Making room for religion in the classroom, in the wrong hands, can end up making room for only one religion to the exclusion of others.

Clearly, studying religion must be accomplished in ways that avoid running afoul of the Constitution's prohibition against establishing religion. Educators and parents must be attentive to methods that do not violate Jefferson's separation of church and state or cross Madison's line of distinction between religious and civil authorities. But teaching religion can be faithful to the founders' intentions. They were careful that the government not establish a religion or religions so as not to privilege one religion over another or religion over nonreligion and also so that religion would *not* be a liability for citizens who enter the public arena.

Church-state separation traditions give good reasons for citizens to be careful about introducing or expanding subjects like religion in tax-supported public institutions. Religion is bad stuff from the word *go*, say some, and the more we can leave it out of the classroom and curriculum, the better off we will be. Put it on the shelf with astrology and other subjects that millions care about but that are not appropriate for serious pedagogy.

5   Introducing religion on curricular terms, say others, only opens the way for proselytizing and witnessing groups to get a foot in the door and to introduce elements of competition to the school scene. The aggressive groups, these critics note, are best poised to take part in religious discussion, and they will exploit the opportunity. Meanwhile more tolerant, ecumenically minded groups will be pushed into the background, and their children will be subjected to pesky and assertive witnesses.

Shouldn't the religiously minded stop clamoring for more attention to religious concerns and be a bit more generous about the republic? This scene is already overrun by competing interest groups: parochial schools, voucher advocates, released-time proponents, textbook revisers, critics of any governmental involvement in education—just to name a few. Why encourage more disruption in a locale that is already being overrun by competing forces? Why beckon the activities of these interest groups, who don't always care that much about the common good? Controversies in society can and should be pursued on the basis of "secular rationality," argue some, and introducing approaches congenial to religion will only complicate the proper, "reasonable" approach to everything.

Criticisms come from all sides. Some religious people will have trouble dealing with religion as a subject one can teach the young "about." When teachers teach "about" religion, faith may either get reduced to something so bland that it leads to a misreading of religion or become something so volatile that it will disrupt school and community life. And anyway, we should not expect the school to do everything. Moral education, to which religion in part relates, is accidental, incidental, and diffuse in schools. Putting it on the agenda weighs a school down. We already ask the schools to be babysitters, entertainers, and recreation leaders. Why make them do more? What, after all, are families and houses of worship for?

Moreover, the curriculum is already overcrowded, the textbooks are too long, and homework is too burdensome. You just can't keep piling on more. Colleges and universities have enough trouble handling the philosophical questions sparked by religion. How and why burden junior and senior high schools with such subjects and problems?

Another related difficulty is that religion deals so much with texts. How can education relate the different ways the academy and religious communities approach such texts? Even high school sophomores would necessarily be thrust into the rudiments of literary and historical criticism of ancient scriptures, and there'd be hell to pay when they report back home on how this does not square with what they've previously been taught.

In the end, many observers ask, won't you be contributing to   10
relativism among children? In public schools, teachers and texts would have to give a basically positive spin to most features of most religions. Won't students then conclude that all religions are nice, that they are all about the same business? Won't they be led to think that it does not and will not make any difference what religious choices people make or what traditions and truth-claims they have inherited?

THE MORAL DIMENSION

The last and probably most important complicating factor in debates about religion and education is that of *morals*. The nation's founders and creators of common schools were uncommonly concerned with morals and civic virtue. Having just "killed the king" in the War of Independence, they were fashioning a constitutional republic under the rule of law. To succeed, the people could not be made to behave simply for fear of punishment, for there would never be enough police to ensure compliance. The founders believed that the new republic depended on a virtuous citizenry. People had to be responsible, and to be so, they had to be moral.

Echoes of this connection between morality and citizenship can be heard in more recent American cultural disputes. Many conflicts take place against the backdrop of widespread concern over perceived moral decline. For many people, public education is the place to inculcate morality, sharpen moral sensibilities, and undergird ethical action. This assumption informs the public division over the performance and potential of public education, and citizens also divide over which available instruments should be used to teach morals and civic virtue.

Like debates over devotion, these moral disputes have a long history in American life. Citizens sometimes appeal to the nation's founders as defenders of religion-friendly philosophies. However, while the Reason and Nature they appealed to sometimes suggested an integral connection to God, this was a God accessible to all people, not just those who claimed particular revelations or scriptures. A republic could not be built on the basis of particular and conflicting revelations; instead, a more general, common-denominator religion would suffice.

Others point to George Washington's famous Farewell Address or the Northwest Ordinance of 1785 to argue that the founders considered morality and religion indispensable to the republic's health. Washington called morality and religion the "twin pillars" of the republic. The Northwest Ordinance provided for morality and religion as part of schooling, including the universities that would soon dot the landscape. There are other examples and occasions of the nation's political and educational leaders appealing to specifically Christian or Protestant affirmations, which supports the historical argument that public education was not to be value- or religion-free.

15   This common view was easier to achieve in the days of a more homogeneous society; in our time, citizens of all sorts agree that it has become more and more difficult to teach a uniform morality. Why? There are just too many competing worldviews. Each voice has something to say about the common good, the true, the beautiful, and these voices often contradict each other. How can schools negotiate this metaphysical and moral pluralism without implying the inferiority or superiority of certain worldviews?

One solution to pluralism is to place all contending beliefs on equal footing, but many observers claim that this relativism creates a bigger problem than it solves. We can define relativism as having one foot on a banana peel, morally speaking—and the other foot also on a banana peel. Everything becomes slippery. With morality as a matter of personal preference, there is nothing secure to hold on to, and no one can gain a sure moral footing. "You have your values and I have mine," people say. "Who am I to judge your morals, and who are you to judge mine?" Some college teachers report that when trying to place boundaries around this moral relativism, they might introduce an extreme example: if morality is a matter of mere preference, with no value system better than another, then what about judging the values of Adolf Hitler? And the shocking answer comes, not always cynically: Well, what about his values?

If all standards for judging right from wrong are relative, moral claims seem to be rooted only in feeling, experience, or personal preference. Gone from the moral scene, say critics, is any sense of God as Absolute Truth. Only with God anchoring morality can there be an objective standard, they argue. Only then can people know *exactly* what is right or wrong.

Only by objectively knowing right from wrong can adults instruct children in the moral life. Here Aristotle's influence shows: people do not become moral just by discussing the good or the ethical; they become so by practice. People must find appropriate models and pattern themselves after those models. They must put into practice the pursuit of "the good" until it becomes a habit. And if the habit is rooted in belief in God, then you can at least have a good argument about how all this works out in society. Throw the divine anchor overboard, and people are left to drift on the open waters of relativism.

People legitimately concerned about the moral situation can add in one more dimension to the discussion: government and the courts are far too responsive to pluralism and diversity, especially the religious variety. Most Americans respond to the Judeo-Christian tradition, which means that they derive morality from the same sources. Most believe that somehow God speaks to us through the Ten Commandments and that indeed God may have literally provided the commandments on stone tablets to Moses on Mount Sinai long ago. So why have the courts disallowed the display of the Decalogue in public school classrooms? Not only do most Americans believe in the importance of these moral guidelines, but these laws put forth moral principles on which almost everyone agrees. Hence there is a majoritarian argument embedded within the issue of morals.

20   The more ecumenically minded may suggest lifting parallel teachings from other major religions and then teaching those distilled values in a combined form. For example, many leaders of interfaith groups argue that something like the Golden Rule belongs not just to Christianity but to almost every religious tradition. Treat others as you would like to be treated, and do not treat others as you would not like to be treated. It sounds very simple and commonsensical, and of course this principle can be taught as common sense or good advice. But what one cannot do is ask children to obey the Golden Rule because God wants them to do so. Yet dropping the transcendent reference, for many people, means dropping the main reason for following such a principle. The Ten Commandments become watered down into the Ten Suggestions—or less. So what begins as a well-intentioned debate over morals in education soon turns into a theological debate that divides school boards, teachers' groups, and parent-teacher associations.

Short of abandoning moral education completely, others have tried to negotiate ethical pluralism by promoting "values clarification." It certainly sounds like a good idea: teachers and students bring their own value systems, and in the classroom they clarify them, to see what might or might not motivate valuable action. But critics swoop in at once: students not only bring to school competing value systems, which leads to confusion, but they might also bring in ideas and behaviors that most of polite society finds unacceptable. No matter how antisocial, fanatical, or dogmatic, in this system those values cannot be discouraged, only "clarified." Won't the child who has undergone values clarification not only be more confused but even less likely to act morally?

Through all these debates and behind all these questions are strong religious interests. While you can have interesting public debates about educational philosophy and moral development, people who pursue philosophical options are not as well organized into competing camps as religious groups are. The religious landscape has many polarities: fundamentalist and liberal in Protestantism, Orthodox and Reform in Judaism, conservative and liberal in Catholicism. It is no wonder that school boards and textbook authors tread cautiously when dealing with moral education. But they often fail to realize that treading cautiously is its own kind of religious or metaphysical commitment. To many religious adherents, it looks as though a competing worldview—such as "secular humanism"—has become the established or privileged religion by default, while the regular voices of the "ordinarily" religious are shut out.

What is clearly needed is more awareness of what motivates the courts and more public discussion about the wisdom or folly of their actions. Many options have been foreclosed already. Arguing for "equal time," no matter how reasonable and practical it sounds, does not seem to offer a clear way to a solution. Present both evolution and creationism and let the students decide? Scientists will contend that the language of their discipline has a different intent than religious critics suggest, while many religious people will resist having the language and claims of their faith converted into something that sounds scientific. Better alternatives must be sought, and conversations can help us reason toward them.

Questions for Discussion

1. What are some of the "illegitimate fears" associated with introducing religion into the public school?
2. What do Marty and Moore mean by the following statement? "When teachers teach 'about' religion, faith may either get reduced to something so bland that it leads to a misreading of religion or become something so volatile that it will disrupt school and community life."
3. How does the issue of morality fit into the debate of religion and public schools?
4. What do Marty and Moore mean by the following statement? "The religious landscape has many polarities: fundamentalist and liberal in Protestantism, Orthodox and Reform in Judaism, conservative and liberal in Catholicism. It is no wonder that school boards and textbook authors tread cautiously when dealing with moral education."

Questions for Writing

1. Marty and Moore contend, "Teachers and students bring their own value systems, and in the classroom they clarify them, to see what might or might not motivate valuable action." Analyze this quotation in an essay.
2. Should church and state coexist in a public institution of learning? Consider the pros and cons of this question in a persuasive essay.

What Sidetracked Choice Advocacy?

John Merrifield

The modern voucher debate began with Milton Friedman's 1955 proposal that was first read widely in chapter six of his 1962 book *Capitalism and Freedom*. He proposed that "parents who choose to send their children to private schools would be paid a sum equal to the estimated cost of educating a child in a public school" (1962, 93)—in effect, a universal voucher or refundable tax credit proposal that does not discriminate against private-school users. Friedman was not trying to shift the worst victims of the status quo to another part of the system. He argued that turning the allocation of public K–12 funds over to parents would allow product differentiation and introduce competition, which would make the school system much more efficient. And it would end the unfair treatment of private-school users.

The voucher concept enjoyed enormous initial popularity. "Liberal" scholars were especially enthusiastic about the general idea: "In the late 1960s, educational vouchers were generally regarded as a progressive proposal" and "All liberal faculty members would wish to be associated with it [education vouchers]" (Senator Patrick Moynihan qtd. in Kirkpatrick 1999, 9). So what shifted the voucher debate from Milton Friedman's simple reform proposal to complicated and limited programs that move only a few children within the system? Each set of voucher proponents unfortunately had its own unique, strongly held views about how the devil could emerge from poorly conceived details (Center for the Study of Public Policy 1970; Cohen and Farrar 1977; Coons and Sugarman 1978; Friedman 1962; Jencks 1966; Levin 1968, 1992; Rand Corporation 1977; Salganik 1981; Sizer and Whitten 1968; West 1967). Everyone found devils in everyone else's details. The voucher concept was popular, but no specific proposal was. The Friedman proposal has few details, and the details subsequently invented were a major evolutionary step in the wrong direction.

The invention and discussion of details transformed the voucher concept from a simple substitute for the current governance and funding system into an addition to it. That transformation of the voucher idea helped opponents depict voucher programs as raids on public schools and as new costs that would lead to tax increases. The scarlet "V" was born. The widely held presumption that voucher programs would be only additions to the existing funding and governance system led eventually to assertions that a voucher program would increase a school system's expenses by up to 25 percent, perhaps more (Levin and Driver 1997).[1]

Voucher became a word that many choice advocates avoid as much as possible (Fox 1977; Kronholz 2000; "School Reform Blooms" 1999). Vague and misleading substitute terms such as *school choice* and *scholarship* further confuse the public debate and reduce the likelihood that an actual program will establish market forces. And the post-Friedman proposals, including the few that became actual programs, unfortunately amounted to limited escape hatches.[2] Such programs can't transform the system through competition or by any other means, though much of the discussion still pretends that they are potential reform catalysts.

Equity concerns dominated the voucher proposals that followed during the 1960s and 1970s. Because there are no standard definitions or formulas, the focus on equity greatly complicated voucher discussions. Equity typically meant income redistribution beyond the amount inherent in the taxes that raise money for K–12.[3] Many reform advocates also wanted to grant (and still do) poor families a disproportionate share of the revenues.

In addition, the gap between the educational opportunities available to the rich and poor seemed to be a greater concern than maximizing progress. Even though Friedman argued that the poor stood to gain much more from competition than the affluent, his proposal's indifference to potential gains by the wealthy created the belief that voucher programs should be reconfigured to deny the wealthy any benefits. For example, in an influential 1970 report from the Center for the Study of Public Policy (CSPP), John Coons and Stephen Sugarman recommended a ban on add-ons and greater funding for the disadvantaged so that disadvantaged children would gain relative to affluent children. The CSPP report did not recognize that add-on bans torpedo market forces (recall that a ban on add-ons amounts to a price control) or that market forces play a critical role in improving the system for all. Furthermore, the CSPP report did not recognize that discouraging private spending on schooling might diminish directly the gains for all children or that the losses for affluent children might exceed the gains for disadvantaged children.

In the 1960s and 1970s, concerns about racial diversity were especially compelling reasons to oppose or limit parental choice. Concern that racial homogeneity would be many parents' top priority led to a sense of distrust that still exists, even though area-based public-school admissions foster de facto segregation. Parental choice today is actually a tool for racial integration because demand for specialized services often surpasses interest in student body homogeneity. But concern that programmatic interests will not adequately suppress racism or in the right proportions restricts parental choice to public-school choice that the authorities can control. Magnet school programs and other forms of "controlled" public-school choice—such as the program in Cambridge, Massachusetts—aim to create racially heterogeneous student bodies. However, the authorities often deny parental choices and substitute their own preferences. Public schools' inability to specialize to nearly the extent that would result from market forces minimizes the integration benefits of public-school choice, but at least it also reduces the scope of the mismatches between student and school characteristics that occur when the authorities veto parental choices and substitute their own. Tony Wagner, a Cambridge resident and prominent educator, confirms my pessimism about the potential for specialization by public schools: "The majority of the thirteen [Cambridge K–8 schools] seem virtually interchangeable and are mediocre" (1996, 71). Furthermore, Wagner found that "School choice has not produced significant improvements in the schools," a statement that illustrates the limited potential of restriction-laden choice and the political risks of lumping diverse programs under the general "school choice" heading and of applauding every program enthusiastically without qualification.

The confusion that grew out of the competing, complicated, restriction-laden plans no doubt contributed to the huge electoral defeats of parental choice ballot initiatives. People tend to vote against things they do not understand. The wide margins of defeat convinced many choice advocates to lower their expectations, which led to futile attempts to appease choice opponents. And advocates celebrate and support every promise to give anyone another choice, even if it might delay or jeopardize more meaningful reforms. Choice advocates typically hype every program as a choice experiment, even though no existing program can show how choice might prompt reform. An incremental strategy has evolved that basically assumes that any extra choices will unleash irresistible pressures leading to a gradual repeal of restrictions until a version of "full school choice" evolves. For many choice advocates, "full school choice" sadly can still contain many key restrictions. For example, one strong voice for reform, the *School Reform News*, called the restriction-laden Milwaukee program a working model of "full school choice" (Clowes 1998).

Chester Finn and Rebecca Gau claim that adequate choices are at hand or that we're moving there quickly and that all that is needed is a slight increase in the accessibility of current private schools. "For all the noise around vouchers, public dollars already underwrite private school attendance in a variety of ways" (1998, 79). Every use of tax money, however trivial, that makes private schools more affordable is called a "virtual voucher." Finn and Gau ignore big differences between where we are—with scattered, tiny "virtual vouchers"—and a true universal choice program that would unleash market forces. Indeed, Finn and Gau do not mention competition, not even as an important force, much less as an objective.

Because an incremental strategy is vague, slow, and even a little deceptive by definition, the strategists can deceive themselves. Many seem to have done so. Through the passage of time, changes in leadership, and slow progress, many choice advocates seem to have forgotten every goal but the ones they might achieve quickly. Despite the potentially terrible consequences of short-term pragmatism, it is easy to sympathize with such thinking. The view from the trenches is often quite limited. The fog of war forces the combatants to focus on the struggles at hand, and it obscures linkages between current and future battles.

10

Such confusion is typical among those who believe that they are well informed, so we are lucky that they are rare. A 1999 poll found that "a vast majority of the American public claims to have little or no knowledge about charter schools, education vouchers, or for-profit schools" (Education Policy Institute 1999). According to Terry Moe (2001), 65 percent of the American public have never heard of school vouchers. That's good because it is much easier to inform people than to dispel their misconceptions. That the semi-informed faction seems to believe in the "escape hatch," "addition to the current system" definition of parental choice is a big enough problem.

Most of the activists and K–12 analysts I encounter speak and write on this issue as if the tiny, restriction-laden current programs are legitimate, ultimately informative, or catalytic "experiments." That is certainly the media mindset. One example is a *Wall Street Journal* front-page article on the conflicting interpretations of test score data from Milwaukee's voucher users. It included this incredible statement: "Education scholars were hoping the Milwaukee experiment would finally settle whether vouchers help poor kids academically" (Davis 1996, A1),[4] a recurring plea that speaks volumes about persistent, deeply ingrained misperceptions of voucher uses and parental choice issues. Voucher systems are seen widely as only additions to the current system, a way to allow a few low-income children to attend private schools—because the system supposedly serves only poor children badly. Based on the recent expansion of Milwaukee's still restriction-laden program, the *Wall Street Journal* proclaimed that the "choice debate is over"

("Choice Debate" 2000). Choice is working as a limited escape hatch in a few places, so the debate is over? Though it would be tragic, they may be right. The persistently narrow scope of the parental choice debate may harden the public's view of parental choice enough so that policymakers use small parental choice programs only selectively as an escape hatch.

PRICE CHANGE

. . . Schools must be free to charge whatever they want without worrying about jeopardizing the parents' eligibility for direct government support or indirect support through vouchers or tax credits. Efficiency requires that prices reflect changing production costs and consumer priorities. Price change maintains the balance between supply and demand, and it is through temporarily higher prices that rising demand prompts the appropriate supply increase. The price hike is usually temporary because the resulting rise in profitability sows the seeds of its own destruction. Higher profits motivate expansions and an influx of new producers. The influx lowers prices, returns profits to more typical levels, and prevents overexpansion.

The current education system lacks the critical price movement process because the 88 percent of K–12 children who attend public schools pay a tuition price of zero. Many existing voucher programs and prominent proposals unfortunately curb price change by forbidding private schools to cash vouchers unless they accept them as full payment.

15 Many prominent choice advocates and conservatives (I prefer not to name them) are too willing to accept a ban on add-ons. Some even actively support them. This is one of the few issues in which the instincts of freedom-loving choice advocates are not good enough. To succeed, we need a deep appreciation for the role of prices in market economies. Price change is not an optional part of the market mechanism. It *is* the market mechanism. Price movement regulates market participation, including how many businesses participate in each market, how they specialize, and how they change over time. For example, higher prices are often necessary to motivate as well as pay for research, development, and the costly early stages of a product's life cycle. Price flexibility—permission to add on—is a nonnegotiable element of system transformation through parental choice.

The critical add-on issue deserves much more attention. Because of the importance of the add-on option, I want to review the example I provided earlier. A tax-funded voucher worth $3,000 means that $3,000 worth of private schooling would cost a family nothing beyond the taxes they already pay. But if families cannot combine their own money with the government subsidy (i.e., add on), $3,001 worth of instruction would cost a family $3,001 more than $3,000 worth of instruction. A huge change in cost to buy a little more amounts to a price (tuition) ceiling at the taxpayer-funded amount. Universal parental choice without the right to add on would wipe out mid-price-range formal schooling options. It would limit private spending to after-school programs, tutoring, and premium schooling (i.e., elite prep schools). For example, with a $3,000 no-add-ons-allowed voucher there probably wouldn't be any $4,000 services and very few $7,000 services. Many of the families who would be willing to buy the $7,000 services by supplementing the $3,000 voucher with $4,000 of their own money would not pay the full $7,000 themselves if add-ons were not allowed. Instead of paying an extra $7,000 for an additional $4,000 worth of schooling, many parents would settle for less schooling of lower quality than they actually want and for which they are willing to pay.

Add-on bans—price controls—stifle experimentation and innovation. The opportunity to charge high prices for innovative practices is an important incentive. In addition, high initial prices may be necessary. New practices and products are often costly. Wealthy individuals' purchases of new goods such as DVD players, cell phones, and computers often sustain such innovations until experience and competition drive prices and costs down enough to make former luxuries the norm.

The right to add on also promotes responsible shopping, and it is arguably a simple matter of fairness. Why should parents lose their child's share of public funds just because they want to do more for their own child than can be done for every child?

Additional schooling for affluent children doesn't make less-affluent children worse off. Society benefits when the affluent devote their earnings to the education of their children. Attempts to go beyond the appropriate and feasible level of equal public funding (a high minimum level of education opportunity)—to equalize gains rather than to maximize them—have few if any equity benefits and high efficiency costs. The trade-offs are severe. The wealthy are always going to have advantages. Efforts to minimize such advantages will torpedo key market forces and distort the political process. Programs that target the poor are inevitably poor programs.[5]

Endnotes

1. Assuming a very restricted version of school choice, Levin and Driver estimate cost increases of up to 25 percent or more.
2. Some of the recent proposals are arguably exceptions; for example, some of Gary Johnson's voucher proposals and California's Proposition 38 would have been more than limited escape valves.
3. Lower-income families pay less than the cost of educating their children, whereas affluent families pay more than the cost of educating their children.
4. A similar article and headline appeared in the August 5, 1998, issue of *Education Week*.
5. This insightful phrase surfaces frequently. Milton Friedman (1998) said he heard it in a 1972 debate on Social Security from Wilbur Cohen, secretary of health, education, and welfare during the Johnson administration.

References

Center for the Study of Public Policy. 1970. *Financing Education by Grants to Parents*. Washington, D.C.: U.S. Office of Economic Opportunity.

Choice Debate Is Over (editorial). 2000. *Wall Street Journal*, April 6.

Clowes, George A. 1998. Five Steps to Full School Choice. *School Reform News* (September): 10–11.

Cohen, David K., and Eleanor Farrar. 1977. Power to the Parents. *The Public Interest* 48: 72–97.

Coons, John E., and Stephen D. Sugarman. 1978. *Education by Choice*. Berkeley: University of California Press.

Davis, Bob. 1996. Dueling Professors Have Milwaukee Dazed over School Vouchers. *Wall Street Journal*, October 11, A1.

Education Policy Institute. 1999. New Poll Finds Public in Dark About Charters and Vouchers. *EPI Update*, November 19.

Finn, Chester E., and Rebecca L. Gau. 1998. New Ways of Education. *The Public Interest* (winter): 79.

Fox, Michael. 1997. Remarks of Ohio State Representative Michael Fox. In *State Legislator Guide to Teacher Empowerment*. Washington, D.C.: American Legislative Exchange Council, 1997: p. 17.

Friedman, Milton. 1962. *Capitalism and Freedom*. Chicago: University of Chicago Press.

Jencks, Christopher. 1966. Is the Public School Obsolete? *The Public Interest* 2: 18–27.

Kirkpatrick, David. 1999. School Choice Choir Has a Broad Range of Voices. *School Reform News* (July): 9.

Kronholz, June. 2000. In Michigan, Amway Chief and Wife Give School Vouchers a Higher Profile. *Wall Street Journal*, October 25.

Levin, Henry M. 1968. The Failure of the Public Schools and the Free Market Remedy. *Urban Review* 2: 32–37.

Levin, Henry M., and Cyrus E. Driver. 1997. Costs of an Education Voucher System. *Education Economics* 5, no. 3 (December): 265–83.

Moe, Terry. 2001. *Schools, Vouchers, and the American Public.* Washington, D.C.: Brookings Institution.

Rand Corporation. 1977. *A Study of Alternatives in American Education* IV, VII. Santa Monica, Calif.: Rand Corporation.

Salganik, Laura H. 1981. The Fall and Rise of Education Vouchers. *Teachers College Record* 83, no. 2 (winter): 263–83.

School Reform Blooms (editorial). 1999. *Wall Street Journal*, May 5.

Sizer, Ted, and Phillip Whitten. 1968. A Proposal for a Poor Children's Bill of Rights. *Psychology Today* 58: 59–63.

Wagner, Tony. 1996. School Choice: To What End? *Phi Delta Kappan* 78, no. 1 (September): 71.

West, Edwin G. 1967. Tom Paine's Voucher Scheme for Public Education. *Southern Economic Journal* 33: 378–82.

Questions for Discussion

1. How have race and cultural diversity fueled the debate in the past several decades over the use of vouchers to finance students' education?

2. What percentage of Americans surveyed in Terry Moe's 2001 poll claim not to have heard of vouchers?

3. According to Merrifield, "additional schooling for affluent children doesn't make less-affluent children worse off. Society benefits when the affluent devote their earnings to the education of their children." What does the author mean by this statement?

4. What conclusions does Merrifield draw concerning school vouchers? Do you agree or disagree with these conclusions? Explain.

Questions for Writing

1. Write a persuasive essay, arguing for or against the use of school vouchers. Examine both the pros and cons related to this topic.

2. Is it ethical to use vouchers in situations that may produce predominantly segregated schools, more than fifty years after federal and state laws declared these schools unconstitutional? Analyze this question in an essay.

Student Essay

Changing the World One Child at a Time

SARAH HUTCHINS

No one has fully been able to realize the abundance of compassion, kindness, and talent hidden in the soul of a child. The effort of every true educator is to unlock that treasure inside each child. Education has been in practice since time began. In our society, teachers sometimes have the sole responsibility of educating and preparing a child for the future. Each child's individuality should be taken into account when educators teach. A child should be taught according to his or her strengths and learning style. The aesthetics of teaching involves catering to the different learning styles and identifying the struggles that teachers have to deal with in their classroom.

A teacher is responsible for teaching many different subjects throughout the school day, one of the most important subjects being reading and the language arts. While there are many ways to teach reading, educators will find that the whole-language-classroom approach is one of the best approaches. The whole-language approach integrates reading, writing, listening, and speaking in a learning experience in the classroom. Educators must develop lessons making use of such learning; for example, designing thematic units, which integrate one theme into all of the other subjects so students can make connections in their learning processes. When students direct their own learning, they are able to go at their own pace and express their individuality.

A teacher needs to understand the different learning styles so that they can adapt the instruction to each student's individual needs in the classroom. Familiarity with learning styles helps a teacher to "become more sensitive and understanding to the differences, strengths, and weaknesses that students have in learning classroom material" (White 1). For example, some students are better auditory learners, while others need visual representations. A teacher can cater to these different learning styles by lecturing and using visual aids. Teachers can also allow students to help choose their own projects. In an American history unit, students can choose to draw a Civil War battle map, while another can write a short story about a character living during that time. This allows the student to work with their strengths and interests and stimulates them to learn. When students are given a choice in their education, they feel more involved and responsible.

A teacher has the power to influence a child and help shape his or her life. Many men and women who have changed the world speak of how their lives were changed by one teacher. Educators must not only teach the curriculum, but also help guide each child to become a strong and confident adult. A teacher should find time for personal meditation before school. While prayer is not allowed in the public schools, "most think that school prayer, properly implemented, is a good way to shore up the crumbling values of today's kids" (Walsh 13). A teacher in his or her classroom can pray silently for all of the students throughout the day. Some teachers even help sponsor independent student-led Bible studies before or after school. In terms of curriculum, many school districts do not have courses that directly address ethics and values, but educators can integrate activities on ethics and values as they relate to units covered in the class. Hence, in Language Arts, students can write business letters to their Congressional Representative advocating a policy reform or write letters to their principal concerning the dress code.

The main struggle faced by teachers is trying to meet the needs of every individual child in the classroom. Many children do not receive the proper care and instruction in their homes. The U.S. Education Department "estimates that there are 322,000 school-age homeless children" (Portner 2). Many of these children are in school, and teachers should not only teach such children about their math, reading, science, and social studies, but also create lifelong-learning experiences that promote character development. A practical way to do so would be to create procedures and rules in the classroom that give the child structure, love, and security. While at-risk children are harder to teach than the average or overachieving students, for some teachers, at-risk kids are the most rewarding in the end because of the multiple challenges many have to overcome.

Another struggle for many teachers is helping students deal with environmental or social traumas, like the tragedy of September 11th. Many children are emotionally upset by the current circumstances occurring in our country, and some parents assume that the schools will handle the child's emotional needs. Teachers and schools should "help children locate themselves in widening circles of care that extend beyond self, beyond country, to all humanity" (Kohn 2). A teacher can help students cope by conducting group discussions where the students can share their feelings concerning the state of our nation.

"A hundred years from now," observes Kathy Davis, "it will not matter what my bank account was, the sort of house I lived in, or the kind of car I drove . . . but the world may be different because I was important in the life of a child" (qtd. by Leigh Baker). Teaching is not only a job; it is changing the world, one child at a time.

Works Cited

Baker, Leigh. *Miss Baker's Favorite Quotes and Sayings*. 16 April 2002.

Kohn, Alfie. "Teaching About Sept. 11." Rethinking Schools Online. 16 (2001); 1–3. 8 April 2002.

Portner, Jessica. "Schooling the Homeless: Few Programs Address the Daunting Challenge." *Education Week*. 2 April 2002.

Walsh, Mark. "Public Sees Role for Religion in Schools." *Education Week*. 8 April 2002.

White, Beverly. "Learning Styles." *Journal for Christian Educators*. 10 April 2002.

Questions for Discussion

1. According to Hutchins, what does the aesthetics of teaching involve?
2. Is Hutchins's view on teaching logical and practical? Explain.
3. What role should a teacher play in a student's life in and out of the classroom?
4. According to Hutchins, what classroom struggles do teachers face with students?

Questions for Writing

1. Do you agree with Hutchins that teaching "is changing the world, one child at a time"? Is it possible for teachers to change their students, or is the role of the teacher to provide tools by which students arrive at sound, ethical intellectual choices? Write a persuasive essay defending your view on this topic.
2. According to Alfie Kohn, teachers and schools should "help children locate themselves in widening circles of care that extend beyond self, beyond country, to all humanity." Assess the pros and cons of this statement in an essay.

Questions for Making Connections Within the Chapter

1. Should education be a moral agent commited to graduating students who are ethically sound? Consider in your answer the ideas of Marty and Moore, Hutchins, and Moe et al.
2. Examine the works of Byron and Moe et al. to show how history and archaeology, respectively, can be used to teach ethics and good citizenship.
3. Is it possible to provide a quality education that is equitable for all students? Consult Merrifield's and Hutchins's works. What does each author conclude?
4. What role should educators, parents, politicians, community, and so forth play in the quality of students' education? Consider the ideas expressed by any of the authors in this chapter.

CHAPTER 2

Ethics and Journalism

Though it be honest, it is never good
To bring bad news;
Give to a gracious message
A host of tongues, but let ill tidings tell
Themselves when they be felt.

Williams Shakespeare, *Antony and Cleopatra*

Since the media have a great influence on American culture—
our perceptions of people, politics, foods, music and entertainment, cars, and so forth; should we hold them responsible for the quality of their work? Some journalists avoid compromising the integrity of a story with half-truths or exploiting human life just to hype up the story: this is good news reporting. Problems occur, however, when we fail to hold the media accountable for bad news reporting. The essays in Chapter 2 address issues of ethics related to the world of journalism and communication.

In the first essay, Howard A. Myrick examines the issue of objectivity in journalism. Myrick suggests that journalists' reporting is the compilation of "experiences, socialization, beliefs, and indoctrination—in brief, their culture, augmented by race, ethnicity, sex, and myriad other intervening variables."

Looking at media taboos, Caryl Rivers looks at the effects of bad news reporting and its ability to influence public opinion in the wrong way. The author probes the idea of objective reporting and argues that journalism is more subjective than objective: "We are at heart storytellers, not scientists. Journalism is more art than science, and the notion that we are androids, collecting, weighing, and measuring 'facts' that are as fixed and intractable as moon rocks, is a chilling one."

In his article Benjamin Radford posits that journalism has undergone a number of changes over the past several decades. He explains that journalists are often influenced by the legal antics of corporate lawyers who threaten to sue networks for broadcasting news stories that put corporations in a negative light, even if the story is factual. Radford points to one such high-profile case involving *60 Minutes*. He goes on to discuss media tactics such as those used to boost ratings.

From a different perspective, Matthew Robinson documents how much influence media-conducted polls have among some politicians. Opinion polls test the heartbeat of a sampling of American voters on a number of issues. Robinson writes, "Many politicians attempt to influence polls as much as polls influence them." The author further contends that some politicians appear to make decisions that go contrary to popular opinion.

Brendan Smith, a media student, examines the influence of capitalism in advertising and advocates that ethics, not capitalism, should play a greater role in the media industry. He calls for greater media accountability.

As you can see, the articles in this chapter are diverse in topics but connected by the common thread of ethics. After reading the chapter, you can draw your own conclusions about a number of these issues, and others, involving ethics.

The Search for Objectivity in Journalism

HOWARD A. MYRICK

The definition of the word "objectivity"—expressing or dealing with facts or conditions as perceived without distortion by personal feelings, prejudices, or interpretations—is so clear and uncomplicated that to begin this article with it would seem at first glance to be gratuitous or, worse, superfluous. On closer examination, objectivity is easier to define than it is to attain in practice. Were that not the case, there would not be the unending allegations of biased reporting leveled at the news media. As any newspaper editor or broadcast news director will attest—and a reading of letters to the editor will confirm—the news media industry and its individual practitioners (i.e., journalists and television news anchors) are assailed constantly with complaints regarding distortion, bias, and lack of objectivity.

Complaints about the lack of objectivity in the electronic media are as frequent, if not more so, than in the print media. Comparisons between print and electronic media aside, the net result is a loss of confidence on the part of the news-consuming public in what is reported to them. Since the Sept. 11 terrorist attacks on the U.S., such concerns about objective reporting have taken on a new level of importance, both with regard to the assuaging of personal fears and about the implications the availability of reliable information can have on the participation of the nation's citizens in the formulation of important decisions facing the government. Public participation in the affairs of state at this juncture in the country's response to these cataclysmic events is becoming increasingly important as various people and organizations (including "political watch" groups, individual politicians, and Congress) question the effectiveness, appropriateness, and legality of some of the government's actions in the war against terrorism.

To avoid the easy temptation to engage in media bashing myself, and for the sake of objectivity, this article is begun without accepting at face value damning accusations against the news media. Moreover, the subject of objectivity in the news media deserves, itself, to be analyzed with as much objectivity as is humanly possible. Emphasis on the word "humanly" is deliberate and essential, for (returning to the definition of "objectivity") it is clear that it is the interposition of the human element in the business of perceiving, processing, and interpreting information through the prism of personal feelings and, yes, prejudices that determines objectivity.

A viable starting point is the posing of a pair of questions: Is the achievement of objectivity in news reporting even possible, and is the expectation of objectivity on the part of the news-consuming public a reasonable one? These are questions that must be asked if we accept that journalists' intervening prism of perception and, ultimately, reporting is the product of the sum total of all of their prior experiences, socialization, beliefs, and indoctrination—in brief, their culture, augmented by race, ethnicity, sex, and myriad other intervening variables.

In the words of communications scholar Ben Bagdikian (in his seminal book, *The Media Monopoly*), "News, like all human observations, is not truly objective. . . . Human scenes described by different individuals are seen with differences." The differences to which Bagdikian and other similarly disposed scholars refer are not only the variables cited above, but numerous others falling under the heading of psychosocial and behavioral factors conditioned by mankind's proclivity to receive, process, and respond to stimuli (and information) selectively and not in a one-to-one, immutable way from one person to another.

Walter Lippmann, the dean emeritus of every school of journalism, provided exceedingly incisive insight into the "asymmetrical relationship of fact and the presentation of fact" (to use the terminology of D. Steven Blum in his book, *Walter Lippmann, Cosmopolitanism in the Century of Total War*). Lippmann is credited with concluding that "the mechanism of human perception itself was a prime culprit in the distortion of information. . . Mechanisms of obfuscation operate within the mind as well as without, and perception was made as problematic by the tricks one's own mind played on itself as by the willful contrivance of others."

Lippmann's conclusion points out a kind of double bind that both the news provider and news consumer face. On one hand, journalists, irrespective of their commitment to the pursuit of objectivity, are likely to have their reportage attenuated or skewed by the inherent psychological function of their own minds and by the "willful contrivance of others"—e.g., editors, news directors, "spinmeisters," et al. Finally, news consumers, policymakers, and the electorate all fall prey to the consequences of distorted journalism.

The psychosocial phenomenon expostulated by Lippmann is exacerbated when the subject matter of the reportage is itself sensitive and/or emotionally charged. In America, for example, race is such a subject, even as the nation moves inexorably to the highest level of racial and ethnic diversity in history. As journalist, author, and media critic Ellis Cose observed in *The Media in Black and White*, "For reporters, race can be a treacherous subject, raising questions that go to the heart of the journalist's craft." Cose comments, "Is objectivity (or, even, fairness) possible when dealing with people from different racial groups and cultural backgrounds?" After all, he continues, "perceptions vary radically as a function of the very different experiences members of various racial groups have endured."

Directing the attention of journalists to the fact of their inescapable susceptibility to the phenomenon of selective perception—and thus their chance of failing to meet the requisite standards of objectivity—is not a cause for self-flagellation or becoming paranoically defensive when confronted with evidence of their failure. In many instances, in fact, it would be sufficient, instructive, and healthy for them simply to imagine their interviewee or information source reciting the adage, "I know you believe you understand what you think I said, but I am not sure you realize that what you heard is not what I meant." The willingness on the part of the journalist or newscaster to accept the wisdom of this adage could prevent further errors of distortion, bias, and various other injuries to objectivity in their reporting.

I hasten to emphasize that to accord some degree of latitude   10
to the journalist in this connection is not to condone transgressions. Also, it is not to engage in what philosopher C.P. Snow refers to as the "intricate defense of the status quo"—that is, to provide an excuse to practice sloppy and irresponsible journalism without regard for the critical need to rid the profession of the mounting number of egregious infractions committed in the name of press freedom and First Amendment rights. Rather, this is but the first of several recommendations I would offer to whomever is privileged to work in the profession of journalism, print and electronic.

To broadcast journalists, for example, who rely on the use of video clips from syndicated news services and/or their own electronic news gathering and field production units—a common and unavoidable practice in the fast-paced world of broadcast journalism—it would serve them well to be reminded that failure to analyze the "word" (the narrative) without paying close attention to the "picture" (the visual) can lead to some grievous distortions or misinterpretations. The picture (video) is an iconic code or stream of iconic codes exceedingly subject to variable interpretation, as has been found in research in culture and visual perception.

The term "iconic" in an audiovisual context refers to meaning embedded in the visual or pictographic component of an audiovisual communication or message. It includes, importantly, what can/may be vital nonverbal cues or messages. Facial expressions and other body language cues, for instance, can be highly communicative, often serving to clarify the depth of affective (feeling) components of a message or interview.

It may be argued that asking journalists to engage in such analysis invites them into the realm of even greater subjectivity. In responding to such arguments or fears, suffice it to say that the truly experienced journalists—those who are willing to go to the greatest lengths in pursuit of truth and objectivity—have worked at honing their skills (or have achieved facility) in polyphasic perception and analysis, to the ultimate benefit of the product of the practice of their craft.

POST–SEPT. 11 REFLECTION

At the time of this writing (coinciding almost to the day with the first-year anniversary of the terrorist attacks on the World Trade Center and Pentagon), reflection on the quality, importance, and role of the news media in society could not be more timely. The public's interest in this horrific story remains high, due to the cataclysmic nature of the events, in terms of the thousands of lives lost, the millions in property damages, and the sheer psychic shock suffered by a population that still has not come to terms with the catastrophe and what it portends for the future. Interest remains high as well because of the continued focus of the mass media, not at all surprising, given the convergence of Americans' appetite—indeed, manifested need—for information that might assuage their sense of disequilibrium and the media industry's insatiable need for content to fill their program schedules and the blank pages of newsprint paper that also carry, indispensably, the advertisements their profits depend on.

15   What is notable, if not surprising, about the media-sustained public interest is the fact that the media (especially television) have not only set the public's news-consuming agenda—that is, determining what subjects the public thinks about, but also, in large measure, how the public thinks about, for example, Muslims, Arabs, and even Arab-Americans. Indeed, until most recently, the news media industry has been a near-collaborator in fomenting a fundamental agreement between the public and the Federal government in determining what the nation's response to the threat of terrorism should be and who the perpetrators are.

An admittedly anecdotal, but telling, manifestation of the electronic media's unabashed expression of its sentiments on the government's war against terrorism is the wearing on camera of miniature American flags as lapel pins—a symbol of national pride, if not necessarily of support of national policies. Arguably, the wearing of a miniature flag should not be a cause for concern or be regarded as inappropriate in a society that espouses the virtues of free speech, especially in a time of national suffering and pain. There is the fact, though, especially since Pres. Bush's "Axis of Evil" speech and his apparent "go it alone" attitude concerning launching a preemptive military strike against Iraq, lively and important public debate and some serious anti-Administration criticism have surfaced involving different branches of the government and by influential and ordinary citizens. It would seem, therefore, that the cause of objectivity in the news is not well-served by this gesture on the part of some television journalists.

It would be a missed opportunity and, indeed, an error on my part if I failed to acknowledge my emotional reaction to the tenor of the times—i.e., the public's persisting anger over the events of Sept. 11, deployment of the nation's military forces in search of redress against the enemy and reclamation of national pride, and desire of no one to be guilty of harboring or displaying unpatriotic sentiments. These are all developments that have had a chilling effect on this author's willingness to attempt to be objective. The same feelings of restraint must influence more than a few journalists who would not like to find themselves in a widely discordant position with the prevailing sentiments of their viewers, listeners, and/or readers. The implications of these considerations on objectivity in the news are obvious, for journalists, too, are citizens, members of communities and political parties, and connected with numerous other affiliations that can have influence on their beliefs and perceptions.

VAGARIES AND TEMPTATIONS

Having dealt with the psychosocial and problematic nature of the mechanisms of the human mind and their impact on objectivity in reporting the news, the point must be made that there is no intent on my part to give short shrift to the "willful contrivances of others" or the willful contrivances of journalists themselves in distorting the news—or what passes as news. As with all humans, journalists are susceptible to the vagaries and temptations of the material world. There are editors and publishers to please if one is to keep one's job. Editors, publishers, news directors, station managers, and owners, in turn, are not impervious to the influence of politicians and business interests.

News organizations—print and electronic (though they often are one and the same in the current deregulated media industry)—are first and foremost businesses. The notion that such organizations exist to provide news and public service is one that still too frequently is espoused in classrooms in journalism schools. The abject and uncomfortable truth is that the profit incentive is the force that guides the daily activities of news organizations. The reality of the profit motive and its impact on the character, quality, and, especially, objectivity in the news is inescapable—and usually negative. As noted by Michael Schudson in *Discovering the News,* "Objectivity is a peculiar demand to make of institutions which, as businesses . . . are dedicated first of all to economic survival. It is a peculiar demand to make of institutions which, often by tradition or explicit credo, are political organs. It is a peculiar demand to make of editors and reporters who have none of the professional apparatus which for doctors or lawyers or scientists is supposed to guarantee objectivity."

20   As the nation—indeed, the world—watches the current implosion of the telecommunications industry, brought on in part by bigness, merger-mania, and the volatility of the market forces unleashed by near-unbridled deregulation, the struggle for survival intensifies. What is becoming increasingly evident is the fact that, like all entities whose survival and profits are threatened, the media industries will do whatever it takes to stay afloat—although staying afloat in their milieu does not mean simply paying the rent and making a modest profit, but paying exorbitant wages to media "stars," granting astronomical salaries and stock options to executives, and engaging in business practices which often cross the line into the realm of criminal conduct.

The loser in this equation is the news media–dependent public and, by extension, the nation. Referring to the Jeffersonian vision of the role of the press in a free society, it is not outlandish to subscribe to the proposed remedy of Lawrence K. Grossman, former head of NBC News and president of PBS, who concludes in *The Electronic Republic—Reshaping Democracy in the Information Age* that the way to "discourage inaccuracies and encourage more responsible reporting is to make the press pay for its own mistakes that unfairly damage reputations, even if the victims are government officials or public figures." In Grossman's view, the rise of "utterly irresponsible, scandal-driven, sensationalist tabloid and television press" is totally unacceptable since, among other injuries, it inhibits citizens' ability to "make sound and reasoned judgments," thus negatively affecting the functioning of participatory government in a government "of the people, by the people and for the people."

After consideration of all the obstacles which stand in the way of achieving objectivity in the news, one's response might be like that of a participant in a debate (actually, in response to my testimony in a legal deposition involving alleged libel and defamation). The participant, the deposing attorney, raised his arms in feigned despair and demanded vehemently, "If this is the way journalists are to be criticized, why not just shut down all the newspapers?" This was not just lawyer histrionics. Rather, it was a case of one person strenuously suggesting that objectivity is an unattainable goal. Therefore, why not forget about it?

Trying not to be dismissive, I set about trying to explain why the pursuit of objectivity—however elusive—was not only worthwhile, but indispensable. Conceding that often the case is not patently clear and that journalists sometimes make honest mistakes, but, to the extent that they move in a positive direction on the continuum from speculation, innuendo, yielding to extraneous pressures, and the sloppiness of depending on press releases and staged press conferences which too frequently are designed to manipulate public opinion rather than inform, to that extent they will be regarded as responsible journalists. When they reach the point on the continuum that is defined by accuracy, integrity, and honesty, to that extent the prerequisites of objectivity will be achieved. It is a goal well worth pursuing, for the good of the profession of journalism and, more importantly, the good of the nation.

Questions for Discussion

1. How does Howard A. Myrick define objectivity in journalism?
2. What does Myrick mean by the following question: "Is the achievement of objectivity in news reporting even possible, and is the expectation of objectivity on the part of the news-consuming public a reasonable one?"
3. How does Myrick define "iconic"?
4. Myrick argues that for the post–Sept. 11 generation, the media "have not only set the public's news-consuming agenda . . . but also, in large measure, [determined] how the public thinks about, for example, Muslims, Arabs, and even Arab-Americans." What are the ethical ramifications of the media's propaganda?

Questions for Writing

1. Myrick postulates that "ultimately, reporting is the product of the sum total of all of their [journalists'] prior experiences, socialization, beliefs, and indoctrination—in brief, their culture, augmented by race, ethnicity, sex, and myriad other intervening variables." Is his view fallible or accurate? Analyze this topic in a synthetic essay, bringing in two to four other media sources to support your view.

2. According to Myrick, journalists will attain objectivity when they "reach the point on the continuum that is defined by accuracy, integrity, and honesty." Do you think that this goal is humanly possible? Explain your response in an informative essay.

Totem and Taboo: The Culture of the News Media

CARYL RIVERS

The news media are usually thought of as agents for change, and sometimes this is true. The intense coverage of the civil rights movement, with images of southern sheriffs setting dogs on nonviolent protesters, shocked and shamed the nation and helped get new antidiscrimination laws enacted. But just as often the staccato of bad news bolsters the status quo and a conservative agenda. Why? Because people tend to believe that the world was once more orderly and just, especially when today seems chaotic and disordered. It's easy to think that if we could only return to some vanished Eden, all would be well again. If only we could make the world like it used to be, by restoring family values or throwing more people in jail, we'd all be better off. But the past was rarely as good as we thought it was nor the present so bad.

Bad news can in fact persuade people that the world is much more dangerous than it is. George Gerbner of the Annenberg School of Communication at the University of Pennsylvania finds that people who watch a lot of television see the world as much more threatening and filled with menace than those who watch less do.[1] James Alan Fox, dean of the College of Criminal Justice at Northeastern University in Boston, says that fears about crime have less to do with actual crime rates than with the perception of crime we get from the news. "The technology of reporting has changed dramatically in the past fifteen years," he says. "With live minicams and satellites, it is possible for any local news outlet to lead every night's newscast with a crime story, including good video."[2] He calls the 11 P.M. report "Crimetime News." Bad news can create panic and distort the public agenda. A case in point: in the spring of 1994 polls showed that the number one issue on the minds of Americans was crime, whereas only a few months earlier it had been health care. Was this change in concern warranted?

Not according to the statistics. Crime had in fact been decreasing in recent years; Americans were less likely than a few years earlier to be the victims of violence. Why were they suddenly terrified? Because the media coverage of crime had intensified. Several shocking high-profile crimes had made the national news—the . . . subway shooter and the killings of tourists in Florida—and coverage of gang violence in the inner city was incessant. The rise in popularity of tabloid journalism—in print or on the many sensational TV shows—also helped to fuel the concern about crime. But the irony is that the profitability of the drug trade—and the involvement of so many inner city gangs in its bloody pursuit—made it *less* likely that the average American was going to be mugged on a city thoroughfare. The gangs had turned inner cities into scenes of carnage, and for the inhabitants of those areas it was a tragedy, but few Americans in other areas were menaced by drive-by shootings. In fact, we are far more likely to be killed by someone we know than by a homeboy with an AK-47. But bad news can reshape the world in unfamiliar and frightening contours.

The bad news syndrome is linked to another characteristic of the news media tribe—its exclusive focus on the present and its tendency to ignore the past. The news media are by definition ahistorical. They have a tendency to reinvent the wheel. Some member of the tribe will come up with a shiny new spherical object, and peers will gather'round, oohing and ahhing at its marvelous shape, its surprising ability to roll along the ground, while in the cave just behind them are dozens and dozens of wheels in all sizes and shapes, fashioned by other members of the tribe in the months and years that have just passed. I am often astonished not only by simple errors of fact that show up in news stories but by the total lack of context. Journalists make flat statements about welfare, about history, about science, about women, about almost everything, that reflect a total ignorance beyond what some expert or some politician has just said.

This tendency has been heightened in recent years because 5 older people—who could supply such context just by having lived for a while—are fast disappearing from newsrooms. The anchorman you see on the evening news may have touches of gray in his hair, but the assignment editor is probably a twenty-three-year-old who doesn't even know who the mayor *was* ten years ago, much less what his policies were. And it is the assignment editor who's deciding what's on the news. Newspapers are offering buyouts to older and more expensive employees in favor of inexpensive, young, energetic talent. If you look around many newsrooms today, you will find hardly a soul who was there twenty years ago. The young journalists often mistake the handy conventional wisdom, or the latest intellectual fad or pronouncement from a media-anointed guru, as actual fact. I did it when I was a cub reporter. Wisdom, perspective—these come only with time. Without them you get uncritical acceptance of such ahistoric ideas as the notion that welfare *created* illegitimacy, to mention a currently popular shibboleth repeated often in the media as if it were so. But one-third of births in pre–Revolutionary War Concord were illegitimate, and our founding mothers were not on food stamps.

Combine the bad news of today with the news media's inability to grasp much beyond the recent past, and it's clear why people believe in a golden past that really didn't exist. You want crime? Try the nineteenth century, when the police were terrified to even set foot in some neighborhoods, and roving bands of violent young men terrorized the populace at will. Worried about how kids are behaving? You may think the fifties were happy days, but in fact the media at the time were filled with stories of unmanageable "juvenile delinquents."

Every era has its problems, but thinking that only *we* are in dire straits, that no people have ever grappled with our problems before, can lead to foolish actions. Fifty years from now, because the news media filled us with terror about crime, will we be straining to pay the bills for housing criminals we sent to jail for life at twenty and are now the most expensive segment of our elderly population? The media drumbeat about drugs a few years back helped create mandatory sentences that filled the jails with dealers. It turned out that we had to let murderers and rapists out to keep the small-fry drug dealers in.

In any event, take what you read and hear in the media with a grain of salt. We tend to believe what is spread before us, because the media have such an air of authority. Television news comes with the cadence of urgent-sounding music, sets of bright colors, and words like *Action News* flashing across the screen; the stentorian tones of the anchors can make a late-day snow storm sound like Armageddon. Newspapers have thick black type and pious editorials and labels that announce *Commentary* in commanding tones on their op-ed pages. All this is the wrapping, and it's easy to provide if you have a good deep voice or a throbbing theme song or a computer that makes nice graphics. But try to ignore all this and remember: it may not really be the gray-haired anchorman who chose the news he brings us today but somebody who is still using acne medicine.

The news media clan, like tribes who live in forests or by rude streams, has its own "anointed ones," Those-Who-Speak-with-Gods. Now we all know that the guys (I use the word advisedly) who speak with gods have a good deal of power in the tribe. But the anointed ones—be they sources or columnists or Big Foot reporters—tend to be much alike. They are nearly always upper-middle-class white males whose worldview is remarkably similar. Even if they didn't start out as upper class, years of being part of a privileged elite have usually dimmed the sense of what it is like for the rest of us, who live less elevated lives. Whom do you see on *Crossfire*, on *Meet the Press*, on the *McLaughlin Group*, on the evening news, on the op-ed pages of newspapers? The same guys, over and over. A few women, only a handful of blacks and a couple of Hispanics are in this group.

The result is that the national debate tends, day after day, to focus on the interests and experiences of these people. It was not surprising that in the 1992 presidential election the problems of cities and the issues of poverty were barely mentioned, and instead a middle-class tax cut was debated roundly. The Clinton camp didn't want to talk about poor people or blacks, because blacks weren't going to vote Republican, and Clinton knew the election lay with the middle class. George Bush wasn't about to dwell on poverty. The boys (and girls) on the bus didn't push the issues. They grew up for the most part in suburbia and had no memory of being poor or working class. When I criticized the lack of media coverage of such issues, a Washington reporter said to me, "The president who deals with the issues of the cities will be the next president—of Common Cause." That may be good campaign strategy, but reporters should be holding the candidates' feet to the fire on precisely the issues they want to avoid. They didn't, because the press was bored with poverty, which had no personal effect on them. Nobody got off the press plane and drove home to Bedford-Stuyvesant.

Working-class voices—not to mention those of poor people—are rarely heard on op-ed pages. The exotic minutiae of foreign policy, the endless inside-the-beltway battles, are the stuff that interests elite journalists. Rarely do such people face layoffs or downsizing, whereas millions of Americans are facing an economic crisis as companies get meaner and leaner, young people can't get jobs, and older workers are being laid off. Couples trying desperately to juggle home and work are struggling to find affordable day care. Yet these issues hardly dominate coverage and comment. Whitewater, however, with its hints of insider intrigue and power players, becomes a megastory.

10

Because the media tend to be fascinated with games men play—politics, war, sports—and the reader is generally assumed to be male, you get an overabundance of news of interest to white men and surprisingly little that is of interest to others. Also, white guys tend to assume white males are individual voices, whereas blacks, women, Hispanics, and others always speak for the entire group. Thus you may see fifteen columns on Bosnia or Whitewater on op-ed pages—sometimes two on the same subject on the same day—but one piece by an African American journalist on a "black issue" is assumed to have covered the subject fully. The same goes for women. How often do you see two pieces on day care by two women on the same op-ed page? Editors will say, about a "women's issue" piece, "Oh, Ellen Goodman did that already." But day after day, page after page, white men pontificate on Bosnia or the arms race or crime, and no one says the subjects have already been done.

Like all groups, the news media clan has its traditions and rituals that it assumes are shared by one and all. They have been written down by Those-Who-Speak-with-Gods. But they tend to exclude many of the not-so-elite, which is why many of us do not strongly identify with what we see or read. For instance, newspapers are losing female readers. Perhaps it is because women do not see themselves when they open their morning newspaper. Studies show that since 1985 women have been disappearing from the front pages of newspapers[3]—and their appearances there were never terribly frequent. A female point of view is even rarer.

In our society maleness is the norm and whiteness is the "norm." The set of viewpoints, ideas, and attitudes that often comes with being male or being white is seen as neutral and unbiased. At the same time, people with a different set of attitudes are nearly always seen as being biased or as being "advocates." This sense is pervasive in the news media, despite the inroads that women and members of minority groups are making. I was fascinated by a conversation I had with a male reporter from a major East Coast newspaper. He complained that his paper had been taken over by women and blacks and that white men were afraid to speak out. He also complained that he didn't like to speak at colleges because students got angry at him when he said that blacks and women didn't really have it so bad anymore and that it was white men who were being discriminated against. He was clearly a man who had strong emotions on the subject.

15   I asked him about the ways in which women had too much influence over the news at his paper, and he cited the story about a study claiming that teachers in school were biased against girls.

He remarked that he thought it absurd to think that in this day and age girls still faced such discrimination, and he said he thought the story was overplayed.

As it happened, this was a story I was quite familiar with, having reviewed much of the research for a book I had written and having fairly recently looked at the newer studies. I found the research to be compelling, because the findings were replicated time and again—found in more than one study, a good indication that bias against girls is a real phenomenon. I had seen videos in which female teachers, unaware of their behavior, ignored the waving hands of little girls in the front row time and again to call on boys in the back. I knew about all this prior research. I judged from the reporter's remarks that he did not.

The swirl of personal experience was the thing that drew me to . . . journalism; in fact I think it's what draws most journalists, male or female. We are at heart storytellers, not scientists. Journalism is more art than science, and the notion that we are androids, collecting, weighing, and measuring "facts" that are as fixed and intractable as moon rocks, is a chilling one.

Transcending personal experience is an impossible goal at any rate. Among those who argued in the 1920s for a new scientific journalism was Walter Lippmann. He called for journalists to remain clear and free of their irrational and unexamined biases. Lippmann, a German Jew who was so assimilated that he hardly remembered he was Jewish, wrote hardly at all about the Holocaust, one of the great tragedies of the twentieth century. Could he not face the vulnerability of a group to which he belonged, however marginally? You have to suspect that the omission had nothing at all to do with "scientific journalism" and everything to do with the swirl of personal experience.

The consequences of the reporter as android are many; Theodore Glasser sums them up this way:

> Objectivity is biased in favor of the status quo; it is inherently conservative to the extent that it encourages reporters to rely on what sociologist Alvin Gouldner describes as "the managers of the status quo"—the prominent and the elite. Second, objective reporting is biased against independent thinking. It emasculates the intellect by treating it as a disinterested spectator. Finally, objective reporting is biased against the very idea of responsibility—the day's news is viewed as something journalists are compelled to report, not something they are responsible for creating.[4]

The idea of objectivity can combine with the white male norm to keep the parameters of what is considered legitimate   20 opinion quite narrow. Objectivity often does not mean a hard examination of all "facts" but only of those that the gatekeeper suspects. Once I was doing an article for a newspaper in which I used as my major sources a black academician and a female professor. But an editor asked me to add another source, a white male professor who had no history of research in the area. Clearly, the editor simply did not have confidence in the "facts" offered by the woman and the black, believing—probably subconsciously—that they were somehow suspect. When my source was a white male, I have never been asked to go and find a woman or a black to bolster the credibility of the information, but the reverse has often been true.

The canon of objectivity is one reason that the voices of blacks and women are not quite trusted. They are suspected of either special pleading or of fuzzy emotionalism. Several women journalists I know have heard editors make remarks indicating that women, although able to turn a nice phrase, are just not as objective in their way of thinking as men.

Objectivity fosters another illusion: that the journalist has no connection to—or, as Glasser says, responsibility for—the subjects of his or her inquiry. Pressure to achieve that detachment is one reason journalists drink too much. We are often put in difficult situations regarding other human beings. We criticize them. We sometimes reveal that they are doing things that are wrong. We invade their private worlds in times of pain. Our job—to find and report the truth as best we can—may indeed result in harm to others. We ought not to pretend that all we feel is the buzz and clang of electronic gears when this happens. We ought to agonize over that. It will keep us honest—and human. We can try to be unbiased; we can try to be fair. But we will never really be *objective*. And we should not dodge moral responsibility in the name of this impossible goal.

And last is another sacred assumption I would like to address in this look at the rituals of the news media—the myth of the liberal press. It was always overdone. When I came into the business during the Kennedy era, the press bus did stop at many places it no longer goes. Many reporters came from working- or lower-middle-class backgrounds and identified at a gut level with the underdog. Although publishers and newspaper owners tended to be staunchly conservative, the rank-and-file did not identify with wealth or privilege. During the Kennedy era liberal ideas often drove public policy initiatives. Michael Harrington's *The Other America*, read by Kennedy, was the wellspring of what became Lyndon Johnson's War on Poverty.

That has changed dramatically during my years as a journalist. Today, as I've noted, journalists tend to lead upper-middle-class lives, often far removed from ordinary people. Indeed, Washington journalists today give speeches, star on TV panel shows, and are far more glamorous than many people they cover. As *Washington Post* media critic Howard Kurtz points out, the pundits of both right and left warmly embraced the North American Free Trade Agreement, almost off-handedly dismissing fears of working-class Americans who felt their jobs were threatened. Kurtz says, "What was striking to me was how casually many journalists dismissed these concerns, comfortably secure in a business that is not among those threatened by foreign competition."[5]

I have seen the political winds shift significantly from left to right, and journalists have swung with them. The media always go where the power goes. Today policy is driven by an energetic and powerful right funded by well-financed think tanks. When I covered the Goldwater convention as a young reporter, it seemed to many reporters that what we witnessed there was a strange and radical force that was alien to us. Today those ideas are in the mainstream, and it is the liberal ideas that often seem alien. In fact, much of the domestic agenda of John F. Kennedy would today be considered quite radical. The darlings of the media today are black conservatives, not the civil rights activists who were at center stage when I was a young reporter.

The political climate in America can only be called stunningly different from my early days in journalism. As sociologist Herbert Gans says, one of the great victories of the Reagan years was the creation of "a cadre of ideologically driven right-wing social scientists and intellectuals. Even now, the cadre's highly vocal presence helps keep liberals out of the media. For example, the so-called liberal position on media op edit pages and television panels is usually occupied by a moderate Democrat."[6]

Consider the case of Charles Murray, the co-author of *The Bell Curve*, now a media superstar, a frequent guest on talk shows, quoted by newsmagazines, asked to speak for considerable fees. Murray argues for the compete abolition of welfare, and his success, as historian Michael Katz points out, "illustrates the role of big money in the marketplace of ideas."[7] William Hammet, president of the Manhattan Institute, read a pamphlet by Murray he liked and supported him for two years while Murray wrote his welfare book, *Losing Ground*. Hammet then invested in the production and promotion of the book, spending some $15,000 to send more than seven hundred free copies to power brokers and journalists, and paid a public relations specialist to manage Murray, booking him on TV shows and the lecture circuit. The institute held a seminar on the book to which it invited journalists and intellectuals to participate, offering honoraria of $500 to $1,500. It was not Murray's brilliance that earned him entrée to the marketplace of ideas but the power of money and influence.[8]

A more affluent press corps identifies more easily with the attitudes and instincts of such a cadre, traditionally associated in America with the wealthy upper classes. Journalists no longer afflict the comfortable and comfort the afflicted. We *are* the comfortable.

There is a lot I don't miss from the days when I was a cub reporter—the provincialism, the tendency to play ball with elected officials, the high levels of alcoholism, the male chauvinism, the near-total absence of minority reporters, the lousy pay, to mention a few. But I do believe journalism was a more compassionate business when I entered it, if only because more journalists came from the working classes. I worry that journalists have become too comfortable, too far removed from the daily struggles and the little terrors of getting by that so many people experience. I'm not sure we should be supping so casually at the tables of wealth and ease. It's too easy to forget what it was like out there, beyond the warmth of the fire where we always used to stand with the hired help, rubbing our hands and cursing, saying that if *we* were inside, surely we would do things differently.

30   Today's conventional wisdom in the media is created by a comfortable suburban press corps on whose ears the arguments of the right may fall with a pleasing ring. But what my thirty years as a journalist have taught me is that everything changes. When I stood inside the Cow Palace in San Francisco listening to the Goldwater minions roar, I could not have imagined that the political landscape would change so radically. It was chic to believe in those days that conservatism had died along with Bob Taft and the America Firsters and would never be seen again in our lifetime. It's chic in media circles today to embrace the neoconservative creed, and journalists often write that liberal ideas are dated and shopworn. But today's shopworn goods can become tomorrow's haute couture. You never know.

. . . [T]he culture of the news media will play a background theme—like Muzak in an elevator—to the discussion of wider cultural myths that create journalistic distortions. Careful, thoughtful journalists can often avoid the pull of mythology and the conventional wisdom. . . . The problem is that the nuanced, careful piece too often simply gets drowned out by the clamor of the chic trend stories of the moment, and misinformation and half-truth blare from headlines and TV sound bites and nest in "background" paragraphs of otherwise competent stories. Most often the biases I discuss are subconscious and unintentional. I believe most journalists are conscientious and want to do a good job. That their thinking has been shaped by forces and ideas they do not realize they possess is no more an indictment of journalists than it is of all Americans—except that what journalists write and say is so important. "The first rough draft of history," as journalism has been called, needs to be corrected.

Endnotes

1. George Gerbner, Michael Morgan, and Nancy Signorielli, *Living with Television* (Hillsdale, N.J.: Erlbaum, 1986), pp. 17–40.
2. James Alan Fox, "A Nation with Peril on Its Mind," *Los Angeles Times,* February 14, 1994.
3. Readership figures come from Media Watch, the watchdog group based at University of California at Los Angeles, 1990.
4. Theodore L. Glasser, "Objectivity Precludes Responsibility," *Quill,* February 1984.
5. Howard Kurtz, "When the Press Out classes the Public," *Columbia Journalism Review,* June 1994.
6. Herbert Gans, *People, Plans, and Policies* (New York: Columbia University Press, 1993), p. xix.
7. Michael Katz, *The Undeserving Poor* (New York: Pantheon, 1989), p. 5.
8. Ibid., p. 152.

Questions for Discussion

1. What does Caryl Rivers mean by the following: "The news media are usually thought of as agents for change, and sometimes this is true"?
2. Why does Rivers criticize the media, white male journalists in particular, for being biased in terms of race and gender? What points does she use to support her claims? Are her points valid?
3. How does the author weigh in on objective versus subjective journalism? Which one does she favor? Why?
4. "The nuanced, careful piece too often simply gets drowned out by the clamor of the chic trend stories of the moment, and misinformation and half-truth blare from headlines and TV sound bites." What does Rivers mean by this observation? Do you agree? Why or why not?

Questions for Writing

1. According to Rivers, "The news media have the power to frame the news, and the frame makes all the difference." Is her claim accurate and fair? As you respond to this question in a persuasive essay, think about a number of news stories you have seen, heard, or read lately on television, radio, the Internet, or newspaper. Do they support or refute Rivers's claim?
2. Is the role of a journalist more like that of an artist or a scientist? Consider Rivers's view as a springboard for a persuasive essay defending your view.

The Changing Face of News

BENJAMIN RADFORD

As the nation's television networks and newspapers are owned by fewer and fewer parent companies, the quality and breadth of news coverage has been compromised. Due to the incestuous nature of the various media outlets, companies tend to be reluctant to cover or criticize corporations with which they are affiliated.

In his book *The Media Monopoly*, Ben Bagdikian found the problem of advertisers trying to influence the news to be pervasive. He cites a 1992 Marquette University poll in which the vast majority of newspaper editors—93 percent—claimed that advertisers tried to influence their news. Worse,

> a majority said their own management condoned the pressure, and 37 percent of the editors polled admitted that they had succumbed. A recent Nielsen survey showed that 80 percent of television news directors said they broadcast corporate public relations films as news "several times a month."[1]

Bagdikian puts the crux of this problem concisely:

> It is normal for all large businesses to make serious efforts to influence the news, to avoid embarrassing publicity, and to maximize sympathetic public opinion and government policies. Now they own most of the news media that they wish to influence.[2]

Not only do corporate decisions influence what gets on the news, they also influence what doesn't get on the news. Mark Crispin Miller, professor of media ecology at New York University, discussed former *60 Minutes* producer Lowell Bergman's comments on the media in an issue of *Free Inquiry* magazine. Miller wrote:

> Bergman offered a wry commentary on the kinds of revelation that the TV news will *never* bring us, regardless of how many ratings points they might rack up. From the journalists of General Electric, Disney, News Corporation, Viacom, and AOL/Time Warner, there will never come a word of troubling news about the ownership of any franchise in the National Football League because that game is simply worth too much to TV's own proprietors.[3]

Media critic and activist Ronnie Dugger wrote in a 2001 article that

> on the Sunday morning political talk shows, according to a recent study, topics loosely related to corporate power made up only four percent of the discussion topics. When your employer is owned by a just-indicted worldwide price-fixer, how much airtime do you give the story, if any? When your boss is a weapons merchant, what do you report, if anything, about the case against the war?[4]

Disney chairman Michael Eisner is clear on his policy about Disney media (such as ABC) covering Disney interests: "I would prefer ABC not to cover Disney," he said on National Public Radio's September 29, 1998, program *Fresh Air.* "I think it's inappropriate. . . . ABC News knows that I would prefer them not to cover [Disney]." Presumably this policy is intended to facilitate, not stifle, objective reporting, but of course it doesn't work that way. When Eisner speaks of ABC not covering Disney, that obviously does not apply to ABC covering Disney media and promotions, and likely does not apply to positive news about the company.

A report studying the content of the network morning shows conducted by the Project for Excellence in Journalism found that much of the content was infomercials, frequently for products of parent companies. Shows such as CBS's *The Early Show*, NBC's *Today*, and ABC's *Good Morning America* were heavily commercialized. On average, a third of the content is devoted to selling a film, television program, book, or music CD. In one example, the project found that nearly a third of the products promoted on CBS's *The Early Show* are owned by communications giant Viacom—which also owns CBS, as well as Paramount Pictures. As Associated Press reporter David Bauder found, the morning show producers are unapologetic:

I think that Jennifer Lopez being on the "Today" show to talk about her concert on NBC is a completely legitimate view of what morning television is all about, and I don't think you should be criticized for it," said Steve Friedman, a morning show executive producer.[5]

True enough, in our day of ever-larger media companies, some cross-promotion is not only unavoidable but to be expected. Morning shows would be remiss to ignore talent that happened to be working for a parent or sister company. But this approach can also be taken too far, and the lines between legitimate news and in-house promotion easily blurred.

This is not just an academic problem; corporations are becoming more and more powerful and important in our society. With billions of dollars in assets, huge companies can rival small governments in the power and influence they can wield. Many of the protests against the World Trade Organization . . . address this very issue. One of the complaints against the WTO is the enormous power it has, in some cases the power to effectively nullify the laws of a sovereign country. The organization can ignore inconvenient laws restricting environmental pollution, minimum wages, labor laws, and other such regulations that might limit profit, trade, and commerce.

10   Each year, Project Censored, an ongoing investigative sociology project at Sonoma State University, publishes a book of the previous year's top twenty-five censored news stories. These are news stories that were largely ignored by the mainstream press for various reasons, but that have important implications for the public and solid documentation to back them up. Though a distinctively liberal bias sometimes emerges from their works, it is an invaluable project, and essential reading for anyone interested in media criticism.[6]

At times the corporate influence on local news is more subtle. Even when corporations have no direct power over the news media, they can still manipulate the news in other ways. In 1994 the computer chip maker Intel was fined for allegedly violating its air pollution permit at its largest plant in Rio Rancho, New Mexico. Intel agreed to pay $40,000 in fines to the New Mexico Environment Department.

The company, long accused by locals of contributing to respiratory and health problems because of its toxic pollution, had a public relations problem on its hands. In a blatant and preemptive attempt to divert attention from the news of its fine, Intel pulled an inspired media sleight-of-hand trick.

Instead of addressing the fact that it was found guilty of pollution for months on end during 1992 and 1993, Intel basked in a well-publicized "Intel Appreciation" event put on by business bigwigs from throughout the Albuquerque metropolitan area. The luncheon was held Wednesday, January 26, 1994, and Intel's press releases to the media stated that the purpose was "to thank Intel for bringing 3,000 construction jobs and 1,000 permanent jobs to the Albuquerque and Rio Rancho areas."

Intel also placed large newspaper ads thanking itself for bringing jobs to the area and listing dozens of locals who expressed their appreciation, including the governor, two senators, and two local mayors. To counter local activists who protested Intel's environmental record and lack of paying gross receipts or property taxes, Intel employees were given signs with slogans like "Intel is a safe place to work" and "Thank you for our jobs!" and held a counterprotest.

Two days later the fine against Intel was quietly announced. The media effort was clearly orchestrated to use corporate clout to drown out bad news with praise and accolades. *Albuquerque Journal* writer Christopher Miller covered the story in an article titled "Applause for Intel," and began with, "It was a show of appreciation seldom witnessed in Albuquerque."[7]

CORPORATE LAWYERS AS NEWS EDITORS

Another impediment to independent journalism is the legal dangers and threats of lawsuits by powerful and litigious corporations. The corporate reminder to keep an eye on the bottom line makes some news departments wary of running in-depth stories that may incur potentially monumental legal bills if their subjects are unhappy with the way they are portrayed.

One of the highest-profile cases of this was the controversy surrounding a *60 Minutes* segment featuring a former Brown and Williamson tobacco company scientist. The scientist, Jeffrey Wigand, was one of the first to publicly confirm what many had suspected for decades: Tobacco companies knew that their product was addictive, and they conducted research into ways of manipulating the nicotine content in cigarettes.

The evidence was solid and corroborated. Yet the problems with airing the piece came not from editors but from lawyers. Concerned about protracted and very expensive lawsuits that might be incurred if *60 Minutes* ran the story, the decision was made to air the segment without Wigand's damning testimony.

The fact that the story was essentially gutted by the excising was apparently of little consequence. The story was later made into the Academy Award–nominated film *The Insider.*

Certainly, the lawyers themselves were just doing their jobs, and any news department should be concerned about the potential for lawsuits, making sure that anything that airs is factually correct and legally airtight. The larger issue is the decision not to air important, accurate, and damaging information about a public health threat. *60 Minutes,* in many people's eyes, backed down.

NEWS AS WIDGET: TED KOPPEL, DAVID LETTERMAN, AND MICKEY MOUSE

20   In early 2002 executives at the Disney-owned American Broadcasting Company (ABC) approached late-night talk show host David Letterman to try to lure him away from CBS, where he had worked for several years. ABC, hoping to raise its flagging ratings, was looking for a way to capture a younger demographic, which in turn would bring higher advertising revenues. If Letterman accepted the $31-million offer to jump networks, he would run in approximately the same time slot—thereby jeopardizing the venerable and award-winning hard-news show *Nightline,* hosted by Ted Koppel.

ABC made it clear that *Nightline* (widely recognized as one of the best broadcast news shows, with a twenty-two-year history and a shelf full of journalism awards) would be happily pushed aside if David Letterman wanted the slot. Thus arose a near-perfect example of how entertainment programming can drive out news programming and of the corporate mindset applied to news reporting.

The *Washington Post* ran an insightful commentary by Tom Rosenstiel and Bill Kovach in which they point out that "what Disney executives are really arguing is that journalism is just another kind of content; that communication is communication."[8]

To the corporate mindset, television content itself is far less important than who will watch that content, and in what numbers. From *Seinfeld* reruns to *60 Minutes,* from *Wheel of Fortune* to *Nightline,* all programs are essentially identical and interchangeable blocks of time. News is turned into widgets. It is not that the networks are actively against programs that serve to inform and educate the public; perhaps worse, they are indifferent.

Frazier Moore of the Associated Press wrote that "after years of media consolidation, concepts like 'market niche,' 'branding,' and 'multiple platforms' are what matter to the bosses in the content they dispense. A thoughtful, older-skewing newscast has become a marketing albatross, not a public trust and a source of pride."[9]

ABC tried to justify its decision by claiming that *Nightline* was losing money (an assertion since proven untrue). Even more disturbing was a quote from an unnamed Disney executive that *Nightline* was no longer relevant. Ted Koppel answered his anonymous critics with a statement in the March 5, 2002, *New York Times:*

> I would argue that in these times, when homeland security is an ongoing concern . . . when, in short, the regular and thoughtful analysis of national and foreign policy is more essential than ever—it is, at best, inappropriate, and, at worst, malicious to describe what my colleagues and I are doing as lacking relevance.[10]

In the end, Letterman decided to stay with CBS, though ABC was widely and rightfully criticized for its inability or unwillingness to recognize the value of *Nightline* when the opportunity arose to replace it.

Ed Bishop, editor of the *St. Louis Journalism Review at Webster University,* writes that

> NBC, CBS and ABC—where most people get most of their news—are all owned by conglomerates which make more money in jet engines, theme parks and movies than they do delivering the news. In fact, the corporate bosses of the network news departments often see their employees more as pitchmen than journalists.[11]

Endnotes

1. Ben Bagdikian, *The Media Monopoly,* 5th ed. (Boston: Beacon Press, 1995), p. 138.
2. Ibid., p. 26.
3. Mark Crispin Miller, "Censorship Inc.," *Free Inquiry* (spring 2000): 12.
4. Ronnie Dugger, "Corporate Takeover of the Media," *Free Inquiry* (winter 2001/2002): 24.
5. David Bauder, "Study: Shows Peddle Products," *Albuquerque Journal,* November 29, 2001.
6. Project Censored is online at www.projectcensored.org.

7. Christopher Miller, "Applause for Intel," *Albuquerque Journal,* January 27, 1994.
8. Tom Rosenstiel and Bill Kovach, "'Nightline' Island of Intelligent Fare," *Albuquerque Journal,* March 10, 2002.
9. Frazier Moore, "'Nightline' Remains Along with a Problem," Associated Press [online], www.augustachronicle.com/stories/031402/fea_1246669.shtml March 14, 2002].
10. Ibid.
11. Ed Bishop, "They Were Only Half Right," *St. Louis Journalism Review at Webster University* 32, no. 243 (February 2002). Available online at www.stljr.org/pages/archives/february2002.htm.

Questions for Discussion

1. According to Benjamin Radford, since television networks and newspapers are increasingly owned by fewer parent companies, "the quality and breadth of news coverage has been compromised." Is Radford's point fair and accurate? What examples have you seen from current newspapers and television news programming that illustrate Radford's view?
2. What influence do some corporate lawyers have on news editors? Consider the story that was to air on *60 Minutes.*
3. Are the media more interested in reporting stories that entertain and arouse emotions than stories that educate and instruct audiences? Explain.
4. What does Ted Koppel mean by the following statement: "In these times, when homeland security is an ongoing concern . . . when, in short, the regular and thoughtful analysis of national and foreign policy is more essential than ever—it is, at best, inappropriate, and, at worst, malicious to describe what my colleagues and I are doing as lacking relevance"?

Questions for Writing

1. According to Ed Bishop, "NBC, CBS, and ABC . . . are all owned by conglomerates which make more money in jet engines, theme parks and movies than they do delivering the news. In fact, the corporate bosses of the network news departments often see their employees more as pitchmen than journalists." If Bishop's claim is accurate, how, if at all, would the quality of news stories be compromised? Write an informative essay addressing this question.
2. Benjamin Radford argues that a journalist is more of an artist or storyteller than a scientist. What are your thoughts on this topic? Consider Radford's view as a springboard as you ponder this question in a persuasive essay.

Politicians and Polls: Everything You Say Can and Will Be Used Against You

Matthew Robinson

Winston Churchill, Britain's greatest leader in the twentieth century, once attacked the idea of the craven politician. In the dark days of 1941, he said to the House of Commons, "I see that a speaker at the week-end said that this was a time when leaders should keep their ears to the ground. All I can say is that the British nation will find it very hard to look up to leaders who are detected in that somewhat ungainly posture." The proliferation of public opinion polls has introduced a new dynamic into public discourse. Although polls are popularly derided as a temporary spine for the spineless, the truth is more complex. Many politicians attempt to influence polls as much as polls influence them. The skill with which Washington's politicians employ polls to push their messages shows that they are far more conscious of the power and limitations of polling than are most journalists. Journalists claim that the polls they write are a mirror of the public's views. For politicians, polls are a valuable tool. Politicians use the bandwagon effects of polling and media coverage to gather support for their ideas, and they exploit the journalistic obsession with polls to garner attention. Politicians realize that polls are more a measure of how an issue is framed than a measure of the fixed, well-informed opinion of an ideologically committed public.

"[T]he polling business gives the patricians an idea of what the mob is thinking, and of how that thinking might be changed or, shall we say, 'shaped,' " suggests left-leaning journalist Christopher Hitchens. "It is the essential weapon in the mastery of populism by the elite. It also allows for 'fine calibration,' and for capsules of 'message' to be prescribed for variant constituencies."[1] Such criticisms aren't new to activists on the left or on the right. Political science professor Daniel Greenberg wrote in 1980:

> Given the devastation that opinion surveys have brought to the American political process, we shouldn't be asking how polls can be sharpened but rather why they are endured and how they can be banished. . . . Polls are the life-support system for the finger-to-the-wind, quick-change politics of our time, and, as such, are the

indispensable tools for the ideologically hollow men who work politics like a soap-marketing campaign. . . . The effect of this—on campaigns, as well as on administrations between campaigns—is an obsession with salesmanship rather than governance.[2]

That "salesmanship" gives politicians tremendous wiggle-room for tailoring their ideas to those of the public. Polling isn't the sole cause of issueless "soap-marketing" campaigns, but public polling has mixed with other dominant trends to make it more difficult for political leaders to educate, debate, and persuade the electorate.

"Salesmanship," or the marketing tactics and strategies of political players, has become very important to candidates who must test-market their ideas because they now sell themselves directly to the public. Television and the decline of the influence of political parties have cast politicians adrift to appeal directly to the voter, often without party support. At the same time, politicians must work around a media filter that values conflict and controversy—even before the "new product campaign" begins.

POLITICIANS KNOW POLLS ARE ONLY THE BEGINNING

The ways in which politicians use polls show that they are familiar with the many limitations and gray areas of polling—even if journalists aren't. Political scientists Lawrence R. Jacobs and Robert Y. Shapiro argue that despite popular perception, politicians are not ruled by polls. Jacobs and Shapiro believe that politicians are more apt to use polls to manipulate the public and the media.

5   In the 1993 health care reform debate, Jacobs and Shapiro found that congressional staffers tended to ignore polling that showed support for health care reform. They identified four reasons that staff members of Congress did not buckle before the polls and pass some version of national health care:

1. The polls from media, party organizations, and lobbyists weren't considered credible. Many in Congress believed that "findings were manufactured through the use of slanted question wording and biased sampling."
2. Staffers discounted public opinion polls because they were too crude to pinpoint public sentiment about complex proposals.
3. The public was too uncertain, with as much as a third of the electorate holding no opinion on major policy issues.
4. Legislators believed public opinion was an "inappropriate" guide for governing.[3]

These four points are perfect examples of the limitations of polls, and they all come down to the same core problem: the American voter. Due to ignorance and apathy, the average voter has withdrawn from the political process and only participates in a minimal way, if at all. Members of the House and Senate understand that the world of politics is far more intricate and complex than the polling conducted by left-leaning media.

During the debate about Medicare reforms, the national media hammered away at Republican proposals as a "gutting of the social safety net," "draconian cuts," and "savage slashes." In the common media schema, Republicans are the reactionaries or obscurantists opposing the will of the people. Similarly it seemed at first that national health care would be just another liberal entitlement to sail through Congress in some form or another.

Initial polling, at least in the eyes of the media, contributed to this notion. But polls often fail to present the trade-offs and opportunity costs for certain courses of action, and even when they do, voter reasoning on complex multibillion-dollar ideas can still be quite primitive. So in the beginning, new government programs or rules tend to poll well. But the political process was designed by the founders to modulate and slow the enactment of legislation so the people and their representatives could look more closely.

The relationship among public opinion, polls, and political leadership is complex. For instance, a politician can't just read the polls and expect to succeed. Even the most plastic politician doesn't solely read the polls, because he or she has to choose which polls to read. As Jacobs and Shapiro state, "The efforts of politicians to weigh the costs and benefits of policy and electoral goals are most significantly influenced by their constituents, but constituents do not provide a clear and uniform signal to politicians about which goal to favor."[4]

POLITICIANS SEE THE RECIPROCITY OF POLLS AND MEDIA

While most pollsters reject the idea that polls produce a bandwagon effect among voters, politicians understand there is such an effect in the media. They understand that polls can drive coverage and therefore attract supporters. In seeking office, donors, or ways to advance their favored issues, politicians know that polls play a critical role in convincing journalists and the public that their ideas are legitimate, popular, and politically feasible.

Candidates and officeholders recognize the hypnotic power that polls—even unscientific ones—have over journalists. The media obsession with polling makes the preprimary "straw polls" in Iowa, Florida, and Louisiana nearly as important as any other primary poll. Politicians have come to realize that the media have little or no self-control when faced with irresistible measures of the horse race. Even when reporters add a caveat or two about the unscientific nature of the straw poll, the news coverage is nearly the same as any other poll, no matter which channel you watch or which paper you read. That's why politicians will spend hundreds of thousands of dollars to bus in supporters and pay for votes at straw polls. Phil Gramm in 1995 and Steve Forbes and Gary Bauer in 1999 spent huge sums trying to boost their showings in the straw polls.

Polling has a powerful influence on the type of coverage that politicians get, so naturally they try to control or exploit the polls as much as possible. As Tom Rosenstiel said of the Democratic primaries in 1992, even the most issue-oriented politicians are forced to play to the polls.

For example, 1992 Democratic presidential candidate Senator Paul Tsongas had promised voters that he was "no Santa Claus." He sought to tell a more balanced story about Washington's liberal spending and the need for responsible budgeting. According to Rosenstiel,

> In his own way, Tsongas used the press as well. Campaign manager Dennis Kanin found out when major newspapers would be conducting opinion polls, and timed the first Tsongas commercial in December to air just before them to influence the results. The trick pushed him into an early tie for first place.[5]

In 1995, during the Medicare reform debates with Congress, Bill Clinton aired commercials throughout the country. His plan was to drive up public opposition to the GOP legislation, but in such a way that it seemed spontaneous. Clinton knew that the media focus on tactics and strategy, so the White House "air war" was conducted outside the major media cities of New York, Los Angeles, and Washington, D.C. As the negative campaign progressed, journalists were left with a story that appeared to be built on a spontaneous public surge: Americans opposed the "cuts" and "slashes" in the Republican-proposed reforms.

15   So it was in the 2000 presidential race. Vice President Al Gore, after months of bad press, came out of the Democratic convention with newfound support and a more united base of core

Democratic supporters. As Gore's poll ratings rose, crossover support for Governor George W. Bush naturally faltered. In the zero-sum politics of journalism, reporters and pundits had any number of explanations. Gore's passionate and unexpected kiss of his wife before his acceptance speech received some of the credit, as did Gore's laundry list of favored left-wing ideas. Finally, some of the blame went to Bush's ideas, specifically his tax-cutting plan. Gore had previously attacked the Bush proposal as a risky scheme, and as soon as Bush began to slide, media scrutiny was unloaded on the idea of cutting taxes.

Unknown to many journalists at the time, the Gore campaign had purchased airtime in markets across the country during the convention, but avoided major media markets that might draw attention to the seemingly renewed interest in Gore. Gore suddenly rose to a 10-point lead in the polls. And Bush retreated from his tax plan, admitting he "needed to do a better job of explaining" the effect of across-the-board cuts. Politicians understand how the media read and misread polls, and they understand how to manipulate polls and public opinion to drive journalistic coverage.

POLITICIANS TAILOR THEIR MESSAGE TO IGNORANT VOTERS

Politicians, unlike journalists, do not assume a high level of voter knowledge. They understand the limitations of public opinion polling and the consequences of public ignorance. They know that their job is not to produce long lists of public policy plans—the kind of "specifics" that journalists say the public craves. Rather, most candidates—and especially their consultants—realize that Americans view politics through a prism of gut feelings, impressions, and even prejudice. Therefore reaching voters and attracting their support goes beyond a mere recitation of numbers and data. It is a far more complex process that often leads candidates to tailor their messages to affect the public's impressions.

Polling and focus groups play an important role in giving politicians insight into touching heartstrings as well as crafting language for the voter. For journalists, this manipulation is mere showmanship. But politicians have an incentive to find the best way to communicate to voters. Although the task of the politician is split between talking to reporters and talking to voters, the methods of impressing each group differ markedly.

In appealing to the people and in trying to move the polls, politicians are often forced to dumb down their message. As author

William A. Henry III wrote, there is a vitiating effect on campaigns when candidates conduct "politics by saxophone"—a phrase Henry coined for campaign stunts that try to make presidential candidates appeal to everyone. In 1988, it was blue-blood Vice President George Bush's revelation that he likes pork rinds and country music. In 1992, it was Clinton's reputed love for junk food and his saxophone-blowing appearance on *The Arsenio Hall Show*.

20 Henry's ideas about "politics by saxophone" were prescient. In 2000, both presidential candidates fought for the attention of talk-show host Oprah Winfrey. Bush delighted morning talk-show host Regis Philbin by wearing Philbin's trademark monochromatic shirt-and-tie combination. Likewise Al Gore sought to win over Regis's audience by demonstrating how to hypnotize chickens.

"The problem with fostering a personal link with the electorate is that this kind of pseudo-chumminess makes it difficult to lead or inspire. It is not enough to be elected," wrote Henry. "A President must renew his mandate, in a close equivalent to campaigning, virtually every day—the ultimate triumph of populist egalitarianism."[6] This state of affairs creates an interesting dynamic, as opinion elite lament every election year in political cartoon and written complaint: Are these really our choices? Journalists tend to be harsh critics, driving up cynicism with contemptuous coverage of the two choices facing the voters. Usually such critiques come with acid-tongued commentary about how the candidates "avoid specifics," refuse to "talk issues," or fail to put forward any policy "substance."

But polls have led politicians to view the world of public opinion differently. Politicians are challenged with getting their message out to a tuned-out populace, which even in the closest races cannot correctly identify political candidates according to their proposals. In addition, political coverage during elections or public controversy is often biased, cynical, and lacking in substance; voters willfully helicopter their brains out of the wasteland of this coverage. Of course there is little excuse for voter ignorance in the age of the Internet. The average citizen has tremendous resources at his or her fingertips for investigating and researching candidates.

But if average citizens do not take it upon themselves to find this information, chances are they won't get it from the media. This is because, for the most part, television and even newspapers tend to eschew the responsibility of serious, substantive real-issue reportage in favor of gaffes, one-liners, and campaign blunders. This creates an environment that encourages consultants, candidates, and campaigns to find ways to reach voters without resorting to bold and enterprising ideas that could prove costly in the polls. Instead political players orchestrate tightly controlled publicity events and soft, subtle messages that keep opponents and the media from savaging *any* ideas.

Endnotes

1. Christopher Hitchens, *No One Left to Lie To: The Triangulations of William Jefferson Clinton* (New York: Verso, 1999), 35.
2. Herbert Asher, *Polling and the Public* (Washington, D.C: Congressional Quarterly Press, 1992), 17.
3. Lawrence R. Jacobs and Robert Y. Shapiro, *Politicians Don't Pander* (Chicago: University of Chicago Press, 2000), 125–126.
4. Ibid., 11.
5. Tom Rosenstiel, *Strange Bedfellows: How Television and the Presidential Candidates Changed American Politics, 1992* (New York: Hyperion, 1993), 54.
6. William A. Henry III, *In Defense of Elitism* (New York: Bantam, 1994), 1999.

Questions for Discussion

1. According to Matthew Robinson, politicians use media polls to manipulate voters. What are the four points Robinson cites as to why Congress didn't pass a national health care policy in the 1990s?
2. How did President Bill Clinton work the polls? Weigh the advantages and disadvantages of his doing so.
3. What does Robinson mean by his claim that "politicians realize that polls are more a measure of how an issue is framed than a measure of the fixed, well-informed opinion of an ideologically committed public"?
4. How did the media's handling of the 2000 presidential election influence the candidates and/or the public's opinion?

Questions for Writing

1. Is it ethically wrong for the media and/or politicians to use polls to promote a particular agenda? Write an informative essay in response to this question.
2. According to the author, "politicians understand public opinion and the limitations of polls far better than the media." Analyze this topic in an essay.

Student Essay

Public Relations and Advertising: The Unyielding Juggernauts of Capitalism

Brendan Smith

Some might say that ethics are not as important in the field of public relations and media as they were fifty years ago. However, I, along with many others, disagree with this. Just because society has transformed over the past few decades, and morals and ethics seem to be on the decline, it does not mean they are not as important.

Without ethics, this world could not continue in its present state. Humans would be on the same level as animals, our only purpose in life to survive. We would be driven by our own selfish lusts and desires for self-preservation and gratification. Nothing would be done for the betterment of society as a whole; life would be this never-ending orgy, the inexhaustible desire to fill one's sexual urges, pausing only occasionally to feast upon the other beasts of the earth.

Today the media seem very separated. I know there is much use of music in film and television, as well as the use of some theatrical elements in music. However, what we do not see anymore is the great influence that the various media have on each other, as exemplified with the "Beat" movement of the 1950's going through the "Hippies" of the 1960's. In fact, we can see the great influence the jazz of the '40's had on the "beat" writers and poets, such as Jack Kerouac and Allan Ginsberg among many, and the effect their writing had on the folk music of the '60's, seen in Bob Dylan and the Grateful Dead (George-Warren 342).

I plan to create a medium for artists with a true art form and talent to work in the media/film industry without sacrificing their artistic integrity. By not forcing my beliefs upon others and using my talent, skills, and personal integrity as an example, I plan to raise the bar of ethics in the workplace and ultimately influence the media industry in general.

5   I much adhere to the words of Tom Caldwell, President of Caldwell Securities Ltd., who once said: "If you tell people you're a Christian, and you base your business dealings on this foundation, you'd better be careful how you behave" (qtd in Reid). Working with those of different beliefs and showing them my beliefs and standards by the way I live my life, I will have a greater impact on their lives as artists and also as individuals.

Works Cited

George-Warren, Holly. *The Rolling Stone Book of the Beats.* New York: Rolling Stone Press, 1999.

Reid, Gail. "Christian Ethics in Business." *Fellowship Magazine* 7 (15 April 2002): 7.

Questions for Discussion

1. According to Smith, what would life be like without morals and ethics?
2. What does the decline of values tell us about the world? How has media played a part in this change?
3. Map out the process of declining ethics from the time of the Industrial Revolution to the 21st century. How have new innovations and creativity influenced these changes?
4. In an era when artistic integrity is not always the norm, is it possible for artists to maintain integrity and achieve success in the media/film industry and/or the workplace, or is Smith's notion merely wishful thinking?

Questions for Writing

1. In an essay, analyze the changes in ethics and moral values in the United States over the past two decades. How have people in the public arena—such as entertainers, politicians, the media, corporate CEOs and so forth—influenced society both positively and negatively?
2. Smith wants to make a positive impact on others in the advertising industry, as well as on consumers. However, can one be noble, professional, and financially successful in advertising? Analyze this question in an essay.

Questions for Making Connections Within the Chapter

1. What influence do the media have on shaping the opinions of the American public? Consider the views of Myrick and Robinson on this issue.
2. Are the media ever guilty of propaganda? Think about the ideas of Myrick and Rivers in your response.
3. Consider objective versus subjective journalism and the effects of both forms of news reporting on morality and/or the demoralization of society. What do Rivers, Myrick, and Radford in their respective articles have to say about it?
4. Does the media industry have a responsibility not only to uphold ethical standards but also to set a moral climate for the country? Explain. Consider in your response Smith, along with any of the other works in this chapter.

Ethics and
Law

A peace above all earthly dignities,
A still and quiet conscience.

William Shakespeare, *Henry VIII*

The essays in Chapter 3 explore issues of ethics related to the field of law and humanities. Should there be more laws to regulate cyberspace crimes? Should there be stricter gun control laws, or should citizens' right to bear arms be protected under the U.S. Constitution regardless of the circumstances? Is the American justice system still plagued by racial profiling? These are some of the questions discussed in this chapter.

First, Walter Olson explores issues arising from state settlements against American tobacco companies. He looks at how settlements are paid, and he questions the legal ethics of attorneys who represent the public, for the law requires that these lawyers do not overcharge their clients.

In her article, Cynthia A. Stark presents the views of supporters and opponents of gun control in the context of what the U.S. Constitution considers fundamental rights of each law-abiding citizen. In the end, Stark argues, "the right to bear arms is not a fundamental right in spite of our fundamental interest in protecting ourselves from harm."

On another issue, Karen Judson looks at the topic of civil liberties in cyberspace against the backdrop of laws that regulate criminal activity in cyberspace. She also takes into account cyberethics concerning such topics as sexual harassment over the Internet, misidentification, and plagiarism.

In their article "All the Court's a Stage," Richard Zitrin and Carol M. Langford expose how some trial lawyers play on the sympathies of the jury by advising their clients to dress or act a certain way. The authors go on to write of some trial attorneys that "often, [they] describe the tricks they've used as if they're trophies on display."

In his essay, Christopher John Alexis, a prelaw student, advocates that racial profiling and other forms of racial discrimination must be abolished. He calls for accountability and equity in the criminal justice system for all people regardless of race.

There is a myriad of laws that are designed to protect law-abiding citizens and punish law-breaking citizens. Even so, some citizens argue that their civil liberties have been infringed on with the enactment of a number of laws designed to protect them. Again, students can come to their own conclusions by the end of the chapter.

Puff, the Magic Settlement

WALTER OLSON

By now millions of words have been spilled on the $206 billion tobacco settlement engineered in late 1998 between 46 states and the major cigarette companies. The deal, which followed settlements with four other states totaling $40 billion, has been called the biggest privately handled redistribution of wealth in world history. It has simultaneously served as a rich source of funds for new state spending programs and as a confirmation of the newly emerging role of entrepreneurial private litigators as a fourth branch of government.

At the same time, many of the tobacco settlement's most curious features have received little public recognition. This was perhaps understandable at the time of the announcement a year ago, when most outsiders still found the settlement's terms sketchy and confusing. Since then, however, a wealth of details has emerged about how the settlement was meant to work, and does work, in practice. These details deserve a close look, if only because it's likely that the "tobacco model" will be replicated in other cases where government eyes some line of business as a source of revenue.

Start, then, with a basic question: Are the payments required by the settlement really an assessment of damages for past misconduct, or are they a tax in disguise? (Cigarette prices jumped by 45 cents a pack almost as soon as the ink was dry on the agreement and have risen again since.) "There'll be adjustments each year based on inflation," an Idaho official told the Spokane *Spokesman-Review,* referring to the state's take. "If cigarette volume goes down, our payments will go down. If volume goes up, our payments will go up even more."

That sure doesn't sound like a damage settlement. Yet the attorneys general take pains not to call what's happening a tax increase, and they have good reasons to maintain this view, one being that they plainly lacked the authority to negotiate an extra-legislative infliction of new taxes on their states' populations. So it's worth looking more closely into the question.

By its nature, a damage settlement for past misconduct could apply only to companies that did business in the past. A start-up tobacco company, or a foreign maker tackling the U.S. market for the first time, couldn't be made to pay based on the failure of U.S. companies to warn of their products' dangers in 1965 or 1980. Likewise, in a damage settlement, a company that was tiny in years past but has lately expanded could be made to pay based only on its old sales, not on any new market success it might enjoy.

But in fact the settlement contains a series of provisions designed to make sure that companies chip in proportionally to their new, and not their old, sales. "The tobacco companies," writes Rinat Fried of Law News Network, "got the states to agree to force small companies not participating in the settlement to fund a 30-year, multimillion-dollar escrow account to be used as insurance against future health-related judgments against the small companies." Contributions to this escrow account will, it seems, be set high enough to discourage small companies from going it alone.

Moreover, small companies can participate in the settlement only if they agree to keep their market share from growing more than 25 percent above what it was in 1998—either that, or pay a prohibitive 35-cent penalty for every pack they sell above that level. This quite effectively deters entry into the market by cigarette discounters who have no liability for past conduct and could therefore undercut the higher prices generated by the settlement.

The word for this process is cartelization, and, the irony is that had cigarette executives met privately among themselves to raise prices, freeze market shares, confine small competitors to minor allocations on the fringe of the market, and penalize defectors and new entrants, they could have been sent to prison as antitrust violators—quite possibly by the very same attorneys general who sued them in this case (they'd also have faced tag-along consumer lawsuits filed by some of the same plaintiffs' lawyers). This way it's all legal.

The effect is that smokers pay generously, while the other parties get cut into a sweetheart deal: State governments quietly turn the same tobacco companies they publicly vilify into captive milch cows for future spending, the attorneys general grab political credit, and the companies get protected from competition. And, not at all by happenstance, the private lawyers who served as middlemen will reap a vast fortune, probably tens of billions of dollars, in what are being called fees.

10   Traditional legal ethics has plenty to say about the role of lawyers who undertake to represent the general public, and one thing it says is that they must not overcharge, even when dealing with a government that (through foolishness or otherwise) is not watching its outlays carefully. Not very shockingly, the reasonableness of a fee depends on the amount of work done to earn it. How much work, and of what nature, did the private lawyers do in the tobacco cases?

There's no doubt that some lawyers representing some states did a substantial amount of work to research the Medicaid cases and engage in various stages of pretrial litigation—though, since only two of the cases reached trial (both were settled before a verdict), the lawyers generally did not have to worry about what is by far the biggest source of costs in an ordinary lawsuit. There were also many states like Illinois, where the law firms hired by the state, as an arbitration panel later pointed out, did "relatively little" to pursue its claims, taking no depositions and submitting no time records of hours spent on the case. Holding back on doing much work may have made sense as a legal strategy—other states were doing the heavy lifting, and Illinois could simply ride on their coattails—but it also meant the Illinois lawyers couldn't expect a huge fee, right?

Wrong. The arbitrators decided to award the Illinois lawyers $121 million, and the lawyers reacted by complaining bitterly that they deserved more like $400 million. According to the *Chicago Sun-Times*, Illinois Attorney General Jim Ryan had "close ties" to one of the two firms he hired to represent the state.

Or consider the case of Maryland, where the state hired asbestos lawyer Peter Angelos, best known as owner of the Baltimore Orioles, to represent it. It isn't clear how much work Angelos did on the case. Yet standing on the terms of a 25 percent contingency fee contract, Angelos now says he's owed a cool billion dollars.

This isn't to say that Angelos did nothing special to advance the state's tobacco suit. His influence is widely credited for one of the most remarkable episodes of the entire affair, in which Maryland lawmakers (like Florida's before them) agreed to change the law retroactively to extinguish legal defenses that would have been available to tobacco companies at the time they took the actions being sued over. "We changed centuries of precedent to ensure a win in this case," explained the president of the state Senate.

As *The Washington Post* reports, Annapolis legislators have   15 grown accustomed to "the proposals known by their yearly short-hand, "the Angelos bill"—legislation that the legal magnate sends over nearly every year to create some new way for him to extract more money from the parties he sues. Among the nation's most munificent Democratic donors, Angelos is, per the *Post* account, "viewed by many political insiders as the most powerful private citizen in Maryland." He sports his own personal lobbyist, glove-close relations with Gov. Parris Glendening, and a host of state-house connections, such as with the president pro tem of the state Senate, who happens to be a lawyer with his firm.

In Massachusetts, Gov. Paul Cellucci called the lawyers' fee request "obscene," and *The Boston Globe* reported that under the eventual $775 million fee award, "attorneys may be paid nearly $5,000 per hour." In Kansas, Attorney General Carla Stovall hired her own former law firm as in-state counsel, claiming she couldn't find another firm to take the work on the terms offered. In Texas, $3.3 billion in fees went to a "Big Five" alliance of trial lawyers, each of whom made *The Houston Chronicle*'s list of the top 10 political donors in the state, all Democratic stalwarts.

In New Jersey, the winning consortium of six lawyers, hatched in a "brainstorm sitting around the convention center having a couple of drinks," included five former presidents of the state trial lawyers' association, ATLA-NJ, though several of its members were very light on experience in either tobacco litigation or mass torts. The team's original proposal for representation was billed as a "public interest" proposal made through a non-profit foundation, "but the foundation's role was later quietly eliminated, if it ever existed," reports the *New Jersey Law Journal*. Meanwhile, nearly $100,000 in campaign contributions was flowing in a six-month period from ATLA-NJ's PAC to Republican lawmakers, including $4,350 in checks written the day after the lawyers got the contract. Expected fee haul: $350 million.

Wisconsin tobacco lawyers retreated from an initial demand of $847 million in fees to accept $75 million plus $2 million in expenses, all the while battling to prevent public disclosure of their billing records (they poignantly cited "ethical issues"). When they lost on the attempt at secrecy, it was revealed that the $2 million in expenses included $7,800 for a chartered plane to fly attorney Robert Habush, former president of the Association of Trial Lawyers of America, round-trip from Florida to Washington (coach fare: $906) and a stack of limo bills typified by an $851 entry to whisk Habush from Milwaukee to Madison and back on May 5, 1997.

As for their claim of hours expended, it consisted in no small part of time spent on such categories as working the press and scoping out the governor and other political players; tasks usually entrusted to office managers, such as lining up bank accounts, office space, and furniture; fee negotiations themselves; and preparing a constitutional challenge to proposed legislation that would have curbed their fees (yep, they get paid for that too). The lawyers' initial demand had amounted to some $32,000 per hour, a figure one may set alongside the $20,000 a year that the median household in northern Wisconsin earned in 1990. (For the lawyers on its own payroll, the state asked $209 an hour.)

20   Far richer rewards went to lawyers who arranged to represent many different states at once. Perhaps the most opulent of these, the firm of Ness, Motley of Charleston, South Carolina, is likely to be in for fees exceeding $3 billion, according to *The Dallas Morning News*. Pascagoula, Mississippi's Richard Scruggs, who happens to be the brother-in-law of Senate Majority Leader Trent Lott, can expect to become a billionaire with plenty of room to spare. (A competitor of Scruggs' who said he didn't want to get "out-brother-in-lawed" cut in as a tobacco suit participant President Clinton's brother-in-law Hugh Rodham, who used his entree to the White House to call his famous relative's attention to the issue. Rodham has now popped up to assist lawyers suing the gun industry, though he told *Time*, "It was totally unforeseen, when we joined that there would be any connection with politics.")

Not long ago, both public sentiment and ethical authority rejected the idea of letting persons clothed with the coercive authority of government use that power to grab instant wealth for themselves by taking a share of the wealth they expropriated. Memories lingered of the evils of "tax farming," in which emperors managed to call forth the most conscienceless class of tax collectors imaginable by according them a share of the funds they extracted from a helpless populace. On a more mundane level, all agreed in deploring occasional reports that rogue police departments were giving traffic cops a share of the proceeds from tickets they wrote. Even when modern forfeiture laws arose with their many evils, there was at least the consolation that the police chiefs and prosecutors were not supposed to convert any of the seized booty to their own personal account.

Now, contingency-fee law enforcement having worked so well for its practitioners the first time out, a veritable gold rush is on to sign up more government clients, who will delegate more and more expropriative powers to the new Fourth Branch. Gun makers were selected as the second target, and trial lawyers are now busily lining up public clients to go after a list of targets that includes lead paint makers, HMOs, latex glove makers, and many others.

Can't we find someone's brother-in-law to stand up and say it's time for this to stop?

Questions for Discussion

1. What occurred in the billion-dollar tobacco settlement in late 1998?
2. Walter Olson questions the ethics of the settlement as follows: "Are the payments required by the settlement really an assessment of damages for past misconduct, or are they a tax in disguise?" What evidence does he provide for his suspicion that the settlement amounts to a tax?
3. What legal ethical guidelines must attorneys follow in representing the general public?
4. How do tobacco tycoons and companies lobby their state legislators and tobacco trial lawyers? Cite some of the examples that Olson alludes to.

Questions for Writing

1. According to Olson, "not long ago, both public sentiment and ethical authority rejected the idea of letting persons clothed with the coercive authority of government use that power to grab instant wealth for themselves by taking a share of the wealth they expropriated." Take into account ethics and morality as you analyze this statement in an essay.
2. Should tobacco products be banned from the United States? In a persuasive essay, address the pros and cons of prohibiting tobacco sales.

Fundamental Rights and the Right to Bear Arms

CYNTHIA A. STARK

Part of what is at issue in the dispute between advocates and opponents of gun control is the nature and status of the right to bear arms. Opponents of gun control tend to see the right to bear arms as, in some sense, fundamental, whereas proponents tend to see the right to bear arms as not fundamental. In what follows I consider Wheeler's and LaFollette's interpretations of the notion of a fundamental right. Against Wheeler and in support of LaFollette, I argue that the right to bear arms is not fundamental.

But first two clarificatory comments are called for. (1) Following LaFollette, I use "gun control" as an umbrella term to cover a variety of regulations that dictate what types of guns can be owned by which citizens under what conditions. I take it that advocates of gun control believe that only a few types of guns (say, hunting rifles) may be owned by certain citizens (say, mentally competent adults who are not felons) under limited conditions (say, provided the citizen has a license, the weapon is registered, and the citizen is not permitted to conceal the weapon or carry it in certain settings). Opponents of gun control, on the other hand, oppose many or most of these regulations.

(2) What is at stake in the dispute concerning the fundamental or nonfundamental status of the right to bear arms is the ease with which restrictions may be justified. Fundamental rights are less vulnerable to regulation than nonfundamental rights. If one can establish that a right is fundamental, one has thereby established that restrictions on that right can be justified only by very compelling reasons. Hence one particularly strong—though certainly not the only—way to argue against restrictions on gun ownership is to show that the right to own guns is fundamental.

In his essay "Arms as insurance," Samuel Wheeler defends Charlton Heston's assertion that the right to bear arms is not only a right but the fundamental right.[1] On Wheeler's interpretation of Heston, what makes it the fundamental right is that the right to own guns is "a condition for the practical existence of other rights."[2] By "practical existence of a right," I take it that Wheeler intends something like "the ability in practice to exercise one's right."

5   Assuming that what is at issue are moral rights, there is a prima facie implausbility about this claim regarding the status of the right to bear arms. For instance, it seems quite unlikely that this right is a necessary condition for the practical existence of our moral right to not be deceived. The claim is more plausible if our constitutional rights are at issue: if the constitutional right to bear arms is our only insurance against tyranny—a claim that Wheeler supports—then that right is necessary to prevent the government from violating all of our other legal rights. The con-

stitutional right to bear arms, then, guarantees the safety of our other legal rights by allowing citizens to resist government incursions upon those rights and by making it less likely that governments will attempt such incursions. In this respect, the right to bear arms is what Wheeler calls a "meta-right."

Yet many of our legal rights, especially our constitutional rights, are underwritten by moral rights. The right to worship as one pleases, the right to own property, and the right to express oneself are all legal rights. They are instituted so that citizens (in democratic regimes) may preserve their moral rights as persons. So, if the right to bear arms is practically necessary for the protection of citizens' legal rights, it is also practically necessary for the protection of those moral rights that are preserved by means of legal rights. It follows that the right to bear arms must itself be a moral right, for one is morally entitled to protect one's moral rights.

And indeed this is born out by Wheeler's defense of the claim that the right to bear arms is the fundamental right. He claims that the right to bear arms is "a special, technology-dependent case of the more general right to be able to resist unjust coercion by whatever means available."[3] Clearly, this general right is a moral right, and so the right to bear arms must also be a moral right.

Yet, one wonders, how can a special case of a more general right be the fundamental right? Surely a general right is more fundamental, at least in a certain sense, than its instances. Wheeler's answer seems to be as follows: "having a right that x entails having a right to take steps to make it more likely that x."[4] He says, moreover; "Making it more likely that x essentially means taking steps to prevent unjust coercions which would prevent x."[5] He offers as an example one's right to enjoy the produce from one's garden: this right entails the further right to protect one's garden by, for example, building a fence around it (acknowledging, of course, that there are limitations on what one is permitted to do to insure one's rights).

Though the right to bear arms is a "special case" of the more general right to resist unjust coercion, it is fundamental in the sense that it is a practically necessary condition for one's exercising some, though not all, of one's important moral rights, such as one's right against assault. It turns out, then, that the right to prevent unjust coercion is fundamental vis-à-vis a range of important moral rights and that the right to bear arms is fundamental vis-à-vis a subset of these moral rights, namely, those rights for whose protection we need guns. Wheeler says: "Among the clearest rights is the right to prevent serious harms to oneself and others by disabling a would-be assailant, at whatever cost to the assailant. A practically useful right to resist criminal assaults entails a right to be prepared for reasonably expected assaults."[6]

10   Thus, on Wheeler's account, it is not the moral right to own guns, but the moral right to prevent unjust coercion that is fundamental because, he says, it is a condition for the exercise of many of our moral rights. The right to own guns is entailed by the right to resist unjust coercion in circumstances in which owning guns is necessary to avert unjust coercion. This view, which can be distilled from Wheeler's 1999 essay, is expressed more succinctly in his contribution to this symposium.[7] He states: "The core 'self-defense' argument for a right to bear arms derives it from a fundamental right to preserve oneself from harm, conjoined with empirical facts about technology, the reliability of police protection, and reasonably expected threats. . . . [G]iven a right to defend oneself against reasonably expected threats, and given that a firearm provides the only practicable means of self-defense, the right to bear arms can be inferred."[8] The "fundamentalness," as it were, of the right to prevent violations of one's moral rights "transfers" to the right to own guns under circumstances in which guns are the only available means to prevent the violation of one's moral rights.

But on LaFollette's account of what makes a moral right fundamental, the moral right to bear arms is not fundamental.[9] According to LaFollette, "a fundamental right is a non-derivative right protecting a fundamental interest."[10] "Fundamental interests," he continues, "are integrally related to a person's chance of living a good life, whatever her particular interests, desires and beliefs happen to be."[11] LaFollette's example of a fundamental right is the right to freedom of expression: "living in a society that protects speech," he says, "creates an environment within which each of us can pursue our particular interests, goals, needs and development, whatever our interests happen to be."[12] On his account, fundamental interests are similar to what Rawls called primary goods—those things, such as liberty and self-respect, that any person needs regardless of her particular conception of the good. For LaFollette, therefore, the right to bear arms is not a fundamental right, for owning a gun is not a fundamental interest. Owning a gun is not vital to one's flourishing no matter what one's particular desires, interests, and beliefs.

Although not a fundamental right, the right to bear arms is, on LaFollette's account, a derivative right. Whereas a fundamental right protects an interest that all of us have independent of our particular interests, a derivative right protects a (legitimate) particular interest. Consuming alcohol, LaFollette asserts, is a (legitimate) particular interest that is protected, all things being equal, by a derivative right. Likewise, gun ownership is a (legitimate) particular interest that is protected, all things being equal, by a derivative right. (LaFollette calls rights that protect particular interests "derivative" because they derive from a general fundamental right of non-interference in the pursuit of one's legitimate particular interests.)

In LaFollette's sense, we have a fundamental interest in protecting ourselves from bodily and psychological harm. Regardless of the nature of our particular interests, our flourishing depends upon our being permitted to protect ourselves from such harm. It follows that we have a fundamental moral right to self-defense. Does it not follow, then, that we have a fundamental moral right to own a gun as a means to self-defense? LaFollette thinks not. He states, "[n]ot every means to a fundamental interest is a fundamental right. That would arguably make most actions protected by fundamental rights."[13] Wheeler, by contrast, thinks otherwise, because there are certain circumstances in which carrying a gun will be the only means of self-defense.

The dispute between Wheeler and LaFollette pivots on the philosophical significance of the claim that carrying a firearm is the only means for defending oneself in certain circumstances. (For the sake of argument let us grant the truth of this claim.) Wheeler seems to hold that if a course of action is the only way in which one can protect a fundamental interest, then that course of action specifies a fundamental right. LaFollette does not deny this claim. But he maintains that something's being the best means to protect a fundamental interest is not sufficient to make it a fundamental right. Thus, LaFollette would not accept Wheeler's argument for the fundamental status of the right to bear arms. That is, he would not agree that something's being the only means to secure a fundamental interest is sufficient to make it a fundamental right.

Two considerations weigh in favor of LaFollette's view. First, since owning a gun is a legitimate particular interest, people have a prima facie derivative right to own a gun. Hence, it does not follow from the fact that gun ownership is not a fundamental right that people will be likely to be deprived of their only means of self-defense in some circumstances. Derivative rights demand protection. Moreover, if in some cases carrying a gun were the only means of protecting oneself, then the protection of the derivative right to bear arms would be especially important. Restrictions on that right would warrant careful scrutiny.

15

Second, the general claim that that which happens to be the only means to securing a fundamental interest is thereby a fundamental right yields some very counter-intuitive results. Bizarre contingencies will result in some strange fundamental rights. If circumstances should make it that the only way in which I can preserve my fundamental interest in self-respect is by mildly embarrassing people at every opportunity, I will have a fundamental moral right to do so. If the only way in which I can exercise my fundamental moral right to worship as I please is by relatively painlessly sacrificing (non-endangered) animals, I will have a fundamental right to do so. And so on.

Thus, the right to bear arms is not a fundamental right in spite of our fundamental interest in protecting ourselves from harm, even if under some conditions carrying a gun may be the only way of protecting oneself. The nonfundamental status of the right to bear arms, however, does not preclude our limiting the restrictions upon that right. Ultimately, the legitimacy of regulations on gun ownership will, as Wheeler and LaFollette both state, depend on a variety of empirical factors concerning the risks and dangers associated with an armed citizenry.

Endnotes

1. Wheeler, Arms as Insurance, 13 *PUB. AFF. Q.* 111 (1999).
2. Id., at 111.
3. Id. at 117–18.
4. Id. at 111.
5. Id.
6. Id. at 113.
7. Wheeler, Gun Violence and Fundamental Rights, *PUB. AFF. Q.*, 19–24.
8. Id., at 19.
9. LaFollette, Gun Control, 110 *ETHICS* 264 (2000), summarized as Gun Control: The Issues, *ETHICS*, 17–18.
10. Id. at 264.
11. Id.
12. Id.
13. Id. at 266.

Questions for Discussion

1. What arguments do supporters of gun control make against the right to bear arms?
2. What do opponents of gun control say in defense of their stand?
3. What does Stark conclude about the gun control issue?

4. Are the arguments of the supporters and the opponents in Stark's essay fairly balanced against each other? Explain.

Questions for Writing

1. Is the right to bear arms a fundamental right—that is, an intangible—like liberty, the pursuit of happiness, and self-respect—that every person needs to flourish and be productive? Stark contends that "owning a gun is not vital to one's flourishing no matter what one's particular desires, interests, and beliefs." Assess the pros and cons of this statement in an essay.
2. What, if any, ethical issues arise from the right to bear arms? Write an informative essay in response to this question.

Laws and Civil Liberties in Cyberspace

KAREN JUDSON

In 1990, law enforcement officers hit hard at suspected crackers. In fourteen American cities in May 1990, Secret Service and police officers staged surprise raids, dubbed "Operation Sundevil." Armed with guns and search warrants, officers seized forty-two computers and 23,000 disks. They also shut down twenty-five electronic bulletin boards. The target of the roundup was a group of youthful crackers, many of them members of the Legion of Doom. They were suspected of trafficking in stolen credit-card numbers, telephone access codes, and other illegally obtained electronic information. At least one suspect, twenty-one-year-old Robert Chandler, later pleaded guilty in federal court in California to a felony possessing fifteen or more telephone access codes.[1] The raids did not result in scores of successful prosecutions, but they did put crackers on notice that law enforcement was serious about computer crime.

While not part of Operation Sundevil, a second raid in 1990 also made history. Two months before, on March 1, 1990, the Austin, Texas, offices of Steve Jackson Games were raided by the U.S. Secret Service. Apparently one of Jackson's employees was under investigation for hacker activities supposedly related to the *Phrack*/E911 incident. Agents had no evidence connecting the employee to his employer, however.

Although Jackson's games were marketed as books and were not sold on computer disks, the agents took computers, laser printers, and photocopy machines, as well as disks containing work in progress. When computers were seized, a bulletin board operated by the business was also shut down. No one was arrested or charged with any crime as a result of the raid on Steve Jackson Games. The business was seriously disrupted, however, and eventually half the staff was laid off.[2]

With the financial and legal help of the Electronic Frontier Foundation, a cyberliberties group formed in 1990, Jackson sued the United States Secret Service. In March 1993 a federal judge ruled in favor of Steve Jackson Games. He said that under the Privacy Protection Act of 1980, the publisher's work product had been illegally seized and held. (The Privacy Protection Act says that it is illegal for the government, while conducting a criminal investigation, to search for or seize "work product" related to books, newspapers, or other "public communication" without probable cause.)

5   The judge also ruled that Secret Service agents had violated the Electronic Communications Privacy Act by unlawfully reading, disclosing, and erasing computer messages on a bulletin board run by Steve Jackson Games. A year after the judgment, Jackson received $52,431 for lost profits and direct costs of the raid. The government also agreed to pay costs of the suit, at $252,405.[3]

After the 1990 raids, several constitutional questions were raised. Were the electronic bulletin boards shut down in the raids entitled to protection under the First Amendment in the same way as the words on a printed page? When computers and disks were seized, were citizens deprived of "life, liberty, or property, without due process of law," as prohibited by the Fifth Amendment?

Electronic privacy and security also emerged as critical issues. How can citizens protect their privacy when every telephone call, credit card charge, and cash-card transaction is recorded electronically? Who owns such information? What happens to property rights when documents can be digitally reproduced to look exactly like the original?

ENCRYPTION

One way to ensure privacy is to encrypt online data. Encryption uses a special chip or software that codes or scrambles computer transmissions so that others cannot read them. The coded data can only be unscrambled by a decode key. Encryption uses either secret keys or public keys. Secret key encryption uses a single decoding key shared by two communicating parties. Public key encryption uses a public key and a private key. The public key is known by everyone, but it cannot be modified. The private key is kept secret. Data encoded with the public key can be decoded only when the private key is supplied.

In 1977 the National Security Agency worked with IBM to create a secret key Data Encryption Standard (DES), which was adopted by the United States Department of Defense for use in coding online data. By 1998 DES had become the most widely used method of encrypting data to protect financial transactions, medical records, and other sensitive information. The key was judged so difficult to break that it was restricted by the United States government for exportation to other countries. The code was difficult to break without the private key, because there were 72 quadrillion or more possible keys that could be used. For each given message, the key was chosen at random. Both the sender and the receiver would have to know and use the same private key.

In a record-breaking feat in July 1998, John Gilmore, a civil liberties activist, and Paul Kocher, a cryptographer, cracked DES. They built a $250,000 computer (financed by the Electronic Frontier Foundation) that searched through 88 billion keys per second and in just fifty-six hours found the one that worked.[4]

In 1993 scientists at the U.S. National Security Agency invented a chip that they claimed could generate uncrackable codes. With computer crime on the rise, the government touted the "Clipper chip" as the answer to secure telecommunications. The catch, however, was that the government would have the key to decode data. This would let law enforcement officials monitor computer and telephone transmissions without the senders' knowledge. The Clipper chip had many critics, and when it was discovered that decoding keys did not always work, it was not adopted for widespread use.[5]

The debate continued over the security of the DES encryption system and the Clipper chip. In the meantime, others were developing alternate methods of making telecommunications more private. Here are two that were in common use in 1998:

- *Pretty Good Privacy (PGP):* A public key encryption code written by Paul Zimmerman in 1991. PGP was free, and by 1998 it was used by private citizens worldwide.
- *Digital Signature Standard (DSS):* Since documents created online cannot be signed by hand, codes were developed for

digital signatures. To identify and authenticate the signer, two codes were used. One code was used when the person "signed" the document; another was used to decode the "signature." DSS assured a receiver that the message was not a forgery, but it did not provide confidentiality of information.

THE STATE OF COMPUTER SECURITY

It is true that computer systems with excellent security are the least likely to be cracked. Yet, despite recent security product developments, some computer networks are becoming more, not less, vulnerable to outside attack:

"I know about 95 percent of [the vulnerabilities] I am going to find at a company before I even get there. I can steal a billion dollars from any [corporation] within a couple of hours," said Ira Winkler, president of the Information Security Advisory Group, a company that contracts to attack business systems to find security holes.[6]

15   "The average system out there uses out-of-the-box software . . . which has extremely poor quality, lack of patches, no security. And these systems are not well maintained or configured. Plus, there is now a wide array of automated hacking tools available. It is pretty much a no-brainer to get into these systems," said Eugene Spafford, director of the Cerias Center for Education in Research, Information Assurance and Security at Purdue University, West Lafayette, Indiana.[7]

"We try to see what we can do when we break into a system. Can we see secret data, can we fake e-mail from the CEO to all employees giving them a day off? Is anyone even aware we are breaking in? In many of the companies we break into, nobody even raises a red flag. In fact, we break in about 80 percent of the time," said Charles C. Palmer, manager of network security and cryptography at IBM's Watson Research Center. Palmer's group is paid by companies to find security lapses by breaking into their systems.[8]

PASSWORDS, BIOMETRICS, AND OTHER HIGH-TECH LOCKS

Passwords can be the first step toward locking out unauthorized computer users. Often they are the weakest link in the security chain, however, because they are too easy to guess. Obvious bad choices are the user's name, birth dates, nicknames, and other easily guessed personal facts.

The most secure passwords, security experts advise, are chosen from a set of random characters such as *(?SOV#! Passwords should never be posted in obvious places, such as near computer workstations or on bulletin boards, and they should be changed often.

Biometrics does not rely on passwords. Instead, it uses physical traits, such as fingerprints, voice prints, or blood vessel patterns in the eye, to identify the computer operator.

Other security measures include software created to detect security holes in a system, and firewalls. Firewalls are powerful Internet gateway computers that protect a network by filtering incoming and outgoing transactions. 20

Vigilant humans are vital to security. System administrators and users should pay close attention to the machine's behavior. Is an account being heavily used? Are there logged messages that someone is exceeding authorization? Is someone logging on who does not have proper authorization? Is someone assigned to read logs and note inconsistencies?

CYBERETHICS

As computer use (and misuse) has increased, ethics, or responsible use of systems, has become more important. Many organizations for computer professionals now have written codes of ethics that members are expected to follow. For example, the Association for Computing Machinery (ACM), the Institute of Electrical and Electronics Engineers (IEEE), the National Society of Professional Engineers (NSPE), the Data Processing Management Association (DPMA), and the International Federation for Information Processing (IFIP) all have professional codes of ethics. Societies in other countries that have written codes of ethics include the Hong Kong Computer Society, the Assistive Devices Industry Association of Canada, and the Australian Computer Society.

Many universities have also begun to deal with the ethics issue. For example, the University of Virginia has posted online an ethics statement for students. It poses these questions: What is sexual harassment over the Internet? Should misidentification, plagiarism, and misinformation be somehow limited or involve punishment? Can these problems be handled without infringing on the privacy of others? Is hacking always wrong? If a student breaks into a system, is he or she obligated to tell the company or institution that they are "crackable"? Should everyone be allotted the same amount of usage/bandwidth, or should it depend on need? Should everyone have the same access to research information? If not, what will determine "information haves" and "have-nots"? When is use of university computers inappropriate? For instance, could a student write a book using school facilities and keep all royalties? And should students play games with their computers, tying up "public" bandwidth in the process?[9]

Most experts claim that the answers to cyberethics questions lie in legal penalties for criminal abuses and in early education of computer users. According to Eugene Spafford, early access to computers does not help teach responsible use, unless young users have guidance. "Access to computers without tradition, without guidance, without understanding can lead some people into trouble."[10]

25   In 1998, IBM's Sarah Gordon noticed a disturbing trend while visiting a theme park.

> One attraction was geared for youngsters to experience computing. A video showed two students breaking away from their classmates on a school trip. They said, "Let's just sneak off and see what we can do." They broke into a locked computer room using a key card, broke into a network, and went through e-mail and personal documents. Then they came back to their group and told their classmates. When the teacher asked them how they had learned all that information, a little girl winked at the camera and said, "It's all out there; it's part of the network." I thought what a terrible message to send to thousands of kids a day. . . . These mixed messages sent to kids as they are learning to interact with computer technologies can be harmful. Students can forget that there are people on the other end of those modems and computers.[11]

GUIDELINES FOR ETHICAL COMPUTING

By following a few simple guidelines, computer users can ensure their own rights to privacy, as well as those of others. The Computer Ethics Institute says never use a computer to:

- harm other people;
- interfere with the computer work of others;
- snoop around in the computer files of others;
- steal;
- issue false statements;
- copy or use proprietary software without paying for it;

- use the computer resources of others without their authorization or without proper compensation;
- steal the intellectual products of others.

When using a computer:

- think about the social consequences of the programs you write or the systems you design; and
- find ways to use the machine that ensure consideration and respect for others.[12]

Like locks on houses, security measures can keep out unwanted computer intruders. But, as is true for all crime prevention, the best barrier to computer crime will always be educated, responsible users.

Endnotes

1. Michael Alexander, "Operation Sundevil Nabs First Suspect," *Computerworld*, February 17, 1992, p. 15.
2. Steve Jackson, "The Top Ten Media Errors About the SJ Games Raid," Electronic Frontier Foundation, February 12, 1992, <http://www.eff.org/pub.Legal/Intellectual_property/Legal/Cases/SJG/media_errors.sjg> (July 18, 1998).
3. Press Release: "Secret Service Pays Damages to Steve Jackson Games," Electronic Frontier Foundation, May 5, 1994, <http://www.eff.org/pub/Legal/Intellectual_property/Legal/Cases/SJG/SS_pays_sjg.announce> (March 10, 1999).
4. John Schwartz, "One High-End PC Cracks Data-Scrambling System," *Washington Post*, July 18, 1998, p. A09.
5. Sharon Begley with Melinda Liu, "Foiling the Clipper Chip," *Newsweek*, June 13, 1994, pp. 60, 62.
6. Tim Wilson, "Profits Embolden Hackers," *TechWeb*, March 23, 1998, <http://www.techweb.com/wire/story/TWB19980323S0013> (March 10, 1999).
7. Eugene Spafford interview with author, May 7, 1991.
8. Charles C. Palmer interview with author, September 8, 1998.
9. "Ethics and the Internet," <http://minerva.acc.virginia.edu/~usem171/feb22/main.html> (September 15, 1998).
10. Eugene Spafford interview.
11. Sarah Gordon interview with author, September 8, 1998.
12. Computer Ethics Institute, "The Ten Commandments of Computer Ethics," December 4, 1997, <http://www.cpsr.org/program/ethics/cei.html> (March 10, 1999).

Questions for Discussion

1. What is the Privacy Protection Act of 1980?
2. Why did the National Security Agency partner with IBM in 1977 to develop the Data Encryption Standard (DES)?
3. What are cyberethics?
4. Along with the legislation that has been passed to monitor the appropriate use of technology, the Computer Ethics Institute has developed a list of user-friendly guidelines. What are they?

Questions for Writing

1. Should there be stricter federal laws for cyberspace crimes? Write a persuasive essay on this topic.
2. Should there be laws that regulate all activities in cyberspace, or would doing so infringe upon your civil liberties? Analyze this topic in an essay.

All the Court's a Stage, and All the Lawyers Players: Leading and Misleading the Jury

RICHARD ZITRIN AND CAROL M. LANGFORD

Abraham Dennison is one of the most successful trial lawyers in Port City. McCabe & Dennison has eighteen lawyers, who handle a wide range of litigation for everyone from wealthy divorce clients and executives charged with white-collar crimes to large corporations that need defending in messy environmental cleanup cases or lawsuits over injuries caused by defective products. Many of Dennison's own clients are among the social elite of town, and Dennison himself is the president of the local country club. The club serves him well for happy-hour rainmaking, or business development, as well as for playing $100 Nassaus on the city's most exclusive course.

Although Dennison is smoother than silk out of the courtroom, in court he takes on a bumbling, aw-shucks persona. He explains to clients and friends that this creates juror sympathy by giving jurors the impression he's just a "hick from the sticks." He wears off-the-rack clothes instead of the Italian designer suits he wears to the symphony. He rarely objects without hesitating, starting over, and making a little speech, which he privately calls "my Jimmy Stewart method." Instead of "Objection, irrelevant," Dennison is inclined to say "I'm sorry, Your Honor, but I don't under . . . I can't put my finger on why . . . I just can't figure out why that question has anything to do with this case." Dennison's persona has earned from his courthouse colleagues the sarcastic sobriquet "Honest Abe."

Dennison also tries to mask the sophistication of his clients, insisting that they too dress down in court by wearing discount-store clothes rather than the expensive outfits they favor. He's even bought subway and bus passes for clients and then placed them conspicuously in his clients' pockets or handbags.

In a rare criminal case, Dennison was hired by a wealthy friend to represent his son, who had been accused of rape. Dennison knew that the jury would be acutely aware of the cross-racial nature of the alleged assault—Dennison's client was white, the alleged victim Chinese-American. In order to defuse this, Dennison recruited an attractive Chinese-American woman from his trial practice class at the local law school to act as his law clerk during the trial. He emphasized to her the importance of being friendly to the defendant during the course of the trial—"complete," as he put it, "with touching."

Dennison tells his young associates that one of the most important tricks of the trade is "selecting a biased jury. Let's get rid of the notion right now that you want a fair and unbiased jury in every case. Nonsense! You want a jury biased in favor of your client. That wins cases." In one recent case Dennison defended two wealthy immigrants from Mexico City in a breach-of-contract action brought by a real estate sales company. He did his best to keep Mexican-Americans off the jury: "To win, we needed to keep alive in the minds of the jurors the stereotype of the poor Mexican farm worker. We didn't want to risk having anyone on the jury who could dispel the stereotype."

Dennison justifies these practices as "trial tactics" necessary to ensure winning verdicts. "My clients don't pay me big money to lose," Dennison says. "They're not here to be bled dry by greedy lawyers. The best defense is a good offense, especially if it's subtle enough to convey my message to the jury without me saying a word. After all," he reasons, "a trial is nothing if not theater, and I've always enjoyed good theater."

Only a tiny percentage of cases go to trial, but it's during those trials that people give lawyers their closest scrutiny. Yet almost all trial lawyers will admit, at least in their more candid moments, that their job is not presenting the truth in any objective or absolute sense, but their client's version of it. This, they will tell you, is what the adversary system is all about: "spinning" the truth and only then letting the jury decide.

In one sense, the courtroom during trial is the great equalizer—the ultimate level battlefield. All the money paid for pretrial discovery and investigation, all the parties' wealth, or the lack of it, may not be worth a damn in the midst of battle. There, lawyers fight on their own, using their abilities to think, talk, and act quickly on their feet. The great trial lawyer has two objectives: to control the courtroom as a director controls a movie set, and to play the starring role as an actor who can also improvise. Usually trial techniques are designed to make the lawyer more persuasive about the facts of the case, the hard evidence. But sometimes, like the snake oil salesmen of long ago, lawyers like Abe Dennison put on a show for jurors in an attempt to distract them from the real issues.

It's impossible to take the theater completely out of the courtroom. Anyone who's ever watched *Perry Mason, L.A. Law,* or *The Practice*—or even the O.J. Simpson, William Kennedy Smith, or Lorena Bobbitt trials on Court TV—expects lawyers to do more than just provide a dry recitation of the facts. Indeed, after Smith was acquitted in his 1991 Florida rape trial, the *Orlando Sentinel Tribune* gave out "Oscars," including one to the "robotic" prosecutor Moira Lasch for her performance, in which she not only read her questions verbatim but "displayed precious little passion." Other awards included "Best Actor" (a tie between Smith and the alleged victim), and even "Best Costume," won again by Smith, the wealthy Kennedy scion who was dressed like a "rejected model from a discount-store catalog." Had a "Best Director" award been given, defense attorney Roy Black undoubtedly would have won. "As TV movies go," concluded reporter Michael Blumfield, "it was an awfully good one. I can't wait for the book."

10   As actors, the best trial lawyers all recognize that a little bit of humanity can be a great asset in the courtroom. If Abe Dennison thinks that adopting an aw-shucks demeanor will help him relate to the jury, who's to say he can't? John O'Quinn, the breast implant litigator whom insurance companies love to hate, cultivates a "down-home" presence in trial in a conscious effort to appeal to jurors. "He could probably say 'polydimethyl siloxane' [the main ingredient in implants] in his sleep," Dow Chemical lawyer Richard Josephson told *Forbes* magazine, "but in the courtroom he kept calling it 'that stuff.' " This role playing tends to set its

own limits: how far a lawyer can go without alienating the jury with something that rings false. When the best trial lawyers teach their techniques to others, one of the points they constantly emphasize is that "you've got to be yourself."

Many trial counsel agree that clothes makes the lawyer, and some agree that, like Abe Dennison, lawyers should avoid fancy dress. "If the unstated accusation is that your client is a rich pig," attorney Jack S. Hoffinger told the *New York Times,* "do you as a lawyer want to come in and look like a rich lawyer?" Post-trial conversations with jurors often reveal that they not only pay close attention to what the lawyers wear, right down to suit and tie coordination, but talk about it amongst themselves, since they are admonished by the judge *not* to talk about the case. Women's attire especially comes in for close scrutiny. When Marcia Clark wore a short red suit one day at the Simpson trial, the suit's color and skirt length got more play in the media than the day's testimony.

Those who teach trial techniques—psychologists, sociologists, and yes, acting coaches, as well as lawyers—often emphasize another point: the art of storytelling. Lawyers learn how to create a clear "image" of the case. They open their arguments with that image—"This is a tale of greed" or "This is the story of a woman who had no choice"—not unlike the sound-bite arguments we hear on *The Practice.* The more graphic the image, the better. Famed New York law professor Irving Younger, who traveled the country teaching the "Ten Commandments of Cross-Examination," explained "demonstrative evidence" this way: "If your client loses a leg in an accident, don't tell the jury about it. Get the leg! And when the time comes, bring it to court and *show them the leg!*"

It's no coincidence that when trial lawyers talk about their triumphs, their tales are called "war stories." Both words say volumes about how litigators think. Often, lawyers describe the tricks they've used as if they're trophies on display. Roger Dodd can hardly contain his pride telling a war story whose point is another lesson often taught budding trial attorneys: how to create an atmosphere or mood—even an aroma—in the courtroom.

Dodd was defending a woman who had killed a man in a barroom fight in full view of other patrons. She plunged a steak knife into the man's chest with enough force to bend the knife 45 degrees. Dodd says he managed to get admitted into evidence a tape of the rap song that was playing on the jukebox, the neon Michelob beer sign that provided the only lighting, and even an open can of beer to convey the stale smell of the bar. In closing argument, Dodd then re-created the barroom as closely as he could in the courtroom. He turned on the Michelob sign and played the rap song tape. He placed the stale can of beer on the jury rail. He told the jury that it was beyond his control to darken the room or to "raise the temperature in this room to the temperature [my client] had felt for two weeks." Then he asked to jurors to close their eyes to simulate darkness.

15   Dodd reports gleefully that his client was acquitted. "Our closing was a direct appeal to the jury's emotions," he says. "We were admonished [by the judge] to be ashamed of ourselves." While Dodd's glee at putting one over on the jury may not be appreciated by many, few judges would do more than scold him.

At least Dodd tied his techniques to the evidence in the case. The irony is that many of the most effective techniques of trial lawyers are those that *don't* directly relate to the facts of the case. The O.J. Simpson murder trial brought us a chief prosecutor who wore an angel pin to signify solidarity with the family of one of the victims, and a defense lawyer who "sanitized" Simpson's home before a jury visit by replacing pictures of his girlfriend with portraits of Simpson's mother. But diverting the jury's attention away from the evidence is hardly new.

This story is attributed to Clarence Darrow: Back in the early part of this century, when people smoked freely in the courtroom, Darrow was sitting at counsel table during the prosecutor's closing argument. He lit a big Havana cigar and started smoking it. As the DA's argument progressed, the cigar ash grew longer and longer. Darrow had placed a straight wire down the center of the cigar, which kept the ash attached. As the prosecutor argued on, the jury paid less and less attention to him and more to whether the cigar ash would fall. The defendant was ultimately acquitted.

It is said that famed Chicago insurance defense lawyer Max Wildman once hired an attractive young woman to sit behind the plaintiff in a case concerning the wrongful death of the plaintiff's wife. The woman's job was to make friendly small talk with the plaintiff during court recesses; the idea was that the jury would observe the plaintiff's "new relationship" and lose sympathy for his loss.

Trial lawyers are always looking for an edge, an angle, with the jury. There are almost as many examples as there are lawyers who try cases. Some efforts seem more desperate, or even silly, than useful, but all are consistent with another lesson repeated by those who teach trial techniques: "Everything that happens in the courtroom counts; you never know what will have an effect on the jury." A few examples:

- One young male lawyer removed his wedding ring during trial and casually flirted from a distance with the women on the jury. According to a colleague, the technique appeared to work, at least to the extent that jurors found him "cute."
- A California lawyer saw a juror he thought was the likely foreman reading the *New York Times* each day during recesses. Thinking that bringing in his own copy of the newspaper was too obvious, the lawyer made sure that he carried needed items into court in the *Times's* familiar blue plastic home delivery bag, complete with distinctive logo. The juror became foreman and the lawyer won the case. But the lawyer sheepishly admits that he has no idea whether the juror even noticed the bag.
- Some lawyers wheel boxes of papers into court each day of trial to send a message to jurors that they have more evidence than can possibly be explained away. They make a display by sifting through mountains of documents to pull out the few pieces of paper that actually have relevance.

Several of Abe Dennison's tactics are similar. Dressing his   20 clients at the Gap or JCPenney instead of the usual fashion boutiques may not descend to the same level as Wildman's hiring an attractive "friend," but in its own way it's just as fake. Planting a bus pass on a client who actually drives a Mercedes creates a deceit; is it less false if Dennison convinces his clients to actually ride the bus for the duration of the trial? Just as important, can—or should—these deceits be prevented if the impressions they leave don't directly relate to the admissible evidence in the case?

In most states lawyers must follow ethics rules, usually based on language written by the American Bar Association, designed to protect the sanctity of trials. These rules say that a lawyer may not "falsify evidence" or help a witness testify falsely, present "material evidence" the lawyer knows is false, or "make a false statement of material fact." But these rules, emphasizing the *legal* concepts of "evidence" and "materiality," or what most of us call relevance, don't directly address the collateral deceits discussed here.

What makes Honest Abe's trial tactics—and others we've described—difficult to prevent under the black-letter ethics rules is that these attempts to sway the jury are *indirect*. Dennison is not attempting actively to misrepresent relevant facts or evidence in his cases, but rather is using back-door techniques to raise subtle issues that are technically irrelevant but which might have a substantial effect on the jury. While lawyers are not allowed to talk with jurors during a trial, other than in the course of presenting evidence or arguing the case, Dennison's techniques allow him to communicate without talking.

The practical reality is that few lawyers are likely to be disciplined for any of these tactics, except for the kind of informal admonishment received by Roger Dodd. Sanctions for unethical behavior won't be meted out if there are no clear ethics rules. One lawyer's "parlor trick" is another's innovative trial technique. People may question the propriety of Abe Dennison's dressing down his clients or making it look as though they ride the bus. But few would take issue with the criminal defense lawyer who gives an incarcerated client a nice shirt and pants to wear at trial instead of an orange jumpsuit that says COUNTY JAIL—a strategy approved by the Supreme Court. Yet without clear ethics standards, the actions of both lawyers will be treated the same.

While law practice is much more closely regulated than it was fifty years ago, trial conduct has been affected less than most other areas of law. Given vague ethics standards, the principal formal regulation comes from the way individual judges run their courtrooms. But a more effective check on the behavior of lawyers is that juries will rebel against tactics that ring false. Smart lawyers know this; they'll try their tricks but be careful not to patronize or underestimate their juries. In the sometimes free-for-all theater of the courtroom, we need the intelligence and common sense of juries more than ever.

25   There is no epilogue to the story of Abe Dennison. He will not be disciplined by the bar or even brought up on charges. A judge is likely simply to warn him, and even more likely to do nothing. His most questionable strategy—hiring the Chinese-American law student—is the one least likely to be sanctioned. So how much Abe has gotten away with will depend on how the jury reacts. And in the long run, the jury's response will determine how much Abe learns to put the brakes on his trial games.

Questions for Discussion

1. According to Richard Zitrin and Carol Langford, "the great trial lawyer has two objectives: to control the courtroom as a director controls a movie set, and to play the starring role as an actor who can also improvise." What ethical concern permeates this notion?
2. Why do trial attorneys look for every "angle" or "edge" to move the jury? What examples do the authors use to illustrate this point?

3. What are the ethics rules lawyers must follow? Which association established these rules?
4. What happened in the case of Abraham Dennison? Why is Dennison's courtroom practice ethically questionable?

Questions for Writing

1. Zitrin and Langford declare, "Almost all trial lawyers will admit, at least in their more candid moments, that their job is not presenting the truth in any objective or absolute sense, but their client's version of it." In an essay, analyze this statement about the role of ethics in the courtroom.
2. The authors contend that lawyers must be good storytellers and actors. With the advent of court programs on daily television, along with the Court TV network, the public is inundated with real-life TV court drama. Does the public, as well as the media themselves, appear to applaud the courtroom tactics of trial attorneys? Analyze this question in an essay.

Student Essay

A Profession of Love

CHRISTOPHER JOHN ALEXIS

Have you ever wondered what would happen to mankind if we were allowed to let loose and run wild? Would the evil inclinations of the flesh take over and change us into sadistic savages? A world without rules or some form of structure is doomed, as is a structured society with perverted legislation.

A standard must be raised in our governmental system. Too long have the beggared hearts of starved humanity been crushed under the rawhide whip of an unjust and perverted judicial system. Someone must reach out to humanity and let them know that honesty and integrity are not archaic words used by eccentric and unrealistic people. This someone is the advocate or lawyer. The job of the advocate according to Merriam-Webster's dictionary is to plead the cause of another. I am called to be a lawyer. I have not chosen the profession, but the profession has chosen me.

I first recognized my call to become a lawyer when it came from my own heart as my family was rent in two, due to the divorce of my parents granted by the courts. The courts did not seek to offer counseling to my parents, but they sought to separate them, realizing that there is no money to be gained through reconciliation.

This cry grew louder after my cousin was gunned down on a street corner in Philadelphia, Pennsylvania. Since he was an African-American male, the courts thought that he was merely expendable. Due process was not sought, and the investigation was botched, even though many witnesses testified to the identity of the killer. These faulty acts led to the eventual release of a murderer.

5   As an African-American male, I know that the odds are not in my favor. Statistics prove over and over again that there is discrimination throughout the American judicial system at the Federal, State, and local levels. For instance, "According to a 2000 study by Human Rights Watch, African Americans comprise 62 percent of the drug offenders admitted to state prisons. . . . Nationwide, black men are sent to state prisons on drug charges at 13 times the rate of white men" (Muwakkil). The general belief of the status quo is that most African Americans are more prone to the baser habits and levels of life, such as poverty, drugs, and violence; however, this is a fallacy.

The truth of the matter is that many African Americans are sought out because of age-old stereotypes and deeply imbedded racism. These unjust sentiments will have a cop pull over a Black man in an expensive car because of the erroneous thought process that says, "How can a Black man afford such a nice car?" These same sentiments give less jail time to power[ful] cocaine offenders, who are mostly White, and more jail time to crack cocaine offenders, who are mostly Black.

As a lawyer, my moral obligation is to even the odds and give a voice to the voiceless, to defend the helpless and the innocent and to seek fair justice and rehabilitation for those who have committed crimes. I am committed to fight against injustice anywhere just as Rev. Dr. Martin Luther King, Jr., was. Dr. King reminds us that "injustice anywhere is a threat to justice everywhere." As a lawyer, I have a platform to fight injustice for all people—Red, Yellow, Black and White.

Not only will I show concern through hard work and preparation as a lawyer, but I intend to show concern for my clients through visiting them in prison, defending them fairly in a court of law, and helping them to get on their feet by offering them affordable housing and work after their release. I will seek to be an ear that they can bend and a counsel in whom they can confide. But I won't stop there; I will seek to change the very legislative system that caters to a privileged class and thereby bring about equal treatment for all people.

Love is the only answer, and only through the power of love and concern will people who have fallen into the grip of murder, stealing, drug abuse, and [other] such habits ever get free. Love can also bring about justice for all. As an attorney, I want to be a catalyst of love, one who brings about a positive change in those who need it the most. After all, laws can't legislate love, but people can legislate love.

Works Cited

King, Martin L., "Letter from a Birmingham Jail." *The Martin Luther King, Jr., Papers.* Stanford U. ed. Clayborne Carson, 23 February 2003. www.stanford .edu/group/King.

Muwakkil, Salim. "Why is Prison Becoming the Norm for Black Males?" *AlterNet.* 20 Feb. 2003 http://www.alternet.org/story.html?StoryID=14077.

Questions for Discussion

1. What does the racial profiling of some young African American males (and some young Latino males) communicate about the ethics of the criminal justice system in America?
2. Discuss the "unjust sentiments" that Alexis mentions in his essay. How might ethics change this unjust system and dispel inaccurate beliefs? Relate your answer to ethics in the criminal justice system, as well as in government policy.
3. Explain Dr. Martin Luther King, Jr.'s statement, "Injustice anywhere is a threat to justice everywhere." Discuss this quotation in reference to the following:
   * education
   * religion
   * democracy and government policies
   * economics
4. According to Alexis, what role should love play in bringing about changes within the individual in particular and society in general? Do you agree or disagree? Explain.

Questions for Writing

1. Is it possible for a lawyer who exhibits unethical behavior to practice law competently and fairly in and out of the courtroom? Defend your answer in a persuasive essay.
2. Do you agree or disagree with Christopher Alexis's argument that the American justice system is plagued by racism? Write a synthetic essay on this topic. Consult two to four sources in defense of your thesis.

Questions for Making Connections Within the Chapter

1. Should Americans have the right to carry arms and surf the Internet without governmental interference? Why or why not? Consider the views of Judson and Stark.
2. Laws are designed to protect and defend victims of crimes and prosecute criminal offenders. What views do Alexis and Olson hold on the issue of legal ethics, defendants, and plaintiffs?
3. What legal ethics do Olson and Zitrin and Langford discuss in their respective articles?

4. Under what circumstances, if any, would one be justified in compromising one's ethics? Consider the issues discussed by the authors in this chapter as you respond to this question.

CHAPTER 4

Ethics and Business

Oh! My fortunes have
Corrupted honest men!

William Shakespeare, *Antony and Cleopatra*

The importance of ethics resounds within corporate hallways and throughout the business world, as is revealed in this chapter. Indeed, corporate immorality corrupts executives and business leaders as well as the public. With corporate scandals like Enron on the rise, consumer confidence is on the decline in America, which in turn affects stock prices and retail sales. In short, when giant financial tycoons go belly up, so does the economy. Some of the writers in this chapter call for a reexamination of business ethics at the corporate level. Others call attention to examples of poor business ethics and the consequences thereof.

In the first essay, Matthew Grimm examines the ethics of marketing to children. He criticizes advertising campaigns that have influenced a generation of young people who are grossly overweight. He cites a study by the Centers for Disease Control showing that the "obesity rates in children, up to 15.6% in 2002 from 6.1% in 1974, stands at 'epidemic' proportions." Much of this problem has been attributed to increased sales to children of "candy, fast food, fatty snacks, and sugary sodas."

In their article Bruce Frohnen and Leo Clarke address the increased number of corporate scandals in America. They suggest that businesspeople's actions affect not only their own fates but also the public's well-being. They argue that laws alone cannot correct this moral dilemma and that businesspeople must change their behavior and their way of thinking about greed-driven, unethical situations so that they can make morally and ethically sound choices for the betterment of themselves as well as the public.

Jeffery L. Seglin in his article raises questions about business, law, and ethics. He claims that just because a business decision is legal does not mean that it is based on ethics. He examines the ethics of businesses' bankruptcy practices. "The number of businesses hiding behind bankruptcy laws rather than repaying their debts is endemic," Seglin contends.

To help businesses avoid the ethical traps discussed in this chapter, John R. Boatright offers a number of pointers for ethical success in international business. He advises companies not to use double standards: "U.S. corporations ought to observe domestic law and a single code of conduct in their dealings everywhere." Boatright also urges businesses to remember the simple rule "When in Rome do as the Romans." American companies doing business abroad should, except in certain cases, respect the local customs "where local conditions require that corporations engage in certain practices as a condition of doing business."

Finally, Blair Masching argues that success in the business world depends on three marketing keys: integrity, tithing, and debt minimization. Masching argues that marketing professionals can reach the height of success when they make decisions with integrity, donate generously to charities, and pay off debts. Marketing professionals, who are in the position to influence others, should use these three principles in day-to-day operations to earn the respect and trust of consumers.

After reviewing these topics, you must decide how important ethics is to the overall success of any business. Can a business be successful without ethics? The topics in this chapter are diverse and offer much for discussion.

Is Marketing to Kids Ethical?

MATTHEW GRIMM

Extra pounds are weighing down American kids in more than just dodgeball. Ever-increasing obesity rates among children mired the overall state of U.S. youth in 2002, sending it 15 points lower than it was in 1975 as measured by Duke University's Child-Welfare Index (CWI), an aggregate of nearly three dozen factors such as crime, safety, community and family environments, as well as suicide rates. The latest index, released two weeks ago by the sponsoring Foundation for Child Development, corroborates last year's alarm by the Centers for Disease Control (CDC) that obesity rates in children, up to 15.6% in 2002 from 6.1% in 1974, stands at "epidemic" proportions.

Those kinds of numbers read starkly in the most advanced consumer society in the world. In consumer business echelons, they hit like a Surgeon General's warning, drawing widespread public scrutiny to the fusillade of images and messages daily influencing the behavior of American youth—specifically those of candy, fast food, fatty snacks and sugary sodas. Such products, not to mention videogame violence, in-school promotional activities—indeed the very notion of selling stuff to soft-headed, non-discerning neophytes—all these raise the dreaded specter of government intervention in the marketplace and, thus, must be discussed part-and-parcel with nearly every marketing program targeting kids, youth marketing professionals say. A prescient new study of their corner of the marketing world by Harris Interactive, obtained exclusively by Brandweek, shows a remarkable degree of candor and critical examination of their own work. And yet, it also reveals no small measure of conflicted ambivalence.

Notably, the overwhelming majority of respondents agreed that marketers today are going overboard in pursuit of kids' dollars and minds—and feel regulation imminent because of it—and yet precious few say that their own employer ever crosses any ethical lines. That chasm could prove problematic, says John Geraci, vice president of youth and education research at Harris, based in Rochester, N.Y.

"That sort of mentality tends to lead to inaction, and these are not issues that are going away," Geraci says. "We can see that their heads aren't in the sand, but they really need to figure out where they should be in this discourse, to take ownership of the problem, or they risk being vilified. Like with the obesity issue—there are many contributing factors to overweight children, but among those are the activities of food marketers. That can make them an easy target for parents and activists, and if you don't take an active role in that dialogue, and do something positive for this group, you risk becoming the next tobacco companies."

Marketers have devoted exponentially increasing resources to young people over the last 20 years, not just for their own consumer spending power. The notion of the "latchkey kid," one given disproportionate time alone and decision making power in two-working-parent households, first cropped up to explain the

5

market savvy (or resistance) of Generation X. With current Gen Y–designated youth, it became a standardized target zone for marketers, who saw chances to emblazon their brands in kids' habitue earlier in life, as well as take advantage of their latchkey access to family-wide consumption decisions.

"Kids are more involved today in a lot of their family purchase decisions," says Debbie Solomon, senior partner and group research director at MindShare, the Chicago-based media unit of WPP, and also the chair of the Advertising Research Foundation's Youth Research council. "Their influence has always been primary in food purchases, but now it extends to things like cars, vacations, electronics. And every year you see new categories, new products, new advertising specifically interested in this market, and there's only so much ad availability."

HAVE MARKETERS GONE TOO FAR?

With the cable explosion, kid-targeted ads proliferated in proportion to kid-targeted programming, from after-school blocks to full networks, then went well beyond it, to in-school vending contracts and even lesson-plan materials that incorporated brands. And when not marketing open-ended toy/merchandise juggernauts like Pokémon, a great majority of the expenditures went to hawking stuff with health consequences attached. One Department of Agriculture study calculated that 95% of the 10,000 food commercials children see each year pitch high-fat, high-sugar products.

Now, however, even those involved in "the trade" evince some wariness of the sheer volume of it, according to the Harris study, conducted in February among 878 professionals from youth marketing and research agencies, educational and non-profit institutions, and traditional ad and PR firms. Certainly, an auspicious list of major food and beverage corporations have recently shifted some gears—or at least said they would—in distribution and product development. Coca-Cola is expelling its sodas from schools, while Kraft and Pepperidge Farm are committing themselves to products freer of the dietary demon trans-fatty acids.

The question is, will such concerns, and such steps, spur actions and products that meaningfully alter the landscape and make for a healthier, more contented collective American childhood? And popping out amid the report's raft of data is a series of curious disconnects that likely will need to be addressed before marketers can, as it were, heal thyselves—and preempt those with designs on doing it for them.

As one respondent put it: "Our industry needs to be much less defensive or we invite regulation. Too often we put our own business needs ahead of the needs of children and the two don't need to be exclusive."

From the get-go, Harris discovered some distinctive differences in purviews, as comparing its marketer sample to its ongoing research of the youth they woo. For example, 51% more of the professional marketers perceive today's kids as "savvy consumers" than do the kids themselves (per a concurrent Harris YouthQuery survey of 643 teens), and 39% more see the target as "powerful" consumers. Meanwhile, . . . teens see themselves as "rebellious," "angry," "depressed" and "distrustful of adults" at far greater rates, measures that do not necessarily make for the discerning, mature or receptive consumer that marketers would prefer.

"Youth marketers' first reaction is to define kids by their characteristics as consumers," Geraci says. "And kids define themselves as kids first."

While, naturally, a different POV is to be expected between developed, adult professionals and, simply, kids, this sharp distinction proves salient to how, when and where marketers approach this troubled cohort and what they think appropriate in doing so. This speaks to the real crux of the youth marketing conundrum: at what point in their development can children really decipher and discern the numerous messages coming at them? More succinctly, at what point can one, in good conscience, consider them appropriate "consumers"?

HOW YOUNG IS TOO YOUNG WHEN REACHING OUT TO KIDS?

There seems to be some discrepancy in marketing executives' perceptions as to when it's OK to start advertising to kids and when, in fact, they can critically appraise these actions as "selling" versus, say, truth or unquestioned commands to action. Asked at what age it is "appropriate to begin marketing to children," the average of all responses was age 7. By comparison, asked when young people can "view advertising critically," the average response jumps to 9.1, whereas the marketers thought kids could begin distinguishing between "fantasy and reality in media and advertising" at 9.3. The average response as to when "most young people can make intelligent choices as consumers" jumps again to age 11.7, closer to accepted estimates in M.D./psych circles.

15   Juxtaposed to those numbers, we see some critical reflection emerging in the concerns of these professionals. A full 91% of respondents say that their colleagues are winging in under that radar, marketing to kids "in ways they don't even notice;" 72% say companies (in general) put pressure on kids to "grow up faster than they should;" 61% say advertising begins at too young an age; and a not-overwhelming, but still eye-opening, 58% say there is too much marketing directed at children.

A curious plurality, 35%, consider the general ethical and moral standards in the industry "lower than in the past," versus 40% who think these about the same.

Here, however, the grass starts to look greener on one's own side of the fence. As a sharp contrast, 67% of respondents say their respective employers maintain higher ethical standards than other organizations in the field. Only 2% say their company rates lower, 91% say their company "treats young people with respect," and 78% say their company "plays a positive role in the lives of children." Most see their companies actively addressing the industry's overall concerns, with 84% saying that people at their company can "openly" discuss ethical issues regarding marketing to kids. And yet, with a minor tweak on that question, only 66% said they "have never been placed in a position where I feel my personal ethics have been compromised." That innocuous 18-point gap may speak volumes to this profound us-vs.-peers juxtaposition.

YIELD AHEAD: MARKETING IN SCHOOLS RAISES SOME CONFLICTS

"There's lot of internal schizophrenia in the industry right now," says survey respondent Wynne Tyree, VP/director of kid insights at Just Kid Inc., a Stamford, Conn., product development and research firm. "We're good people, citizens of the community, we're parents, we're members of school boards, we see the obesity trends and recognize there are societal problems around us. And, at the same time, we love marketing, we believe in what we do and doing the best for our clients, making them more money, which makes us more money. And we're sort of weighing if and where those things contradict each other. We're always looking for the opportunity to make a difference, but we're also people who might in our personal lives do things differently than we sometimes might have to do professionally."

Some ambivalence crops up, as well, on the always-contentious topic of marketing in schools. Few, in this survey or in the general public, would dispute the financial crisis that currently wracks the public school system. The business community has long couched its moves towards the classroom—and cafeteria—as wholly benign attempts to make up where federal or state funding has fallen woefully short, to help pay for books, uniforms, etc. In fact, of the Harris respondents, 64% said that reaching children in schools was "not at all" or "not very" important to them, and in a list of different kinds of school-related marketing/sponsorship activities, the only ones they give majorities of approval to are those designed to help a school's purchasing power. Healthy majorities, meanwhile, deem "inappropriate" such endeavors as advertising on school-book covers, lesson-plan product-placement, and vending snacks and sodas.

Curiously, 47% agree that "schools should be a protected   20
area, and we should not be advertising to children on school grounds," while, at the same time, 74% expect to see more advertising there in the future. MindShare's Solomon, however, isn't among the latter. "There's been a lot of backlash around it," she says. "I haven't seen anybody for a long time try to sell space on cafeteria tray liners. Some of the more frivolous efforts just aren't happening. If [marketers] are going to do something in school these days, it's got to be quality, worthwhile; it has to supply financial aid to schools, either by giving them things they can't afford, or getting them the money to get those things."

Her colleagues in the Harris sample agree, 73% thinking that advertising revenues help "pay for things schools need," and 61% agreeing that "without corporate participation, important school programs would be cut." Still, the pros are split as to the ultimate impact of in-school marketing: asked whether "the benefits schools receive from from in-school marketing activities far outweigh the negatives," 38% agree, 35% disagree and the rest said they don't know.

Survey respondent Dan Acuff, president of Youth Marketing Systems Consulting, Encino, Calif., is similarly divided. "School should be a sanctuary," says Acuff, a Ph.D. currently working on a new book tentatively titled, Kidnapped: How Irresponsible Marketers Are Stealing the Minds of Our Children. "Certainly, marketers can be a source of additional money for schools, and they need it, but it can get out of hand. The best solution is probably education itself, the trade-off being, 'OK, we've got [ad-emblazoned] book covers on campus, let's make that part of the curriculum.' If you're going to let someone market to a 13-year-old, make sure it's one who is discerning about this message on a book cover and those sponsored sports events, and these things aren't going to slip by him unconsciously. This is all supposed to be about choice. You don't get choice without awareness and awareness comes with education." (Indeed, some schools have turned to marketers such as Dole Foods to initiate branded nutrition programs; see *Brandweek,* March 10, 2003.)

That, however, may fly in the face of the more cynical point of marketing to kids: getting them while they're young is easier than when they've matured and built psychological barriers.

On the issue of child obesity, while 97% of youth-oriented professionals feel that youth obesity is at least a "somewhat important" public health issue (with 50% deeming it "extremely important"), a full 68% are reticent to blame food companies as the "primary" factor in the issue, and 69% said "health and well-being" should be a matter of personal responsibility. Assigning such responsibility becomes problematic, however, when advertising begins years before one's capacity for critical thought.

A CALL TO ACTION FOR MARKETERS: MAKE IT HEALTHY FOR A CHANGE

25   This gets back to the quick of the argument; that is, given the flurry of "calls to action" kids receive, can they truly distinguish the truth of the world from the truth of chocolatey or cheeseburgery goodness—especially when so many adults can't seem to?

The hard reality, as one respondent puts it, is that the companies with the money and resources to bring heavy marketing expenditures to bear on this segment are the ones who have made that money via chocolatey or cheeseburgery goodness, and eliminating the "SuperSize" from the menu doesn't make what remains any more nutritional. So, can they come up with some kind of alternative, remotely healthy goodness that can make them money free of all this scrutiny? Of the Harris respondents, 75% think that, should their industries or clients provide healthy food alternatives, consumers won't buy them. Still, some have committed to that course.

"There are [marketers] either fending off attacks with X-Y-Z PR move, or hiding under a rug and waiting for the media frenzy to pass, but there are a lot of them who're genuinely looking for ways to cut calories and reduce fat in products and play a truly positive role," says Just Kid's Tyree.

"The question is, what's going to get kids as excited as talking about chocolate? We're trying to find those messages and trying to find those products, and it's a very big challenge. It's a whole new era. We need to find that nexus of cool and fun and, ideally, beneficial."

Questions for Discussion

1. What do the alarming statistics of the Centers for Disease Control (CDC) reveal about children? Whom does the CDC blame for this problem?
2. Why do marketing teams target children?
3. There is some ambivalence as to how much school-related marketing and corporate sponsorship should be permitted in schools. What are the conflicting views on this subject as revealed in this article?

Questions for Writing

1. Matthew Grimm writes, "Given the flurry of 'calls to action' kids receive, can they truly distinguish the truth of the world from the truth of chocolatey or cheeseburgery goodness—especially when so many adults can't seem to?" Write an informative essay in response to Grimm's question.
2. Should food, toy, automobile industries, and so on target children in ads? Grimm posits that "assigning [personal] responsibility becomes problematic, however, when advertising begins years before one's capacity for critical thought." Where do you stand on this issue? Consider the ethics involved as you analyze this topic in an essay.

Scandal in Corporate America: An Ethical, Not a Legal, Problem

BRUCE FROHNEN AND LEO CLARKE

Scandals within some of America's largest corporations have brought about some long-overdue soul-searching among people in business and government. Presidential speeches and Congressional bills set forth useful ideas and policies regarding heavier penalties for fraud and clearer standards for accounting practitioners. Nevertheless, it would be a mistake to think that some new regulations from Washington will make everything right with the business community. The answer to corporate skullduggery is not more or stronger law. Over 2,000 years of lawmaking and lawbreaking have demonstrated that laws are important, but cannot do the job by themselves.

Statutes will be effective only where the human spirit and will are already attuned to the law's objectives. Law may solve a problem that stems from good-faith differences regarding particular public policies, but it cannot change the attitude that the law itself is something to be overcome as just one more obstacle to making the maximum amount of money in the minimum amount of time. As long as American business executives and their professional advisors believe in their hearts that greed is good and that the appearance of satisfying shareholders is more important than actually satisfying them, more law will be a futile response.

Business is not a machine. We can't simply "fix" it with a new law here or there. The U.S.'s free market economy is made up of real people, acting on the basis of real motivations that include, but are not limited to, the desire to obey the law. People's actions, in business as in all areas of life, are deeply affected by those they deal with every day. Nowhere is this more true than with securities laws. America's complex legal system requires people in business to rely on (and persuade) attorneys and accountants. The securities laws are clearly meant to check individual and corporate greed, limiting it and channeling it to socially useful ends. However, they do so through the persons of professional advisors and experts, and, to put it bluntly, those experts are not doing their job. Why? Because they don't know what their job really is or should be.

Too many accountants and attorneys have come to see their job as helping businesses get around the clear purpose of the law. Moreover, "watchdog" lawyers, claiming to represent "the little guy" and serve as the conscience of the marketplace, continue to file suits against those companies that fail to sacrifice everything else to painting a picture of continually increasing short-term profits. Thus, accountants and attorneys today are undermining business ethics, rather than serving their traditional role—the one anticipated by securities laws—of supporting and encouraging ethics. The results are proving disastrous for the public's perception of business and for the economy as a whole.

5   No economic system can perform as well as free markets, but no economic system depends as much as free markets do on trust. An efficient market requires that parties to transactions trust one another and trust that the information presented to them is accurate. The most efficient method to establish that trust where substantial dollars are at stake is to have the person who is providing the information have it certified, at least in a limited way, by a reliable third party. Otherwise, everybody in-

volved will have to spend money documenting the same state of affairs—principally, the health of a company in which they may wish to invest—and thereby unnecessarily drive up costs.

The largest, seemingly anonymous markets, like America's stock exchanges, are excellent examples of the importance of trust supported by third-party confirmation. If stock analysts and everyday investors cannot be confident that they are being given accurate figures regarding the financial health and prospects of all the companies they are considering buying into, they cannot make informed buying decisions. The result is simply gambling or, more likely, an increasing reluctance to invest. The stock market will plummet and investment will dry up, and without investment, there will be no capital improvements, no research, and no prosperity.

Honesty and ethical behavior are not just goods relevant to Sunday morning and the Hereafter; they are critical to our economic well-being. We have often heard it said that the vast majority of people in business are decent folk who try to act fairly and honestly. This is as true of lawyers and accountants as it is of businesspeople. Yet, what does it mean to act fairly and honestly? This should be an easy question to answer. Don't lie, cheat, or steal, but, for instance, what does it mean to lie? This seemingly simple question has become all but impossible for many of those in business and the professions to answer, just as it has for leading public servants. That is the heart of our ethical dilemma.

We increasingly are losing our understanding of just what it means to act fairly and honestly. To be sure, we have a multitude of laws on the books that say, in essence, "Thou shalt not lie." However, the very number and complexity of these laws, applied in different ways to almost every aspect of economic life, have blurred the basic point: Lies are evil. The very complexity of our laws has encouraged many professionals and business people to find ways of conducting business that arguably fit within the letter of the law while avoiding its true intent. The game is not whether a statement is true, but whether it can be defended as not knowingly false. Moreover, those accountants and lawyers who choose to game the system are seldom caught and punished because their professional associations—those who are supposed to police their conduct—no longer understand what it really means to lie or tell the truth. We have become so tolerant of half-truths, hair-splitting definitions, and the notion that truth is "subjective" that we have lost our ability to enforce basic, commonsense honesty, even where it is crucial to our economic well-being.

Let us look in a very oversimplified way at some of the failings—one might say crimes—the nation has seen recently. The two most notorious (and expensive) cases are Enron and World-Com. The former encompassed a myriad of complex transactions involving mysterious, gossamer partnerships that allowed Enron to book huge corporate profits and payments to insiders, while ignoring any associated financial liabilities. Was there any real business reason to structure those transactions in such a fashion? Of course not—unless one is attempting to make something seem what it's not. Enron was just the New Century equivalent of putting sawdust in the Model T's transmission or changing the brand on cattle.

10   WorldCom was not only bigger, but more surprising. Internal bookkeepers simply accounted for everyday spending (that should have been deducted from income) as expenditures for "capital assets"—as if an appreciable number of pencils and paper clips bought today would still be in use a year from now. That simple adjustment greatly overstated income because expenditures for capital assets are spread over the life of the asset instead of being deducted 100% from income right away. Sure, future reported income would be substantially reduced in the long run, but those WorldCom Keynesians figured that, in the long run, they would all be dead. Unfortunately for stockholders, it was their investments that died.

How did such obvious lying occur? After all, in both cases, the corporate employees and the outside auditors and counsel retained to support the reliability of the internal accounting were all operating under rules that said, in effect, "Thou shalt not lie"— that transactions are to be accounted for according to their substance, not just any seemingly defensible argument concerning how they might be represented on a form.

Here is one answer to that simple question: We have become too sophisticated, as individuals and as a society, to believe that God will punish us if we tell a lie, and that answer is also our problem. Our facile confidence that there are no longer any moral roles everyone must obey no matter what has led us to forget that bad behavior naturally brings bad consequences. It has encouraged more and more of us to behave worse and worse without even realizing it. As author C.S. Lewis observed, "Moral collapse follows upon spiritual collapse." Our refusal to teach our children—and our professionals—that they are answerable to their society and ultimately to God for their behavior has cost us our collective moral bearings. We have lost our ability as a society to pass moral judgment on individual behavior. Indeed, we condemn ethical judgments as just that—"judgmental."

In our drive to be "nonjudgmental" and "multicultural," we have lost sight of the roots of our own morality and our own individual cultures. Just as a child using each of the 64 new crayons in the box ends up with a blot of gray on the page, throwing all cultures into one big pot and refusing to discuss their individual values and truths ends up with a society that recognizes no truth—except tolerance for gray. Whether European or Asian, Hindu, Muslim, Jewish, or Christian, every culture is rooted in a religious vision of life, its meaning, its goals, and the rules by which it must be lived.

Our nation was founded by devoutly religious people convinced that they should be a "city on a hill" shining as an example to all nations of how well religious people would treat one another and of how good a community they could build together. They brought with them the Christian religion and a determination to make their political leaders answer to religious principles, a determination they inherited from the Israelites, whose Ten Commandments they took, quite rightly, to be the foundation of their system of law. These religious ancestors sought to build that city on the basis not merely of laws, but of individual habits and norms of behavior rooted in their religion. Yet, we forbid our children from learning about the Judeo-Christian roots of their nation, and of their way of life. This does not mean that other cultures have no valid truths, but only that this country was built on one ethical system and it will work only if we continually follow that system. Anyone who has ever tried to run a Windows-based program on a Mac should appreciate that point.

We already see the results of ignoring substantive ethics and their religious roots. A recent Zogby International poll of college seniors found that 97% said their college studies had prepared them to act ethically in their future careers, but 73% conceded that what their professors taught them was moral relativism. When our new professionals are taught that truth depends on the facts and circumstances, and that no individual can challenge the conscientious decision of another, we have no right to be surprised that rampant lying is the result. Without substantive moral judgments that we hold and enforce as a nation, we should not be surprised when a senior partner tells a junior lawyer or accountant that, although the reporting of a transaction does not appear to be "absolutely true," it really is in accord with the highly technical requirements of accounting standards and Federal securities regulations. We should not be surprised when most smart,

15

ambitious professionals inculcate that relativism into their own ethical systems.

Today, we refuse to call a statement a lie if it can be defended as a reasonable interpretation of all the underlying facts and circumstances. After all, there is no oath so breached in the business world as the one to "tell the truth, the whole truth, and nothing but the truth." The import of that oath has become lost on the thousands of well-meaning professionals who have succumbed to the "greed is good," "winning is the only thing" and "aggressive advocacy is the highest professional service" mantras of postmodern America.

CHANGING BUSINESS CULTURE

So, how can we change business culture to make the truth both a cultural and economic imperative? Certainly, we must start in primary schools with real values education, but we can also deprogram our current corps of executives, lawyers, and accountants. While the President and Congress would have us scare them into telling the truth, we think the problem will be resolved more quickly and completely with a simple two-step approach. First, those in business need to be assured that telling the truth is not only okay, it is what the people they are working for want. We are already seeing that message being conveyed in the market by investors who are punishing those firms that have been identified as having engaged in so-called "aggressive accounting." We see as well that firms that eschew aggressive accounting—such as Coca-Cola, which announced it will begin reporting stock options as expenses—are being rewarded by investors.

Merely reinforcing the fact that virtue is its own reward is not enough, though. We must overcome two generations of moral relativism and teach executives, accountants, and attorneys how to recognize the truth. For instance, most professional licensing organizations require licensees to participate in continuing education, and a small portion of that requirement is generally satisfied at the end of a long day of "substantive" learning. Now, however, investors and clients are beginning to realize that ethics is a part of substantive business. Lawyers and accountants have so long viewed themselves as being mouthpieces for a particular spin on a client's business that they need to be taught the skills necessary for ferreting out the truth and evaluating the dynamics of business that might—and often do—lead to fraud. More than this, they need to be taught how to counsel their clients objectively and with a view toward helping them meet their obligations. In short, far more than preaching is needed. All players in the disclosure regime must be taught not only how to recognize the truth when they see it, but how to press their superiors and their clients until they find it.

This means very practical ethical training—teaching attorneys how to negotiate honestly, teaching accountants what techniques do and do not accord with an honest balance statement, etc. Yet, even this is not enough. Business and professional schools across the country are making noises about "getting serious" about ethics, but what will this mean in practice? Unless we reconnect with the source of our ethical precepts, grounding moral rules like "don't lie" in deep moral habits and our religious tradition, once the latest crisis of confidence passes, it will be business (and lying) as usual.

To give weight and meaning to seeming platitudes like "don't lie," we need our religious institutions, families, and communities to speak more forcefully about the religious grounding of decent behavior. We need to develop a more positive attitude in our political institutions and public schools toward the religious tradition that is at the root of our system of ordered liberty, and what remains of our habits of moral behavior. We are not suggesting that public schools inculcate students into any particular religion. However, when we ban the Ten Commandments—the font of our legal and ethical system—from our courthouses and schools, we have lost contact with common sense. Does "Thou shalt not lie" become an impermissible command when its origin in religious experience is acknowledged? Does the prohibition against stealing become oppressive when we admit that, in every civilization on this planet, it stems from the religious belief that we owe a duty to our God to treat others as we would have them treat us?

In the appendix to *Mere Christianity,* Lewis recounts moral strictures common to every society on Earth. This moral code, which can be summed up in the Golden Rule or, more extensively, the Ten Commandments, is, in every instance, rooted in religious belief. Without that belief in God and a rational universe ordered by Him on moral principles, nothing makes sense finally, and everything is permitted. Divorced from the story of their origins, of the meaning and necessity of moral conduct, people cannot make sense of their lives and will fall back on selfishness and the will to dominate others. As we work to reestablish an ethical structure to business behavior, we had best remember our need for religious moorings. Otherwise, we will continue to see more Enrons and WorldComs, whether new laws are put on the books or not.

20

Questions for Discussion

1. What do Bruce Frohnen and Leo Clarke mean by the statement "Business is not a machine. We can't simply 'fix' it with a new law here or there"?
2. Frohnen and Clarke write, "No economic system can perform as well as free markets, but no economic system depends as much as free markets do on trust." What do you think about this claim?
3. What percentage of college seniors polled felt that their college education offered the ethical preparation needed to succeed as business professionals?
4. What do Frohnen and Clarke recommend for changing the business culture in America? Do you think that Frohnen and Clark's recommendations can influence the business culture of the future?

Questions for Writing

1. Consider the following statement of Frohnen and Clarke: "Law may solve a problem that stems from good-faith differences regarding particular public policies, but it cannot change the attitude that the law itself is something to be overcome as just one more obstacle to making the maximum amount of money in the minimum amount of time." What do the authors mean? Do you agree? Why or why not? Analyze this topic in an essay.
2. At the end of their article, the authors call for a moral code of conduct, connected to God and his absolute truths, in the business world. Should a Bible-based universal moral code be designed that would not offend people who base their moral code on some other holy book or on no holy book at all, or should business leaders who design and establish the Christian-inspired code care whether if offends non-Christians? Write an informative essay addressing this topic.

Just Because It's Legal, Is It Right?
JEFFREY L. SEGLIN

It's very possible for an owner or manager of a company to make a perfectly legal decision without ever exploring the ethical aspects of the decision. That's not to suggest that making a decision that is legal is inherently unethical. It's just that sometimes the law gives us an excuse to ignore whether the action we are taking is right or wrong.

The bankruptcy laws in the United States are a perfect example. In theory, they're a wonderful tool that gives troubled business owners the opportunity to turn their businesses around rather than go under. When a company files for protection under chapter 11 of the bankruptcy code, it can keep its creditors at bay while it tries to work out a plan to reorganize itself so it can overcome its financial troubles. In theory, this is a good thing, because if the business emerges from chapter 11 protection rather than liquidating its assets in a chapter 7 bankruptcy filing, the chances are that creditors will ultimately be paid and the company itself will continue to contribute to the economy by creating jobs, paying taxes, and engaging in commerce.

There "are many reasons why a business gets sick, but they don't necessarily mean it should be destroyed," observes Judge James A. Goodman, the chief bankruptcy judge for the district of Maine. Hundreds of thousands of businesses that at one time or another had financial difficulties survive today as the result of chapter 11 proceedings. They continue to contribute to employment, tax revenues, and overall growth. It's counterproductive to destroy the business value of an asset by liquidating it and paying it out in a chapter 7 if that company shows signs of being able to recover in a reorganization. As for creditors, one of the provisions of the bankruptcy code is that in order for a reorganization to be confirmed, the creditor must get not less than he or she would have gotten in a chapter 7 liquidation. So why not go through with the reorganization?"[1]

Judge Goodman argues that in spite of the fact that 80 percent of businesses that file chapter 11 protection never make it out of bankruptcy, the fact that 20 percent do makes the bankruptcy laws all the more worthwhile.

"If a doctor had a 20 percent success rate with terminal cancer cases, you'd say, 'That's incredible!' Well, that's what we've got—companies that are terminal. We take the nearly dead and show them how to operate better, and one-fifth survive. What's wrong with that?" the judge asks.

The fact that there are roughly 1.4 million bankruptcy filings a year hasn't helped calm the perception that bankruptcy is being used as a shield to keep those who owe from paying back those who are owed. But the reality is that, of those 1.4 million filings, the vast majority are personal filings rather than business filings.

ARE LAWS ABSOLUTION FROM HAVING TO THINK?

Forget whether or not you should have the responsibility to pay back your debts for a moment. The whole area of bankruptcy protection raises a far more interesting issue. And that's that it's a prime example of how laws and regulations, however well-intentioned, have resulted in a nation of business owners who are forgiven from having to think through the implications of their actions. If the law allows such and such behavior, the argument goes, then that's what I'm obligated to do—no more, no less.

Well, fine. But somewhere along the line, were business owners absolved from having to do some hard thinking on what their actions might mean? What they might say to the business community? What they might say about us and how we want to be perceived? Remember, this business community is likely one in which, post–dead company, you're going to be operating for a long, long time.

Now, don't get me wrong. I'm not suggesting that the laws are wrong or that after thinking through the meaning of your actions you might not decide to do precisely the same thing as you would have done had you just blindly followed the letter of the law.

10   When did we become a nation of people like Ilsa in the movie *Casablanca*, who looks longingly into Rick's eyes and sighs, "You'll have to do the thinking for both of us." Please. Just because the law makes it so doesn't mean we shouldn't have to think long and hard about our actions, just as we'd do in any other aspect of our business.

Be real, I can hear you saying it. (Or thinking it silently to yourself as you roll your eyes.) Who wants to sit around and participate in self-flagellation sessions where you go over in painful detail everything you owe to everybody you've disappointed—your customers, your vendors, your employees, your creditors, and not least, yourself? Especially when you're in the midst of something as painful as losing your business and everything you built? I can think of few takers for the role. It's only when you're on the other side of the fence—when you're one of the ones being stiffed—that you spend time wondering loudly why the bankrupt business owner doesn't think about doing the right thing.

That's pretty much what happened to Daniel J. Driscoll, the owner of Darlyn Development Corp., a $4-million general contracting company in Marlboro, Massachusetts, when he found himself looking at the cover of the November 1995 issue of *Inc.* magazine. There, staring out from the cover with a plate of roasted chicken with all the fixings was George Naddaff, the entrepreneur who discovered Boston Chicken, at the time a fast-growing restaurant franchise success story that in 1993 had become one of the hottest public offerings on record.[2]

Mr. Driscoll was incensed. So he took pen to paper and wrote the magazine a letter. In part, he wrote: "While I find it wonderfully motivating that one business can flourish because of the ideas and actions of Mr. George Naddaff, I also find it infuriating that the same man could flaunt to the business world that he had $14 million to invest in a new venture, when he has not paid small businessmen like myself for his business ventures that failed." When asked about that failed venture in that November 1995 article, Naddaff told *Inc.* senior editor Joshua Hyatt: "I'd like to forget about it."[3]

"Why should a man who has all the money he did be able to walk away from a million-dollar debt?" Driscoll asked. "They should make it illegal. If you have the funds to pay your debt, then you shouldn't be able to walk away. . . . When he realized that his concept wasn't going to be the next Boston Chicken, he pulled the plug on it and fucked everybody."[4]

Naddaff and his partners at Olde World Bakeries, the corpo-   15
ration which owned Coffee by George, had invested roughly $5 million in the drive-through coffee kiosk concept before they realized it wasn't going to work. They decided to liquidate the business and arrived at an agreement to pay their creditors roughly 30 cents of every dollar that was owed. Driscoll was one of the creditors who had agreed to the payout.

Driscoll may have agreed to the payout, but he was none too pleased that it ever came to having to make this choice. What bothered Driscoll had nothing to do with whether Naddaff followed the law. Driscoll doesn't doubt that he did. But in spite of the fact that what Naddaff did was legal, Driscoll thinks he shouldn't have gotten off as easily as he did. Since Naddaff had the resources from his personal wealth or his other business dealings to make good on his debts, Driscoll believes that he should have been made to pay back his creditors in whole.

DIFFERENT SIDES YIELD DIFFERENT PERSPECTIVES

Driscoll, one of those creditors who settled for 30 cents on the dollar, just didn't think Naddaff did enough. But Driscoll doesn't take issue with the laws themselves that Naddaff could have used to protect himself. Nor does he seem to have a real problem with the fact that bankruptcy laws exist. Driscoll's problem, it seems, was that Naddaff hadn't suffered as much as he did when, back in 1989—six years before Coffee by George went bust—he'd filed for bankruptcy himself. As it turns out, Driscoll's earlier venture—Emerald Electric, a 50-employee, $7-million electrical contracting business—had failed. He filed for chapter 7 bankruptcy, then liquidated all of the company's assets. His problem with what Naddaff did stemmed from the fact that Naddaff didn't suffer as much as Driscoll thinks he did when he went out of business.

"When I went out of business, I lost everything—my house, the cars, the whole nine yards," says Driscoll. "I didn't shut my doors, walk away from a million dollars' worth of debt, and then go home to a $5-million house and a $100,000 automobile. When I went out of business everything went. I didn't have some 50-odd million dollars behind me and just decide, 'I'm not going to pay these people,' and close down another entity and walk away from it. If someone personally has the money, why should they be able to walk away and screw everybody? Where, when I did it, I didn't have any options. I didn't have choices—you know what I'm saying?"

A common argument among some seasoned business owners is that part of the responsibility for not getting burned by companies that go bust is to do enough due diligence on the companies you're doing business with, so you can gauge how much of a risk they really are. A pool-and-spa industry consultant in California, makes the point that while he feels sorry "for the company that gets nailed with a bankrupt customer, it is, in the final analysis, the responsibility of the supplier to weigh the loss potential against the possible gain in dealing with a corporation. All too often a company will jump at the chance to sell their products and services without due diligence."[5]

20   That might be an honest sentiment, but no matter how much due diligence you do, it's impossible to always determine when a business is likely to go bust owing you money. You do the best you can to trust that the people you're doing business with will stay in business and make good on their debts.

But what about the notion that everyone should suffer equally when a company goes under? The idea of writing a set of laws based on the premise that everyone should suffer equally when a company goes out of business just "doesn't make good common business sense," says Judge Goodman.[6]

That's a good point. For one thing, who's going to make the determination of just how much suffering is enough? And for another, one man's suffering is another man's . . . well, you get the point.

But tell this to a group of business owners and you're likely to get a visceral response on both sides of the argument. After reading the story of George Naddaff and Coffee by George, one CEO was incensed. The founder of a business that goes under should suffer at least as much as the folks owed money, this owner of a software development firm in Denver, argued. "George Naddaff is wrong and he knows it," he said. "The law may be on his side, but he's confusing what is legal with what is right. Just one question for you, George: When the lawyers arranged for your creditors to be paid 30 cents on the dollar, did you adjust your salary accordingly?"[7]

Still, Judge Goodman sees the fact that the U.S. Constitution holds that Congress should provide for a uniform bankruptcy act, where essentially debt is forgiven as a national policy, as a good thing. This "country was founded by debtors," he says. The authors of the Constitution "came from places where they were put in jail because they owed money. Our forefathers didn't want commoners like themselves thrown into debtors' prison if there was some other way out."[8]

You can find an equal number of CEOs who agree with this sentiment as those who don't. A CEO of an asset-management company in Dallas, sees the clear intelligence of a bankruptcy law that forgives failure. "You have to look at each bankruptcy individually," he said. "Too often we look at the past abuses of a few and often end up really hurting the ones that are truly using the system for what it was designed to do."[9]

But that doesn't address the fact that anger is a perfectly normal and common way to feel when it's you who are the one who's being stiffed. "We all want to feel bad for someone or a business that has had to file for bankruptcy," says the president of a Tampa-based debt-collection agency, "but how do you feel when you can't collect on an invoice and your accounts receivable are down the tubes?"[10]

Driscoll's experiences with companies going bust were unhappy ones, to say the least. First, when his own company, Emerald Electric, goes out of business, he takes a huge professional and personal financial hit. And then, when Coffee by George bites the dust, he's faced with not getting total payment for work he'd done for the business.

Given the ire he felt on both occasions, and the exasperating anger he felt toward George Naddaff for not paying him back in full, it's interesting that, unlike Bartmann and Graff, Driscoll didn't feel obligated to pay back Emerald Electric's creditors in full once he found success in Darlyn Development Corp., his new business.

Driscoll certainly had no legal obligation to take such action. But, like Bartmann and Graff, he could have chosen to.

SITUATIONAL ETHICS

30   If ever there was a prime example of *situational ethics* at work, here it is. In the less-then-perfect world of situational ethics, you can adapt what you hold to be ethical behavior based on how each event or circumstance affects you. Say, if you get burned in business and the laws do nothing to make you whole, well, then you can pronounce the person doing the burning as highly unethical or, at the very least, of questionable ethics. But if your business goes under and there's simply no cash left to pay back the folks to whom you owe money, why then you can hide behind the protection that the laws afford. Ah, sweet vindication. Using situational ethics allows you to miss the inconsistency between the way you behave, which you hold to be perfectly reasonable, and the way others are when they behave exactly the same way and you hold them to be wildly unethical.

One of the problems with situational ethics is that it gives people the ability to elevate and label unfortunate situations to the status of unethical ones. If he's been wronged, the wronged party may feel better if he can toss accusations of ethical misbehavior around. People in business find themselves in situations like this all the time. If you've got to fire a problem employee, that employee quickly becomes, at least to your mind, guilty of all sorts of unethical behavior. If your creditors are knocking on your doors for cash because you've been late paying or because they know your company's down on its luck and they'd better get their payments now, you start viewing these creditors as unethical vipers beating at the doors to pile on when you're down. And those customers who owe you money, but keep telling you they'll have a check in the mail as soon as their cash flow improves get elevated to the status of no-good, unethical deadbeats. But the truth is that just because something feels unfair to you at some particular moment in time, doesn't mean that it's the result of an unscrupulous, unethical pattern of behavior. You just may not like it.

PERSONAL DECISIONS DEFINE BUSINESS BEHAVIOR

Much of how you behave in business comes down to personal decisions you make about what you believe is the right thing and the wrong thing to do. If you have to shut down a business, you might make the same choice that Naddaff and Driscoll did and liquidate its assets and then pay back creditors not a penny more than whatever agreed-upon percentage you arrive at. You could also follow suit with Bartmann and Graff and decide that you believe the right thing to do is to pay creditors back in full regardless of what the letter of the law requires. Driscoll is entitled to his strong opinions about what Naddaff did and how he should have behaved—even if Driscoll himself behaved almost exactly the same way when faced with a similar situation—but that doesn't by any means suggest that what Naddaff did when he shut down Coffee by George was unethical.

"This is a man who is upset, and rightfully so," says Naddaff. "Especially if it hurt him in other ways. But it was a decision that was made by the board, who said, 'This business is not viable.' A brave man does it with a sword. The coward with a kiss. And that's the way it's done in business."

Indeed, when a company goes bust and there's no legal agreement to make full restitution to creditors, then it's up to the owner or founder how much he is going to go beyond the law. Does he think it's right to make good on debts? Like Bartmann and Graff, does he think there might even be an upside to future business dealings if he goes beyond the law and makes folks he owed money to whole?

Driscoll is hardly alone in feeling one way when he's owed money and another when he's the one doing the owing. We're all capable of taking a strong, yet diametrically opposed stand depending on what side of the issue we're on.

When Naddaff, for example, was asked what he looked for in entrepreneurs to invest in, he responded: "I look for the passion. I look for the commitment. I look for where this guy has been in his life. Is this a guy who has hocked his wife, his firstborn, his teeth, his contact lenses, his pacemaker, and his hearing aid? That, to me, is commitment. That's the guy I'm going to back. . . . I can see the sweat on his upper lip. Lots of entrepreneurs hock their houses. What's more sacred than a house? I like it when I hear someone has done that."[11]

George Naddaff may "live by the sword and die by the sword," but, like Driscoll, he's perfectly capable of seeing the same situation differently depending upon which side he's on. If he's looking to invest in someone, then he wants someone who's willing to put his personal assets on the line. But in the case of Coffee by George, when Naddaff's corporation was left owing creditors, that was a different case.

Here's the thing when it comes to situations like this. The easy thing to do is hide behind whichever side of the law or circumstances protects your interests the most. And that's fine. But the ethical thing to do is to acknowledge that that's precisely what you're doing, to give some thought to whether by your actions, you're behaving in a way that you believe to be right. It's perfectly reasonable to believe that business is a game, where sometimes you win [and] sometimes you lose, but in all circumstances you're willing to play by the rules. You have to determine for yourself though, after careful thought, when you arrive at a point where rules be damned, whether you've got an obligation to set things right.

Endnotes

1. Robert A. Mamis, "Why Bankruptcy Works," *Inc.*, October 1996: 39.
2. In what seems to be a classic example of what goes around comes around, Boston Chicken filed for chapter 11 bankruptcy protection in October 1998. By the time of the filing, George Naddaff was not with the management team running the company. See Mike Hofman, "Boston Chicken Files Ch. 11 as Troubles Come Home to Roost," Inc. Online, October 7, 1998.
3. Joshua Hyatt, "The Next Big Thing," *Inc.*, November 1995: 62.
4. Jeffrey L. Seglin, "Brother, Can You Spare 30 Cents on the Dollar?" *Inc.*, April 1998. The case study told here was originally told in a different form in this article in *Inc.* magazine. Unless noted otherwise, while the telling of the story is new, the quotes from the subjects in this case are drawn from this article.
5. From "Readers' Debate: Is It 'Right' to Go Bankrupt?" in "Would You Lie to Save Your Company?" *Inc.*, July 1998: 53.
6. Interview by the author with Judge James A. Goodman, January 1998.
7. From "Readers' Debate: Is It 'Right' to Go Bankrupt?" in "Would You Lie to Save Your Company?" *Inc.*, July 1998: 53.
8. Robert A. Mamis, "Why Bankruptcy Works," *Inc.*, October 1996: 39.
9. From "Readers' Debate: Is It 'Right' to Go Bankrupt?" in "Would You Lie to Save Your Company?" *Inc.*, July 1998: 53.
10. From "Readers' Debate: Is It 'Right' to Go Bankrupt?" in "Would You Lie to Save Your Company?" *Inc.*, July 1998: 53.
11. Joshua Hyatt, "The Next Big Thing," *Inc.*, November 1995: 62.

Questions for Discussion

1. What did Judge James A. Goodman discover about businesses and their bankruptcy practices? What ethical concerns are revealed by Goodman's data?
2. According to Seglin, even though "the laws about how much of your personal assets are protected when a company goes out of business vary from

state to state, some business owners ... believe the right thing to do in such circumstances is to go beyond what's required by the law to make good on your debts." Is this an ethically appropriate stance? Measure some of the examples in this article against Seglin's standard.

3. Is a uniform bankruptcy act in which "essentially debt is forgiven as a national policy" the answer to the financial woes of American businesses? Consider this question in the context of the examples in this article, as well as current businesses that are facing financial hardships.
4. What does Seglin have to say about situational ethics in business?

Questions for Writing

1. According to Seglin, "Much of how you behave in business comes down to personal decisions you make about what you believe is the right thing and the wrong thing to do." Do you agree or disagree with this observation? Defend your response in a persuasive essay.
2. As a businessperson, should you ever sacrifice the interest and well-being of your employees for the sake of money and/or the interest of your business? Analyze both sides of the issue in your essay.

Ethics in International Business
JOHN R. BOATRIGHT

Transnational corporations [face a quandry,] namely, deciding which standards of ethics to follow. Should TNCs be bound by the laws and prevailing morality of the home country and, in the case of American corporations, act everywhere as they do in the United States? Should they follow the practices of the host country and adopt the adage "When in Rome, do as the Romans do"? Or are there special ethical standards that apply when business is conducted across national boundaries? And if so, what are the standards appropriate for international business?

Unfortunately, there are no easy answers to these questions. In some cases, the standards contained in American law and morality ought to be observed beyond our borders; in other cases, there is no moral obligation to do so. Similarly, it is morally permissible for managers of TNCs to follow local practice and "do as the Romans do" in some situations but not others. And even if there are special ethical standards for international business, they cannot be applied without taking into account differences in cultures and value systems, the levels of economic development, and the social and political structures of the foreign countries in which TNCs operate. The existence of special standards, in other words, does not require us to act in the same way in all parts of the world, regardless of the situation. Local circumstances must always be taken into consideration in conducting business abroad.

"NO DOUBLE STANDARDS!"

Let us consider, first, the position taken by some critics of TNCs: that business ought to be conducted in the same way the world over with no double standards. In particular, U.S. corporations ought to observe domestic law and a single code of conduct in their dealings everywhere. This position might be expressed as, "When in Rome or anywhere else, do as you would at home."[1] A little reflection suffices to show that this high level of conduct is not morally required of TNCs in all instances and that they should not be faulted for every departure from home country standards in doing business abroad. Good reasons can be advanced to show that different practices in different parts of the world are, in some instances, morally justified.

First, the conditions prevailing in other parts of the world are different in some morally relevant respects from those in the United States and other developed countries. If Rome is a significantly different place, then standards that are appropriate at home do not necessarily apply there. Drug laws in the developed world, for example, are very stringent, reflecting greater affluence and better overall health. The standards embodied in these laws are not always appropriate in poorer, less developed countries with fewer medical resources and more severe health problems.

5   In the United States, the risk of prescribing an antidiarrheal drug such as Lomotil to children is not worth taking. But a physician in Central America, where children frequently die of untreated diarrhea, might evaluate the risk differently. Similarly, the effectiveness of Chloromycetin for massive infections might offset the possibility of aplastic anemia in a country where some people would die without the drug. A missionary in Bolivia who spoke with doctors about the extensive use of chloramphenicol (the generic name for Chloromycetin) reported: "The response was that in the States, because of our better state of general health, we could afford to have the luxury of saving that drug for rare cases. Here, the people's general health is so poor that one must make an all out attack on illness."[2]

Second, some aspects of American law and practice reflect incidental features of our situation, so that not all U.S. standards express universal moral requirements.[3] The fact that a drug has not been approved in the home country of a transnational or has been withdrawn from the market does not automatically mean that it is unsafe or ineffective. A drug for a tropical disease might never have been submitted for approval, since there is no market for it in the country where it is manufactured. Other drugs might not be approved because of concerns that are unfounded or open to question.

The FDA acted conservatively in initially refusing approval for Depo-Provera, for example; many countries of Western Europe and Canada, with equally strict drug-testing requirements, permitted the use of this drug as a last-resort contraceptive. In borderline cases, there is room for legitimate debate between competent, well-intentioned persons about the correctness of FDA decisions. Also, the approval of drugs in the United States is a lengthy process. Companies convinced of the safety of a drug might be justified in rushing it to market in countries where it is legally permitted, while waiting for approval at home, especially if there is a pressing need abroad. Finally, some critics charge that the long delay in the FDA's approval of Depo-Provera was based on political considerations arising from the opposition of some groups to birth control.

Third, many factors in other countries, especially in the Third World, are beyond the control of TNCs, and they often have little choice but to adapt to local conditions—if they are going to do business at all. This position can perhaps be expressed as, "We do not entirely agree with the Romans, but we sometimes find it necessary to do things their way." For example, physicians in the Third World often prefer to prescribe multiple drugs for a single ailment. Hence, the demand for combination antibiotics. Although this practice is disapproved by the American medical community, extending the U.S. ban on such drugs to the rest of the world is unlikely to bring about any significant change. If combination antibiotics were not sold, many doctors would continue to issue prescriptions for several different drugs to be taken simultaneously, very possibly, in the wrong proportions.

As another example, consider the ethics of marketing prescription drugs directly to consumers. Deep opposition to this practice exists in the United States, and drug companies are severely criticized for ad campaigns that appeal to patients over the heads of physicians. In much of the Third World, however, self-medication is a deeply ingrained practice, since many people are too poor to consult a doctor, if, indeed, one is available. And many drugs that are available only by prescription in the United States are freely dispensed by pharmacists in the Third World—and even by street corner vendors. Under these conditions, drug companies contend that advertising cannot be effective if it is aimed only at physicians. Drug companies are accused, however, of encouraging self-medication and inducing the population to spend scarce resources on pills, tonics, and other medications when they have so many more pressing needs.

"WHEN IN ROME . . ."

10   The opposite extreme—that the only guide for business conduct abroad is what is legally and morally accepted in any given country where a TNC operates—is equally untenable. "When in Rome do as the Romans do" cannot be followed without exception. In order to see this, however, we need to distinguish at least three different arguments that are used to support this position. These correspond to the objections to the first position just examined and can be sketched briefly as follows:

1. *There really are morally relevant differences.* The justification for holding a double standard and marketing a drug in a host country that is not approved at home, for example, is that the conditions that prevail in the country are different in morally relevant respects.
2. *The people affected have a right to decide.* Where different standards exist, the right of a host country to determine which to apply should be respected. The primary responsibility for setting standards properly rests on the government and the people of the country in which business is being conducted.
3. *There is no other way of doing business.* Where local conditions require that corporations engage in certain practices as a condition of doing business, then those practices are justified. This is a version of the argument "We do not entirely agree with the Romans, but we sometimes find it necessary to do things their way."

The first argument presupposes the existence of general principles of justification, such as the utilitarian principle that justifies practices in terms of their consequences for benefit and harm. As a result, it is possible that no ultimate conflict exists in some cases of apparent double standards; whatever principles are employed simply justify different practices when conditions are different in morally relevant respects. Many of the criticisms directed against TNCs fail to recognize the extent to which the practices in host countries are capable of being justified by the same principles that justify different practices at home. We have already noted some of the relevant differences that might justify different marketing practices for prescription drugs, but there are many other cases that illustrate the point.

Consider whether a double standard is involved, for example, when TNCs pay wages in less developed countries that are a fraction of those in the developed world. One possible position is that although there are vast differences in the actual wages paid by a TNC in the United States and, say, Mexico, the disparity is not unjust *if the same mechanism for setting wages is employed in both cases.* Thus, the wage paid to a worker in the Third World must provide a decent standard of living in that country and be arrived at by a process of fair bargaining that fully respects workers as human beings. In order for these conditions to be satisfied, unions might also be necessary to ensure that workers are adequately represented.[4] What is morally objectionable about the wages paid by many TNCs in the Third World, then, is not that they are lower than those in the home country but that they are imposed on workers in violation of their rights.

How far this argument is able to justify the use of different standards in host and home countries is a matter for speculation. Although a few of the marketing practices for which the pharmaceutical industry is criticized can perhaps be justified in this manner, it is difficult to believe that the differences between countries are sufficient to justify extensive double standards. A serious effort by TNCs to apply the ethical principles underlying home country standards to the varying conditions they encounter in different parts of the world would be a welcome development—and one that would result, most likely, in many changes in current marketing practices. . . .

THE NEED TO "GO ALONG"

The final argument, "There is no other way of doing business," like the other two, has some merit. As long as they have a right to operate abroad, corporations ought to be permitted to do what is necessary for the conduct of business—within limits, of course. American firms with contracts for projects in the Middle East, for example, have complied in many instances with requests not to station women and Jewish employees in those countries. Although discrimination of this kind is morally repugnant, it is (arguably) morally permissible when the alternative is to risk losing business in the Arab world. Attempts have been made to justify the practice on the ground that American corporations are forced to go along.

15   A more complicated case is provided by the Arab boycott of Israel, which was begun by the countries of the Arab League in 1945.[5] In order to avoid blacklisting that would bar them from doing business with participating Arab countries, many prominent American transnationals cooperated by avoiding investment in Israel. Other U.S. corporations, however, refused to cooperate with the boycott for ethical reasons. An executive of RCA, which is now part of General Electric, declared:

> We're a worldwide communications company that has done business with China and Romania, and we'd like to do business with the Arabs. But we are not going to end relations with Israel to get an Arab contract. This is a moral issue that we feel strongly about.[6]

(The position taken by RCA is now required by law. An amendment to the Export Administration Act, signed into law in June 1977 over vigorous objections by segments of the business community, prohibits American corporations from cooperating with the Arab boycott against Israel.)

As with the other arguments, "There is no other way of doing business" cannot be accepted without some qualifications. First, the alternative is seldom to cease doing business; rather, the claim that a practice is "necessary" often means merely that it is the most profitable way of doing business. Drug companies might lose some business by refusing to market combination antibiotics, for example, but the amount is not likely to be substantial, especially if the changeover is accompanied by a promotional effort to educate doctors about the proper use of drugs. Similarly, direct marketing is less likely to be objectionable if advertising is used to educate consumers about drugs in a way that genuinely contributes to their well-being instead of the profit of the transnationals. The Arab embargo against Israel greatly complicated the problems of doing business in the Middle East, but some companies were able to avoid cooperating with the boycott and still have business relations with Arab countries.

Second, there are some situations in which a company is morally obligated to withdraw if there is no other way to do business. At one time, any company with plants and other production facilities in South Africa was required by law to observe the rigid segregation imposed by apartheid. Some critics held at the time that if the only alternative to participating in racial oppression is to cease all operations there, then the latter is the morally preferable course of action. Subsequently, the South African government allowed U.S. subsidiaries to integrate their work force and abide by the so-called Sullivan Code, which bars discrimination in employment.

However, the Sullivan Code does not address the charge that American firms were still contributing by their presence to the survival of a country that systematically violated the rights of its own people. Also, critics charge that some of the products sold in South Africa contributed to the maintenance of apartheid. Several computer companies in the United States, including IBM, for example, were accused of selling equipment that enabled the South African police to enforce the hated passbook and to keep track of dissidents. American banks have also been criticized for making loans that helped to preserve the economic stability of the white regime. These critics contend that such involvement in an immoral system cannot be justified and that the only moral course was to cease doing business there.

Defenders point out in reply that American companies provided high-paying jobs for blacks in South Africa and that their presence encouraged a gradual process of liberalization. If they had withdrawn, the condition of the oppressed majority would, most likely, not have improved and pressure on the government to make reforms would have been eased. The main consequence would probably have been that other foreign investors and white South Africans would take the place of the departing American firms with worse consequences.

The difficulty with both of the qualifications just discussed lies in finding the appropriate cutoff points. When is conforming to the local way of doing things absolutely necessary and when is it a matter of convenience or mere profitability? When is it morally permissible for a corporation to remain in a country such as South Africa under apartheid and when is a corporation morally obligated to withdraw? Answering these questions requires a careful consideration of the hard realities of the situation and the possibility of justifying each practice. The argument "There is no other way of doing business," therefore, does not settle the matter in any given case but only serves as a starting point for further ethical inquiry.

SPECIAL STANDARDS FOR INTERNATIONAL BUSINESS

Our results so far have been largely negative. The two extreme positions—"When in Rome, do as the Romans do" and "When in Rome or anywhere else, do as you would at home"—are both inadequate guides in international business. However, the discussion of these positions suggests some principles that can be used to make decisions in difficult cases. These principles recognize that the world of the TNC requires a slightly different approach to issues than the one appropriate to a corporation operating wholly within a single nation-state. This is so for several reasons besides those already mentioned.

First, some of the conditions that create a social responsibility for corporations in a country such as the United States are absent elsewhere. The basis for many of the obligations of American corporations to employees, consumers, and the public at large lies in the extensive powers and privileges that we have conferred upon them. Their responsibility to society rests, in other words, on an implicit "social contract," and that contract does not exist to the same degree when corporations operate abroad. The role of TNCs is often limited to marketing goods produced elsewhere, participating in joint ventures with local companies, and so on. Thus, they are not full-fledged "corporate citizens" of a host country, so to speak, but are more like guests. Hence, they have less reason to exhibit the good citizenship that we expect of domestic corporations, although they should still be good "corporate guests."

Second, the lack of effective international law with comprehensive multinational agreements, codes of conduct, and the like creates a less regulated, more competitive environment for international business. One benefit of a legal system is a uniform system of enforceable rules that provides a level playing field for all firms. Business competition within a single country with an extensive set of laws is thus like an athletic competition. International business, by contrast, is more akin to war, which cannot be conducted by the detailed rules of a boxing match, for example. Even war is bound by moral limits, however, such as the concept of a just war and rules such as the Geneva Convention.

Because of these features of international business, it is not appropriate to hold that TNCs have all the same obligations abroad that they have at home and to use the same principles of justification to determine the extent of their obligations in foreign operations. Still, there is a minimal set of obligations that every corporation is morally bound to observe no matter where the activity takes place. An ethical framework for international business consists in part, then, of the moral minimum for corporations operating abroad.

MINIMAL AND MAXIMAL DUTIES

Thomas Donaldson suggests that we distinguish the minimal and 25 maximal duties of corporations and come to some agreement about the former. A maximal duty or obligation, he says, is one whose fulfillment would be "praiseworthy but not absolutely mandatory," whereas a minimal duty is one such that "the persistent failure to observe [it] would deprive the corporation of its moral right to exist."[7] The requests of Third World countries for help in improving living conditions and developing the local economy, although often expressed as demands for justice, are, in Donaldson's view, pleas for a kind of "corporate philanthropy" that is, at best, a maximal duty and not a moral minimum.[8] Further impoverishing a people or violating a fundamental human right, such as employing child labor, is, by contrast, a failure to observe minimal obligations that apply to all business enterprises.

What principles might serve to justify the minimal duties or obligations of corporations engaged in international business? Two have been proposed. One is the principle of *negative harm*, which holds that in their dealings abroad, corporations have an obligation not to add substantially to the deprivation and suffering of people.[9] The utilitarian injunction to produce the greatest possible benefit to people creates a set of maximal obligations of TNCs, but a concern with consequences can take a number of progressively weaker forms that include preventing harm and merely avoiding the infliction of harm. William K. Frankena distinguishes four versions of an obligation of beneficence: (1) One ought not to inflict evil or harm, (2) one ought to prevent evil or harm, (3) one ought to remove evil, and (4) one ought to do or promote good.[10] The negative-harm principle, which is the weakest form, is (arguably) a moral minimum, so that regardless of what other obligations corporations have in foreign operations, they have this one. The only morally justified exceptions to the obligation not to inflict substantial harm on a people are to avoid violating an important right of some kind or to produce a greater benefit in the long run.

A second principle, proposed by Thomas Donaldson, is that corporations have an obligation to respect certain rights; namely, those that ought to be recognized as *fundamental international rights.*[11] TNCs are not obligated to extend all the rights of U.S. citizens to people everywhere in the world, but there are certain basic rights that no person or institution, including a corporation, is morally permitted to violate. Fundamental international rights are roughly the same as *natural* or *human* rights, and some of these are given explicit recognition in documents ranging from general statements, such as the United Nations Universal Declaration of Human Rights, to the very specific, such as the World Health Organization (WHO) Code of Marketing Breast Milk Substitutes.

Of course, the main problem with a principle to respect fundamental international rights (or fundamental rights, for short) is specifying the rights in question. Even undeniable human rights that create an obligation for some person or institution, such as the government of a country, are not always relevant to a transnational corporation. Everyone has a right to subsistence, for example, but TNCs may be under no obligation to feed the hungry in a country where it operates. It has an obligation, however, not to contribute directly to starvation by, say, converting cultivated land to the production of an export crop. To deal with these complications, Donaldson says that a right must meet the following conditions:

1. The right must protect something of very great importance.
2. The right must be subject to substantial and recurrent threats.
3. The obligations and burdens imposed by the right must be (a) affordable and (b) distributed fairly.[12]

The "fairness-affordability" criterion, expressed in condition 3, serves to relieve corporations of an obligation to do what is beyond its resources and more than its fair share. Although a more extensive list could perhaps be justified by Donaldson's conditions, he suggests the following as a moral minimum:

1. The right to freedom of physical movement.
2. The right to ownership of property.
3. The right to freedom from torture.
4. The right to a fair trial.
5. The right to nondiscriminatory treatment.
6. The right to physical security.
7. The right to freedom of speech and association.
8. The right to minimal education.
9. The right to political participation.
10. The right to subsistence.[13]

Sample applications of these rights, according to Donaldson, include failing to provide safety equipment, such as goggles, to protect employees from obvious hazards (the right to physical security); using coercive tactics to prevent workers from organizing (the right to freedom of speech and association); employing child labor (the right to minimal education); and bribing government officials to violate their duty or seeking to overthrow democratically elected governments.[14]

Endnotes

1. Norman E. Bowie, "The Moral Obligations of Multinational Corporations," in *Problems of International Justice*, ed. Steven Luper-Foy (Boulder, Colo.: Westview Press, 1987), p. 97.
2. Quoted in Ledogar, *Hungry for Profits*, pp. 46–47.
3. This point is made by Richard T. DeGeorge, "Ethical Dilemmas for Multinational Enterprise," in *Ethics and the Multinational Enterprise*, ed. W. Michael Hoffman, Ann E. Lange, and David A. Fedo (Lanham, Md.: University Press of America, 1986), p. 40.
4. For an argument of this kind, see Henry Shue, "Transnational Transgressions," in Tom Regan, *Just Business: New Introductory Essays in Business Ethics* (New York: Random House, 1984), pp. 271–91.
5. For a history of the Arab boycott, see Dan S. Chill, *The Arab Boycott of Israel* (New York: Praeger, 1976).
6. Walter Guzzardi Jr., "That Curious Barrier on the Arab Frontier," *Fortune* (July 1975): 170.
7. Thomas Donaldson, *The Ethics of International Business* (New York: Oxford University Press, 1989), p. 62.
8. Ibid., p. 63.
9. For an application of the negative-harm principle to business in South Africa, see Patricia H. Werhane, "Moral Justifications for Doing Business in South Africa," in Hoffman, Lange, and Fedo, *Ethics and the Multinational Enterprise*, pp. 435–42. The principle is applied to hazardous wastes and technology in Henry Shue, "Exporting Hazards," in *Boundaries: National Autonomy and Its Limits*, ed. Peter G. Brown and Henry Shue (Totowa, N.J.: Rowman and Littlefield, 1981), pp. 107–45.
10. William K. Frankena, *Ethics*, 2d ed. (Englewood Cliffs, N.J.: Prentice Hall, 1973), p. 47.
11. Donaldson, *The Ethics of International Business*, chap. 5.
12. Ibid., pp. 75–76.
13. Ibid., p 81.
14. Ibid., pp. 87–89.

Questions for Discussion

1. Boatright contends that one key to practicing good ethics in international business is to avoid double standards. What does he mean?
2. In what circumstances would it be appropriate, according to Boatright, to abide by the local standards of a foreign country in which one is doing business?
3. What are the ten suggestions that Donaldson proposes as "a moral minimum" with respect to international or fundamental rights?
4. What does Boatright mean by the adage "When in Rome . . ."?

Questions for Writing

1. According to Boatright, "The conditions prevailing in other parts of the world are different in some morally relevant respects from those in the United States and other developed countries." Is Boatright's claim valid? Why or why not? Analyze his statement in an essay.
2. Is it always possible to follow the advice "When in Rome . . ." when one is pursuing international business? Assess the pros and the cons of following local ethical standards in an essay.

Student Essay

The Three Keys to Marketing Success

BLAIR MASCHING

Some believe that the ideas of a country can be distinguished from its advertising. By studying a country's advertisements, many are certain, "you can tell what lifestyles people lead, their aspirations, their fears, and you can even tell a country's future" (Leonard 1). This gives those in the field of marketing a huge responsibility. Unfortunately, laws are often stretched to the limits and reputations tainted in the area of marketing without even the knowledge of wrongdoing. Although there are indeed many corrupt persons in the realm of business, a number of talented marketing professionals are actively combining three keys for success in the field of marketing.

Unfortunately, many corporate firms concern themselves more with profits at the expense of their customers. Some practices that should be illegal or unprofitable are in fact not. However, I believe that even, at times, when the law is not restricting "questionable business tactics," business professionals should avoid partaking in unethical practices. After all, your deed does not go unnoticed, because it usually attracts a like response. Zig Ziglar, an American motivator, has said it like this: "Life is an echo. What you send out—comes back" (98). His statement describes my passion for the field of marketing.

As a marketing professional, I will have a hand in creating campaigns and promotions that "send out" positive messages, and therefore, positively influence the population and society as a whole. I want to see the United States in a position in which other countries can positively identify our country by the family values displayed in our advertising strategies.

However, some of America's advertising strategies have not promoted family values. For example, Calvin Klein, a well-known United States garment designer, frequently presents next-to-naked models that appear to be underage in his advertisements. Over twenty years ago, young actress and model Brooke Shields was featured in commercials all over the world wearing Calvin Klein denim jeans while erotically claiming, "Nothing gets between me and my Calvins." Klein has stood behind his marketing since the day he began promoting his clothing line by assuring, "We're not trying to shock and we're not trying to create controversy" (qtd in Boone and Kurtz 289). Although Klein may think of his commercials and photos as artistic expressions merely used to sell products, pedophiles and pornographers, for example, prey on images of this kind.

Three principles, which are justly applied to the realm of business and a career in marketing, are integrity, tithing, and being debt-free. Having integrity in business includes not lying, bribing, or hiding facts from unsuspecting customers. By applying the principle of integrity to the day-to-day pragmatics of a career in marketing, professionals can be assured that remaining upright and not compromising their morals to increase sales or company revenue will allow them to truly succeed. The second important principle is tithing.

Tithing is voluntarily contributing one-tenth of one's annual income to a cause, for example, support of a nonprofit organization. However, selecting a charitable organization worthy of company donations is essential and should be done with ethical consideration. Aside from gaining community [respect], when a business executive donates a percentage of his company's revenue, he should expect a return in future business endeavors.

Another principle that can be followed daily by those in all fields, including marketing, is to remain free of debt. Owing others money, especially if there is not an intent to repay the debt, is unethical. Utilizing a company's finances efficiently should always be that company's objective. In addition to freeing one's company from debt, there is importance for those in the business world to remain in the black in personal financial standing in order to be examples to those they advise.

Although many marketing professionals, for instance, use ads of deception to entice consumers, some marketing professionals work to apply ethical principles to the day-to-day pragmatics of the business profession in this area. Hence, if the echo that comes back is the reflection of what we send out, then for those business professionals who play by the golden rule, the dividends of fair play and honesty are worth it.

Works Cited

Boone, Louis E., and David L. Kurtz. "Consumer Behavior." *Contemporary Marketing*. New York: Dryden Press, 1999. 264–293.

Leonard, Mark. "Sinister Secrets of the Ad Men." *New Statesmen* 127 (1998): 1–4.

Ziglar, Zig. *Zig Ziglar's Little Instruction Book: Inspiration and Wisdom from America's Top Motivator*. Tulsa: Honor Books, Inc., 1997.

Questions for Discussion

1. According to Masching, what are the three keys to success? What, if any, keys would you add and why?
2. Discuss Leonard's assertion (quoted by Masching), by studying a country's advertisement, "you can tell what lifestyles people lead, their aspirations, their fears, and you can even tell a country's future." Do you agree? Explain.
3. Explain Ziglar's statement "Life is an echo. What you send out—comes back." Discuss the implications of this statement for business ethics.
4. Discuss Masching's statement "I want to see the United States in a position in which other countries can positively identify our country by the family values displayed in our advertising strategies." Relate this to the following:
   - politics
   - education
   - international business and other relations

Questions for Writing

1. Remaining debt free is a challenge for most Americans, especially for college students, who often have student loans, car payments, credit cards, and so forth. How can college students in particular, and Americans in general, devise plans to eliminate their debts? Write an informative paper on this subject.
2. Do you think that Masching's three keys are necessary for success in the business world? Write an analytical essay in response to this question.

Questions for Making Connections Within the Chapter

1. How can ethical behavior be fostered among professionals in the corporate world? Consider the recommendations for higher ethical standards suggested by Masching and Boatright.
2. Grimm as well as Frohnen and Clarke, in their respective articles, explore the consequences that business executives' greed-driven choices have

on the public. What do these authors conclude about the ethics, or the lack thereof, in these instances?

3. What ethical responsibilities do businesses have in relation to their consumers? How do Grimm and Seglin address this question?

4. How important are business ethics in terms of the following topics? Think about the views of the authors featured in this chapter.

- overall longevity of a company
- long-term profits
- employee morale
- retention rate of employees

CHAPTER 5

Ethics and Medicine

The web of our life is of a mingled yarn,
good and ill together: our virtues would be proud if our faults whipped
    them not;
and our crimes would despair
if they were not cherished by our own virtues.

        William Shakespeare, *All's Well That Ends Well*

A number of issues in the field of science and medicine require ethical attention. With more and more research in genetic engineering and cloning, bioethicists are struggling to define the lines between exploitation of humans and the preservation of human life. Should scientists use stem cells for medical research? Should they move forward with cloning human life? Should terminally ill patients have the liberty to end their life? On yet another issue, the Internet has become a black market for the distribution of bogus medicine, and the Federal Trade Commission and Food and Drug Administration are working to crack down on this problem. These are some of the issues that currently plaque the medical community and that are discussed in this chapter.

In his article Peter Singer explores the sanctity of human life, a topic that has been debated by Jews and Christians, among others, for millennia. He looks at not only the religious and moral but also the medical and legal aspects of the definition of death. Singer examines euthanasia in the case of disabled infants and terminally ill patients.

Health insurance is a topic on the minds of many Americans, for a number of them are without insurance. To complicate matters more, Sheryl Gay Stolberg and Jeff Gerth tackle pharmaceutical sales representatives who woo physicians with perks to sway them to prescribe certain drugs to their patients, but advocates of the pharmaceutical industry claim that the industry educates physicians so that they can effectively prescribe medications.

In her article, Margaret R. McLean examines the ethics of shaping public policy concerning stem cell research. The task is daunting and complicated. One major problem is reconciling the number of "moral commitments and belief systems" that often polarize discussion of this topic. Stem cell research can be seen as simply another way for the medical community to maintain human dignity by treating disease and abnormality. However, opponents see this research as the exploitation of human life.

Sparking as heated a debate as stem cell research has, human cloning poses many of the same ethical challenges for the medical community. Dan W. Brock surveys the pros and cons of human cloning. One argument of supporters is that "human cloning would enable couples in which one party risks transmitting a serious hereditary disease to an offspring to reproduce without doing so." One argument of opponents is that "human cloning procedures would carry unacceptable risks to the clone." The author concludes that due to the moral and ethical concerns, much more public debate should occur before human cloning is permitted.

Toni Sanchez, a premed major, explores in her article the medical profession from a scientific view. Then she applies faith-based principles to healing, arguing that some of what physicians do can be traced to medical research while some of what they witness goes far beyond medical explanation: "Even scientific evidence supports the phenomenon that some terminal medical cases and their 'Cinderella' outcomes exceed known medical research and treatment options."

Life is precious, more valuable than anything else, and the more we discover about how to prolong it, the more we are faced with another problem: can we maintain the quality and dignity of life for each individual without crossing ethical, moral, and legal parameters? Then, there is the issue of stem cells, among other hot-button topics. The subject matter in this chapter offers much for stimulating dialogue and much for thoughtful ethical consideration.

Changing Ethics in Life and Death Decision Making

PETER SINGER

The traditional ethic of the sanctity of human life has been central to Jewish and Christian thinking for millennia. I shall argue that the traditional ethic cannot be defended in terms of public reasoning—that is, reasoning that can appeal to people independently of their religious beliefs. I shall do so by discussing two separate issues. First, I shall look at the way in which we have, over the last 30 years, changed our understanding of when a human being is dead. I take up this seemingly settled issue in order to show that the change we have made is in fact an illogical one, and one that already represents a significant erosion of the traditional doctrine of the sanctity of human life—and yet one that few of us would wish to undo. Secondly, I shall consider an issue that shows how secular reasoning might offer a better solution than the traditional ethic to a very difficult problem: the treatment of infants born with severe disabilities.

CHANGING CONCEPTIONS OF DEATH

In 1968 the legal definition of death, everywhere in the world, was based on the cessation of heartbeat and of the circulation of the blood. Since that year, with surprisingly little controversy, brain death has been accepted as an alternative criterion of death, not only in the United States, but in virtually every country of the world. This came about because the change was presented and accepted as an improved scientific understanding of the nature of death. It was therefore seen not as an ethical issue at all, but rather as a matter of medical science. This widely-held view is a mistake. The new criterion of death sprang from the suggestion put by Professor Henry Beecher of Harvard University, who was clearly motivated by the need to make organs available in good condition for the then-new procedure of organ transplantation. The Harvard committee that Beecher subsequently chaired did not claim, in its ground-breaking 1968 report, that its new definition of death reflected some scientific discoveries about, or improved scientific understanding of, the nature of death. It was, instead, because the committee saw the status quo as imposing great burdens on various people and institutions affected by it, and as preventing the proper use of the "life-saving potential" of the organs of people in "irreversible coma" that the committee recommended the new definition of death.

But the judgment that it is good to avoid these burdens, and to ensure that organs can be used, is an ethical judgment, not a scientific one. To think that this definition was either a new scientific discovery, or merely a matter of clarifying a vagueness introduced by modern methods of intensive care, was a widely shared misconception. (As early as 1957, when respirators were beginning to be used, Pope Pius XII had said that it is for doctors, not the Church, to give a clear and precise definition of "death" and "the moment of death" of a patient who passes away in a state of unconsciousness. See "The Prolongation of Life: An Address of Pope Pius XII to International Congress of Anesthesiologists," *The Pope Speaks*, vol. 4, 1957, p. 396.) But it was in no one's interest—not that of doctors, hospitals, families of brain-dead patients, or potential organ recipients—to challenge the reassuring idea that accepting the new definition of death was a matter of taking the advice of experts on a technical and scientific matter. This may explain why the new definition has triumphed in a relatively uncontroversial way. But that situation is already unraveling.

Some patients who can be shown to have no brain function are quite evidently still living human organisms. They have been maintained in intensive care units—or even, in one case, at home—for long periods, and in the case of pregnant women, they have even supported fetuses that have grown to term inside them. If a human organism can "survive," as an organism, for several years after all brain function has ceased, this shows that the brain is not essential for integrated organic functioning. True, the survival of these human beings is dependent on machines, but we do not consider a person on dialysis to be dead because a machine has replaced her kidney function. Similarly, we should not think of people whose brains have irreversibly ceased to function as dead because their brain functions have been replaced by machines or other techniques.

5   Attentive readers will have noted that the passage I quoted earlier from the Harvard committee's report refers to "irreversible coma" as the condition that it wishes to define as death; the committee also speaks of "permanent loss of intellect." "Irreversible coma" is an odd term to use of someone who is dead, and it is by no means identical with the death of the whole brain. Permanent damage to the parts of the brain responsible for consciousness

can mean that a patient is in a condition in which the brain stem and the central nervous system continue to function, but consciousness has been irreversibly lost. Patients in a persistent vegetative state are in this situation, although today they would not be said to be in a coma.

Admittedly, the Harvard committee report does go on to say, immediately following the paragraph quoted above: "we are concerned here only with those comatose individuals who have no discernible central nervous system activity." But the reasons given by the committee for redefining death—the great burden on the patients, their families, the hospitals and the community, as well as the waste of organs needed for transplantation—apply in every respect to all those who are irreversibly comatose, not only to those whose entire brain is dead.

Why then did the committee limit its concern to those with no brain activity at all? One reason may be that the committee believed—as many others have believed since—that the bodily functions of people whose whole brain was dead could only be maintained for a day or two. Where the brain stem survives, the body does not need anything more than food, fluids and basic nursing care to keep functioning indefinitely. A second reason could be that in 1968, the only form of "irreversible coma" that could be reliably diagnosed—with no possibility of a patient being declared dead and then "waking up"—was that in which there was no discernible brain activity at all. Another possible reason for the committee redefining death only as far as those with no brain activity at all is that if the respirator is removed from such patients, they stop breathing and so will soon be dead by anyone's standard. People in a persistent vegetative state, on the other hand, continue to breathe without mechanical assistance. So if the Harvard committee had included in its definition of death people who are in an irreversible coma but still have some brain activity, they would have been suggesting that people could be buried while they are still breathing.

We now know that the bodily functions of those whose brains have entirely ceased to function can be maintained for months or years. So the first possible reason for restricting the definition of death to those whose entire brains have ceased to function is no longer valid. Technology has also eliminated the second reason: although in some cases of patients in a long-term persistent vegetative state, we still lack any completely reliable means of saying when recovery is impossible, in other cases new forms of brain imaging can establish that the parts of the brain associated with consciousness have ceased to exist, and hence that consciousness cannot return.

Thus of the three reasons for limiting the definition of death to those whose brains have entirely ceased to function, only the last—the problem of declaring patients dead when they are breathing spontaneously—remains.

10   One solution to the present unsatisfactory state of the definition of death, therefore, is to couple the implications of the reasons given by the Harvard committee for switching to brain death in the first place with our improved diagnostic abilities, and move on to a definition of death in terms of the irreversible loss of consciousness. With the irreversible loss of consciousness, we have lost everything that we value in our own existence, and everything that gives us reason to hope for the survival of someone we love.

The significance of consciousness, and its link with the brain, answers the fundamental question—"why the brain?"—which supporters of the whole brain death criterion have never been able to answer satisfactorily in any other way. The death of the brain is the end of everything that matters about a person's life. Of course, the death of those parts of the brain required for consciousness, is also the end of everything that matters about a person's life. So the definition of death in terms of the irreversible loss of consciousness means that the criterion for death is the irreversible cessation of function of what is variously referred to as the cortex, the cerebral hemispheres, or the cerebrum. To avoid the need to define this more precisely, I shall use the expression "the higher brain" to refer to whatever parts of the brain are required for consciousness. (For an early defense of a higher-brain definition of death, see Michael Green and Daniel Wilder, "Brain Death and Personal Identity," *Philosophy and Public Affairs*, 9 [1980], pp. 105–133.)

Do we really want to introduce a new concept of death, which implies that warm, spontaneously breathing human beings are dead? I doubt that it is wise to attempt such a revisionist redefinition of a term in common use. "Dead" is a term applied much more widely than human beings, or conscious beings. Living things with no brain at all, let alone a higher brain, can be alive, and they can die. Why fiddle with a term that we all understand quite well? Even the much more modest revision proposed by the Harvard committee has yet to be absorbed into the way most people think about death. It is common to read newspaper headlines like 'Brain-Dead Woman Gives Birth, then Dies." If we try to tell relatives that their loved one is dead when he or she is lying on a bed, with no machines in sight, breathing normally, they are simply not going to believe us. And with good reason: for like the proponents of the initial shift to brain death, we would be guilty of trying to disguise an important ethical decision as a matter of scientific fact.

We cannot go back to the traditional definition of death, for then we would lose the chance to obtain many organs that save people's lives. But equally, we cannot go forward and define death in terms of the irreversible loss of consciousness. But while most people would have difficulty in believing that someone lying on a bed, breathing normally, is dead, they do distinguish between different brain functions, not for the purposes of separating the living from the dead, but because there are some brain functions that we care about, and others that do not matter. If then, we ask which brain functions do matter, I believe that most people would answer that it is, minimally, those associated with consciousness. If it could be shown that vital organs were removed from patients who still retained the capacity for conscious experience, the likelihood of a public outcry would be much greater than if it were reported—as in fact it has been reported—that organs are being taken from patients whose brains continue to secrete hormones, and who thus are not legally dead, in the sense that their brains have not entirely ceased to function.

Stressing the importance of consciousness may suggest that we should move to a higher brain conception of death: but this is not the only possible conclusion to draw. To claim that human beings die when they have irreversibly lost the capacity for consciousness is too paradoxical. Instead we could accept the traditional conception of death, but reject the ethical view that it is always wrong intentionally to end the life of an innocent human being. We could then regard it as ethically acceptable (subject to the appropriate consent being given) to discontinue life support, or to remove organs for transplantation, when there has been an irreversible loss of consciousness. We would thus achieve the same practical outcome as we would achieve by redefining death in terms of the irreversible loss of consciousness. We would, in the terms used by the Harvard committee, have relieved the burden on families, hospitals and those in need of hospital beds, placed by the need to care for those who can never return to consciousness. We would have relieved this burden, not only when it arises from those whose whole brain has ceased to function, but also when it arises from those whose brain stem continues to operate. We would have done this without having to declare dead—in any sense—those who breathe unaided. Last but by no means least, we would have made our ethical judgments transparent, thus advancing public understanding of the issues involved rather than hindering it.

15   The only serious objection I can see to this proposal is the claim that, no matter how logically compelling it may be, it is so out of touch with reality that it stands no chance of success. After all, it is a head-on challenge to the traditional doctrine of the sanctity of all human life. Better, some will say, to do our best to push back the extent of that doctrine's reach, by extending the definition of death to cover those who have irreversibly lost consciousness, than to hurl ourselves vainly against the doctrine's citadel. Better, in other words, to maintain the fiction that brain death really is death, and indeed to try to spread this fiction even wider.

I would not deny that there are occasions when a fiction serves a useful purpose and is better not disturbed. But this does not seem to be one of them. For one thing, the fiction is coming apart anyway; and [for an]other, the traditional sanctity of life doctrine is increasingly being abandoned by medical practice and the law, if not yet in the United States, then in other countries like The Netherlands and Great Britain. Truth is generally a better basis for ethics than fiction.

LIFE AND DEATH DECISIONS FOR DISABLED INFANTS

I have shown that even those who want to hold fast to a traditional view of the sanctity of all human life must face difficult problems in relation to humans whose brains have irreversibly ceased to function. To reach a coherent and consistent solution to these problems, we need to dig deeper, and question something that we ordinarily take for granted, the idea that it is always wrong to take the life of an innocent human being. This is, to many people, a shocking suggestion, for the sanctity of human life is something that we scarcely dare question. Yet philosophers ought to question just those beliefs that we routinely take for granted, including this one, and I hope I have now shown that the questions are already raised even by something that is a matter of broad consensus, namely the shift to a definition of death in terms of the irreversible cessation of brain function. So here is one way to make progress with this problem. Ask yourself: "Is it worse to kill a human being than it is to kill, say, a chicken?"

Unless you are a vegetarian, you are certainly going to say yes, it is. And even if you are a vegetarian—as I am—you are very likely going to think—as I do—that when someone kills people randomly in the street or in a school, that is a greater tragedy than what happens daily at a slaughterhouse. But why? Unless we take refuge in religious teachings, which not all of us share, the answer has to be because of some difference between humans and animals. That difference, however, cannot merely be the fact that we belong to one species and chickens, for instance, belong to another. To think that mere species membership alone could make such a crucial moral difference would be a kind of species racism—more briefly, speciesism. Suppose there were intelligent Martians, very like us, and entirely peaceable and friendly to us, but of a different species. Would it be acceptable to kill them, just because they are not members of our species? Surely not.

So if it is worse to kill human beings at random than to kill nonhuman animals, the difference must have something to do with the kinds of beings that humans are. And I would suggest, more specifically, that it must have something to do with the higher mental capacities that humans have—capacities that nonhuman animals do not have. This cannot be merely the capacity to feel pleasure or pain, or to suffer from the severing of a relationship like that between mother and child, for all mammals have these capacities. To give us a reason for thinking it much worse to kill typical humans than it is to kill beings of other species, the capacities must go beyond these—they might include, not merely awareness, but self-awareness, or possibly the capacity for making plans for the future. Here we have, I believe, a reason for distinguishing between the wrongness of killing beings that is based on something that is clearly morally relevant. The fact that a being is capable of understanding that it has "a life" does make it worse, other things being equal, to end that life. Then, and only then, are we ending the life of a being that knows it is alive, and can see itself as existing over time. Then, and only then, does the being have any conception of what it might lose by being killed, or have any capacity to have desires for the future that are thwarted by being killed.

But at this point it will become obvious that while typical humans—the humans who get killed when a gunman randomly fires into a crowd—have these capacities, and have them to a degree that a nonhuman animal does not, some humans do not have them. Newborn infants, for example, do not have them. And, while you might immediately object that a newborn infant has the potential to become a being with intellectual capacities far superior to those of any nonhuman animal, if this is supposed to be the reason why it is as bad to kill a newborn infant as an older human being, we shall have to acknowledge that the human fetus also has a very similar potential to that of the infant, and hence the same reason would make it very seriously wrong to kill a human fetus. Some, of course, will endorse this conclusion. But let us note here that a lot of people do not, and without the influence of hard-line religious teachings, even fewer would endorse it.

20   I do not think that the potential of a being is enough to make it wrong to kill that being. The world population has now passed six billion, heading for somewhere around 9 or 10 billion—a figure that will strain our planet's resources to the limits of their capacity. We do not think it obligatory, or even desirable, for fertile couples to bring as many human beings as possible into existence, even though each one of them would, in all probability, become a unique, rational, self-aware human being. And on the same grounds, I do not think that the fact that a human fetus would, in all probability, become a unique, rational, self-aware being is a reason against having an abortion.

I can now begin to explain my views on the issue that has caused so much controversy over my appointment to a chair of bioethics at Princeton University—the issue of life-and-death decision making for infants with disabilities. For the reason I have just quickly sketched, I do not think that killing any newborn infant is morally equivalent to killing a rational and self-conscious being. This does not mean, of course, that killing infants is a matter of moral indifference. On the contrary, to kill an infant is normally very wrong indeed, but normally it is wrong primarily because of the harm it does to the parents, who have conceived the child, and already love it and wish to nurture it. The death of a newborn infant is generally a tragedy for the parents, not for the infant who has not even glimpsed the prospects of the life that might have been in store for it.

What difference, then, does disability make to our life-and-death decision making for newborn infants? I became interested in the treatment of severely disabled newborn infants in the late 1970s when I learned that it is common practice for doctors to deal with such cases by "letting nature take its course." This means that no operations are performed, or no antibiotics given, and the babies die slowly over many days, weeks, or even months. Parents are often not consulted, but simply told that there is nothing that can be done for their child. This seems to me an evasion of moral responsibility, and often grossly inhumane. Yet on investigating the prospects for some of the more severely disabled infants. I had to accept that it was not always good to prolong life, no matter what its prospects might be. But who should make this difficult decision? The infant, of course, cannot.

The parents are, in normal circumstances, the people most affected by whether their infant lives or dies, and they should, on the basis of the fullest possible information, have the principal say in the decision whether or not the resources of modern medicine should be used to keep their child alive. I accept that doctors may have an unduly negative view of life with a particular disability. I therefore urge parents in doubt over such a decision not to rely only on information from their doctors, but to contact groups representing those with the particular disability, or their parents or those who care for them, to broaden their sources of information.

Nevertheless, parents will still sometimes decide, on reasonable grounds, that it is better that the child should not live. What should happen then? When the publicity over my views about the treatment of severely disabled newborn infants was at its height. I received a phone call from a doctor who directs a neonatal intensive care unit, and deals with such cases every day. He told me that, after consulting with parents, if they agree that it is better that their child should not be kept alive, he will turn off respirators, and even withdraw the tubes that supply the baby with food and fluids. But he will not give the baby a lethal injection. He said that he sees an important moral distinction there, but he could not explain to me in what it lay. I told him that I can understand why, psychologically, he perceives the two as different, but that I can see no important moral distinction between allowing death to occur by the deliberate withholding of available medical treatment and actively intervening to hasten death and ensure that it comes swiftly and humanely. In fact, I think the latter course, precisely because it does involve less suffering, is often the morally better one to take.

Not all doctors, of course, are as ready as this doctor was to consult with parents and withdraw treatment, even when the prospects for a baby are very poor. Around the same time that I spoke to the doctor, I received an email from a woman I will call Mrs. B:

25

My son, John [not his real name], was born almost 2 1/2 years ago 11 weeks premature and weighing only 1 lb. 14oz. They assured me that because he was already 29 weeks and had no intracranial hemorrhages that he would be fine; he would just need to catch up with other kids his birth age. That is not the case. John has spastic diplegia cerebral palsy with underlying right hemiplegia, . . . has sensory problems, and has speech delays. We don't know what his level of intellectual functioning will be, although people tell me he will probably be of "normal" intelligence with perhaps numerous learning disabilities. He is certainly more functional than some children with CP and has at least a small chance at a reasonably "normal" life, but that is not the issue.

My husband and I love our son (middle of three), but had someone told me, "Mrs. B, your son will have numerous disabilities down the road. Do you still want us to intubate him?," my answer would have been no. It would have been a gut wrenching decision, but it would have been for the best. It would have been in the best interest for John, for us, and for our other children. I am saddened beyond words to think of all he will have to cope with as he grows older.

This is not the only letter of this kind I have received, and I do not think that Mrs. B is an atypical mother. [Mrs. B and other mothers like her] live with children with severe disabilities, and they clearly judge the lives of their children to be such that it would have been better if they had died at or soon after birth.

Mrs. B goes on to make another point that is also relevant to the question of how most of us would act when faced with the option to choose whether to have a child with a serious disability:

This is definitely not the life I would have chosen for myself either. My husband and I have never made it a secret that we were not cut out to be parents of a severely handicapped child, and had always said that if we were to find out we were having one, we would abort. I felt I was not a special enough person to deal with having that kind of a child.

This is, evidently, a common view. Prenatal diagnosis is routinely recommended for women who become pregnant over the age of 35, and the overwhelming majority of women of that age act on the recommendation. If the tests show that the fetus is affected by a condition such as Down syndrome, or spina bifida, almost all women will terminate the pregnancy. Their motivation may be mixed. In part, like Mrs. B, they may not see themselves as cut out to be the mother of a child with a severe disability. But, wanting the best for their child, they may also think that it is better to terminate a life that has started badly, and perhaps try again.

In thinking about these issues, we should not forget that most couples today, at least in the developed world, plan their families. They will have perhaps two or three children. The decision to abort a fetus that has, say, Down syndrome, is not a decision that is "anti-children," still less "anti-life." It is a decision that says: "Since I will only have two children, I want them to have the best possible prospects for a full and rich life. And if, at the outset, those prospects are seriously clouded, I would rather start again."

This is surely a reasonable view to take. Does it reflect a prejudice against the idea that life with a disability can be worth living? No, no more than requiring those who sell alcohol to put warnings on their containers saying: "GOVERNMENT WARNING: According to the Surgeon General women should not drink alcoholic beverages during pregnancy because of the risk of birth defects." That clearly implies that in the opinion of the United States government and the surgeon general, women should avoid causing birth defects in their offspring. In both cases, we are not denying that people with disabilities can have lives worth living, we are just saying that, other things being equal, it is better to have children without disabilities And I haven't noticed groups like Not Dead Yet campaigning against government funds going into research to find ways of overcoming paraplegia.

It is curious that many of us seem to accept such reasoning when it comes to preventing the births of children with disabilities, sometimes even when this involves ending a life during pregnancy, and yet we are shocked by exactly the same reasoning as soon as the baby has been born. I am not sure why. If there is one thing that the opponents of abortion are right about, it is surely that birth does not mark any decisive change in the nature of the being itself. The development of the fetus into infant is a gradual one. Perhaps the most significant difference that birth makes is that the infant can more easily be given up for adoption. That is why, where the disability is not a very serious one, if there are couples keen to adopt a child, that is a better outcome than ending its life.

Apart from that distinction between the late fetus and the newborn, I can see no reason for drawing the line at birth—unless it is the need to have some non-arbitrary line that compels us to take our stand with birth. I have suggested that the real

30

moral dividing line occurs later, when self-awareness begins. But here too there is no sharp line to be drawn. That is why, at one point, my colleague Helga Kuhse and I proposed that a breathing space of 28 days should be allowed after birth, in which parents and doctors together should have discretion to make life and death decisions about a newborn child. But I now think this is too arbitrary to work—so I will merely say that these decisions should be made as soon after birth as the accurate diagnosis of the infant's condition, and the parents' need for due consideration, permits.

I want to conclude this section by emphasizing that what I have been discussing is in the context of infants, and parents' decisions about infants. None of it has any direct application to older children or adults with disabilities. The fact that a person is in a wheelchair, or blind, has nothing at all to do with his or her status as a "person," and therefore is in no way relevant to the seriousness of ending that person's life against his or her will. It is, I admit, true that I would allow parents to end the lives of children who would later grow up to be in wheelchairs, or blind. So people might say to me—as some have—that if my views had been widely followed, they would not be alive today. But that is also true in many cases in respect of abortion, and it might also be true in some cases because of prenatal counseling, since parents may have been advised to, for example, obtain donor semen to avoid a genetic disability. Does anyone see this as a reason to stop prenatal counseling? And no doubt there are many people alive today who would not be alive if their parents had been able to have an abortion, because then their parents would not have had another child.

Finally, I would like to say again, as I have said many times before, that I believe that people with disabilities should be given the fullest possible support from the community in integrating into the community, and being enabled to receive an education, and to live and work as normally as they possibly can. By those standards, the United States still has a long way to go.

EUTHANASIA AND PHYSICIAN-ASSISTED SUICIDE

Another challenge to the traditional ethic comes from the increasing emphasis on the rights of patients to make their own decisions about medical care. In a free society, those with one

ideological position about the wrongness of killing are not entitled to be in a position to prevent an informed, competent, terminally ill patient and a willing doctor from making and acting on
the patient's own judgment about when his or her life is no
longer worth living. It is therefore odd that those who have
claimed to be defenders of individual rights and freedoms have
not all come to the support of the legalization of voluntary euthanasia. How can anyone who thinks that the government
ought not to intrude unnecessarily in the private lives of its citizens hold that the government should interfere in the private decisions of terminally ill patients and their doctors about when it
is time to die?

Voluntary euthanasia will be morally unacceptable to some
members of our society. Their views are, however, implicitly respected in the very idea of voluntary euthanasia—it is an option
(like palliative care and the withholding of treatment) available
to those who want it, and is not a mode of dying that must be
taken up by everyone. Palliative care and non-treatment will remain the preferred option for many people. The fact, however,
that palliative care can give many people the kind of dignified
death they want does not mean that it is appropriate for everyone.

So it is scarcely relevant to argue, as many do, that there are   35
few terminally ill patients who cannot be helped by palliative
care. The figure may be as low as 5 percent. The fundamental
point would still stand even if the percentage were only 0.05 percent: no patient should be made to die in ways that, while meeting the moral or religious precepts of some, are anathema to
their own.

BROADER ISSUES

There are many other things that I would have liked to touch
upon, if space permitted. I would have liked to argue that, just
as we should be critical of the distinction between allowing to
die and intentional killing in the case of the medical treatment
of a severely disabled newborn, so too we should question this
distinction when it comes to our failure to do enough to save the
lives of people in absolute poverty in the world's least-developed
countries. Here we are "allowing [others] to die" by withholding
aid, in order to have more to spend on ourselves. While this may
not be exactly the same as killing, it is uncomfortably close in its

outcome. Since I have on the whole been critical of Christian thinking here, let me try to redress the balance a little by quoting one of the most influential of all Christian thinkers, Thomas Aquinas. Aquinas held that the institution of private property "exists for the satisfaction of human needs, and hence whatever a man has in superabundance is owed, of natural right, to the poor for their sustenance". (*Summa Theologica*, 2, ii, Q 66, Art. 7). Hence those of us who have property in "superabundance"— which I think includes most Americans with average or above average incomes—do wrong to live such comfortable, even luxurious, lives, when elsewhere in the world there are people who are hungry, or malnourished, or dying for want of the most basic medical care. I would also have liked to ask you to reconsider your attitudes to animals, especially those who, at the hands of modern agribusiness, suffer a degree of confinement and exploitation that makes working one's ox on the Sabbath—something the bible prohibits—pale into insignificance. Here it is not so much the death of the animals we eat, as the way they live before they die, that constitutes the strongest argument for change.

Questions for Discussion

1. According to Peter Singer, how have the criteria for the legal definition of death changed since 1968?
2. Is killing a newborn infant who has disabilities ethically, morally, and legally wrong? How does Singer address this delicate topic?
3. What does the author suggest by the statement "Voluntary euthanasia will be morally unacceptable to some members of our society"?
4. In his conclusion Singer brings up a radical perspective on the "allowing to die" issue: Americans' refusal to send necessary food, medicine, money, and so forth to poverty-stricken people in least-developed countries is a form of euthanasia. Is Singer's point valid? Explain.

Questions for Writing

1. Singer affirms, "No patient should be made to die in ways that, while meeting the moral or religious precepts of some, are anathema to their own." Assess the pros and cons of this statement in an essay.
2. Should parents of a disabled infant have the right to end the life of their ill-formed child? Write a persuasive essay considering the different aspects of this question.

High-Tech Stealth Being Used to Sway Doctor Prescriptions
SHERYL GAY STOLBERG AND JEFF GERTH

As a busy internist, Dr. Bruce Moskowitz frequently prescribes cholesterol-lowering medicines and osteoporosis drugs for his elderly patients. Like most physicians, he is no stranger to pharmaceutical sales representatives, and he often chats with them about his preference in medication.

But the drug companies know more about Dr. Moskowitz than he realizes. Over the past decade, with the advent of sophisticated computer technology, pharmaceutical manufacturers have been quietly compiling resumes on the prescribing patterns of the nation's health care professionals, many of whom have no idea that their decisions are open to commercial scrutiny.

These "prescriber profiles" are the centerpiece of an increasingly vigorous—and apparently successful—effort by drug makers to sway doctors' prescribing habits. To create them, pharmaceutical marketers are buying information from pharmacies, the federal government and the American Medical Association, which generates $20 million in annual income by selling biographies of every American doctor.

The profiles do not contain patient names. But they do offer drug companies a window into one half of the doctor-patient relationship. And they are raising important public policy questions, both about the privacy of doctors' prescribing decisions, and how much commercial pressures influence them.

"As an extension of the doctor-patient relationship, doctors are entitled to privacy," said Lawrence O. Gostin, an expert in health privacy at the Georgetown University Law Center.

In describing the profiles as "a fundamental violation" of that privacy, Mr. Gostin said they also raise "an extremely important policy question, which is to what extent are health care prescribing practices influenced by commercial concerns?"

That question is now front and center in the political debate. With the price of prescription medication high on the national agenda, the impact of marketing on the cost of pharmaceuticals is at issue. But while the public discussion has focused largely on the recent trend toward advertising directly to pa-

5

tients, the industry still spends most of its money wooing doctors.

Of the $13.9 billion that the drug companies spent promoting their products last year, 87 percent, or about $12 billion, was aimed at doctors and the small group of nurse practitioners and physicians' assistants who can prescribe some medications, about one million prescribers all told.

"The pharmaceutical industry has the best market research system of any industry in the world," said Mickey C. Smith, a professor of pharmaceutical marketing at the University of Mississippi. "They know more about their business than people who sell coffee or toilet paper or laundry detergent because they truly have a very small group of decision makers, most of whom still are physicians."

10   Pharmaceutical sales representatives have been a staple of American medicine for decades. Their courtship of doctors is intensive and expensive, and their largess runs the gamut, from trinkets like prescription pads and pens, to staff lunches at hospitals and medical offices and offers of free weekends at resorts.

Prescriber profiles play a significant role in the courtship; pharmaceutical marketers say they use the reports to help determine which doctors should be offered certain perks. And the perks themselves worry ethics officials at the American Medical Association, who are trying to discourage doctors from accepting them, even as the association's business side sells information that facilitates the giving of gifts.

Dr. Moskowitz, of West Palm Beach, Fla., is one example. In late August, he received an invitation from two drug companies, the Bayer Corporation and SmithKline Beecham, asking him to a private dinner at the Morton's of Chicago Steakhouse, an expensive chain restaurant not far from his West Palm Beach office, on the evening of Sept. 18.

The topic was high cholesterol, including an update on Baycol, a drug the two companies jointly market. For his feedback, Dr. Moskowitz would be designated a consultant and given a $250 honorarium, along with his choice entree. He declined.

"Drug companies ask me, 'How can we change your prescribing, what would it take, do you want to serve as a consultant?'" Dr. Moskowitz said. "The schemes get more and more desperate."

15   Although most doctors do not believe that such entreaties affect their professional behavior, some studies suggest otherwise.

Dr. Ashley Wazana, a psychiatry resident at McGill University in Montreal, recently analyzed 29 studies on the effects of gifts to doctors.

Published in January in *The Journal of the American Medical Association*, Dr. Wazana's analysis found an association between meetings with pharmaceutical representatives and "awareness, preference and rapid prescribing of new drugs and decreased prescribing of generics."

His conclusion? "We are influenceable," Dr. Wazana said.

In an effort to save money, and also to avoid this influence, some clinics and hospitals have imposed a ban on free drug samples and visits from sales representatives and discourage doctors from taking consulting fees like the one offered by Bayer and SmithKline Beecham.

Among them is the Everett Clinic in Washington State, a group practice of 180 doctors that cares for 250,000 patients. Its officials say that drug costs have declined since the ban.

"Pharmaceutical marketing would often lead to physicians 20 prescribing more costly medicines than are necessary," the clinic's medical director, Dr. Al Fisk, said.

But Dr. Bert Spilker, a senior vice president with the Pharmaceutical Research and Manufacturers of America, an industry trade group, said marketing "serves an essential function in the health care delivery system" by helping to educate doctors, so they can prescribe drugs more appropriately.

Drug companies, however, are often reluctant to disclose details about their marketing efforts, particularly the use of prescriber profiles.

"If we talk about what we do and how we do it," said Jan Weiner, a spokeswoman for Merck & Company, "then our competitors will know a whole lot more than they know now."

THE A.M.A. MASTER LIST

Singling out doctors is not new, but detailed prescriber profiles have been available only since the early 1990's, when most pharmacies adopted computer systems to process insurance claims, said Pat Glorioso, a marketing executive at I.M.S. Health, a leading pharmaceutical market research concern and one of two companies that specialize in collecting records of pharmacy sales.

Through the profiles, a drug company can identify the high- 25 est and lowest prescribers of a particular medicine in a single

ZIP code, county, state or the entire country. They can learn, for example, which antidepressants a particular psychiatrist favors.

"It's very flexible in the way we can slice and dice the information," Ms. Glorioso said. "As technology has improved, we have just ridden that wave."

When pharmacies sell records of prescription drug sales, they do not show names of patients or, in some cases, their doctors. But those records are typically coded with identification numbers issued by the Drug Enforcement Administration to doctors for the purpose of tracking controlled substances. The government sells a list of the numbers, with the corresponding names attached, for fees that can run up to $10,200 a month, depending on how widely the list will be distributed.

The American Medical Association, meanwhile, sells the rights to what it calls its "physicians' master file" to dozens of pharmaceutical companies, as well as I.M.S. Health and other market research concerns. Though only about 40 percent of American doctors are dues-paying members of the medical association, the database has detailed personal and professional information, including the D.E.A. number, on all doctors practicing in the United States.

Pharmaceutical marketers consider the master file the gold standard for reference information about doctors. Combined with the records of pharmacy sales, the file helps create portraits of individual doctors, their specialties and interests. As the nation's largest doctors' group, the medical association has maintained the master file for nearly 100 years, and has licensed it for more than 50. It is so complete, A.M.A. officials say, that even the dead are included.

30   "We're trying to provide a reliable database, which is accurate, so that it can be used appropriately to focus efforts on ways that are beneficial to the patient," said Dr. Thomas R. Reardon, the association's past president, who was designated by the group to address these questions.

There are some restrictions, Dr. Reardon said: the roster cannot be sold to tobacco companies and it cannot be used to deceive doctors or the public. While they say sale of the master file brings about $20 million in annual income to the association, officials would not say what they charge individual companies.

Much of the information in the association's database is available from sources scattered around the country. But one ma-

jor element is not: the medical education number, which the
A.M.A. assigns to new medical students in order to track them
throughout their careers. Most doctors do not even know they
have one.

This number, which enables computers to sort through the
huge A.M.A. master file, is "the core element in the database of
tracking physicians," said Douglas McKendry, a sales executive at
the Acxiom Corporation, a pharmaceutical marketing company
that recently formed a partnership with the medical association
to manage the database.

"The A.M.A. data helps identify the individual physicians that
are being targeted," Mr. McKendry said.

Doctors who do not want their names sent to marketers can   35
ask the association to remove them from the file, Dr. Reardon
said. But in interviews, several prominent doctors said they were
unaware that their biographies were being sold.

Among them is Dr. Christine K. Cassel, a former president
of the American College of Physicians and chairman of the department of geriatrics at Mount Sinai School of Medicine in
Manhattan. In Dr. Cassel's view, information about doctors' prescribing habits may appropriately be used by their health plans
to improve quality of care. She called the commercial use of the
data outrageous, saying, "This is not about quality. It's about
sales."

DINNER AND A MOTIVE

Pharmaceutical marketing is big business not only for drug companies, but also for companies firms like I.M.S. Health and
Acxiom, which cater to them.

Overall spending on pharmaceutical promotion increased
more than 10 percent last year, to $13.9 billion from $12.4 billion in 1998. Experts estimate that the companies collectively
spend $8,000 to $13,000 a year per physician. In recent years,
as demands on doctors' time have grown more intense, pharmaceutical marketers say they have been forced to become
more creative.

"You have to have a hook," said Cathleen Croke, vice president of marketing for Access Worldwide Communications Inc.,
which specializes in drug marketing. "If you offer them $250, that
might get them. Or they are attracted to the prestige of being a
consultant, that a company is asking for their opinion."

40   The offer of dinner and a $250 consulting fee was sufficient to draw about a dozen South Florida physicians to Morton's in West Palm Beach on Sept. 18. They gathered there, on a muggy Monday night, in a back room called the boardroom, where a slide show and a moderator from Boron, LePore & Associates Inc., the market research firm hosting the event, awaited their arrival.

Dr. Moskowitz, who has been in practice in West Palm Beach since 1978 and heads a group of 12 doctors, says he routinely receives—and rejects—such invitations.

The Morton's dinner was not open to the public; had Dr. Moskowitz accepted, he would have been required to sign a confidentiality agreement. Instead, he told the companies he intended to take a reporter for *The New York Times.*

But when Dr. Moskowitz and the reporter showed up at Morton's, the Boron LePore moderator, Alexander Credle, told them to leave.

"This is a clinical experience meeting, a therapeutic discussion," Mr. Credle said. "There is an expected degree of confidentiality."

45   Dr. Moskowitz asked Mr. Credle why he was invited; Mr. Credle had no answer. But in an interview a few weeks after the dinner, John Czekanski, a senior vice president at Boron LePore, said the invitations were "based on databases targeting physicians" who prescribe cholesterol-lowering drugs or who might.

Boron LePore calls these dinner sessions "peer-to-peer meetings," and in 1997, it acted as host at 10,400 of them. Typically, they feature presentations from medical experts, on the theory that doctors are receptive to the views of their peers. With new drugs coming onto the market all the time, physicians are hungry for information about them. Pharmaceutical companies say it is that desire for education, rather than a free meal or modest honorarium, that draws many doctors to the meetings.

But the dinners are creating unease among officials of the American Medical Association's Council on Ethical and Judicial Affairs, which in 1990 published guidelines that limit what gifts doctors may accept. The guidelines, which have also been adopted by the Pharmaceutical Research and Manufacturers' Association, the drug industry trade group, prohibit token consulting arrangements, but permit "modest meals" that serve "a genuine educational function."

Compliance is voluntary, and Dr. Herbert Rakatansky, who is chairman of the A.M.A.'s ethics council, says doctors routinely ignore the rules. That is in part because they are murky, as the dinner at Morton's reveals.

Whether the dinner was intended to educate doctors, or was part of a marketing campaign, or both, is not clear. In the $7.2 billion market for the cholesterol-lowering drugs known as statins, Baycol ranks last in sales, with just $106 million in sales last year. Bayer and SmithKline Beecham recently introduced a new dosage for the drug, and the companies said they used the Morton's meeting to share new clinical data with doctors.

"As far as we're concerned, it's educational," said Carmel   50
Logan, a spokeswoman for SmithKline Beecham. But Tig Conger, the vice president of marketing for cardiovascular products at Bayer, said the company intended to teach a select group of doctors about Baycol, then use their feedback to hone its marketing message. And Allison Wey, a spokeswoman for Boron LePore, said the dinner was "part education and part marketing."

RAISING ETHICS QUESTION

While Dr. Rakatansky, of the A.M.A., could not comment specifically on the Baycol meeting, he had harsh words for these dinners in general.

"We think 99 percent of those are shams," he said. "They are marketing devices and not true requests for information."

As to whether the dinner fit the "modest meal" criteria, that, too, is unclear, because the guidelines offer no specifics. At Morton's in West Palm Beach, the entrees range from $19.95 for chicken to $32.95 for filet mignon—a la carte. The sales manager, Lauren Carteris, said the restaurant frequently was the site of pharmaceutical meetings for Boron LePore.

"Doctors," Ms. Carteris said, "will only go to an expensive restaurant."

To heighten doctors' awareness about the ethics of accepting   55
gifts, the medical association is beginning an educational campaign. In addition, *The Journal of the American Medical Association* devoted the bulk of its Nov. 1 issue to conflict of interest in medicine, including an essay entitled "Financial Indigestion" that

questioned the effects of pharmaceutical company gifts on doctors' professional behavior.

But some prominent doctors say the medical association needs to address its own role, as a seller of information that helps drug marketers select which doctors to target.

"It potentiates this gift giving, and implicitly endorses it," said Dr. David Blumenthal, a professor of health policy at Harvard Medical School who has used the A.M.A.'s data for his academic research.

The sale of the master file to drug companies, Dr. Blumenthal said, "hands the weapon to the drug company that the A.M.A. is saying is an illicit weapon."

Dr. Reardon, the past president of the medical association, dismisses such a connection. Doctors are responsible for their own decisions about whether to accept gifts, he said, adding, "I don't think the database has anything to do with ethical behavior of physicians."

60   Dr. Reardon noted that drug marketers could obtain information about doctors from other sources, including the federal government. But Mr. Gostin, the privacy expert at Georgetown, who is also the health law and ethics editor of *The Journal of the American Medical Association*, said that did not justify the association's action.

"We live in a society where, if you comb long enough and hard enough with sophisticated enough search tools, you can find just about everything," Mr. Gostin said. "That doesn't mean it's all right for people to assemble it, make it easy and sell it."

As for Dr. Moskowitz, he is still receiving invitations from drug companies, despite his longstanding habit of spurning them. One arrived on Oct. 18, from Aventis Pharmaceuticals and Procter & Gamble Pharmaceuticals, who jointly market Actonel, an osteoporosis drug.

Attendance at the meeting, scheduled for Saturday, will be limited to 12 doctors, the invitation said. Breakfast and lunch will be served; in between, there will be a clinical discussion of osteoporosis, with 30 minutes reserved for doctors' feedback. The honorarium is $1,000.

Questions for Discussion

1. What are "prescriber profiles"?

2. Should pharmaceutical companies have access to the prescriber profiles? Consider the advantage(s) and disadvantage(s) to the groups listed below in your response.
   - patients
   - doctors
   - pharmaceutical industry
3. What does Mickey C. Smith mean by the following statement: "The pharmaceutical industry has the best market research system of any industry in the world."
4. What action has the medical association taken "to heighten doctors' awareness about the ethics of accepting gifts"?

Questions for Writing

1. Are there ethical concerns associated with a drug company's "courtship" with physicians who prescribe medication to patients daily? Write your response in an informative essay.
2. Should the American Medical Association sell the rights to its physicians' master file to pharmaceutical companies? Write an argumentative essay for or against this practice.

Stem Cells: Shaping the Future in Public Policy
Margaret R. McLean

A fitting assessment of human stem cell technology mandates that it be seen in light of how it might be used if it meets the bars of safety and effectiveness. Although research involving human embryonic stem (hES) cells will initially improve our understanding of basic human embryonic development and pathology, these cells are harbingers of a revolution in medical therapeutics in which individual replacement cells and tissues will be used to treat myriad degenerative diseases. In addition, because of their ability to undergo prolonged undifferentiated proliferation—so-called immortality—hES cells are potent tools for genetic germ line interventions. The "bigger picture" (Parens 2000) of hES technology, therefore, encompasses both the potential generation of transplantable tissues and, in combination with nuclear and gene transfer technologies, the possibility of reprogenetically shaping children.[1] It is not an exaggeration to say that no corner of medical practice will remain unaffected as medicine shifts its sights from organs and systems to genes and cells.

Stem cell technology's bigger picture presents unprecedented public policy and regulatory challenges. The current genetic revolution and the steady march of biotechnology deeply affect lives, relationships, ideologies, and social structures. How to respond to the challenges of "the biotech century,"[2] including the balance between technologic development in the public and private sectors and extent and type of regulation, is increasingly important to citizens and of increasing concern to governing bodies and regulatory agencies. These policy and regulatory challenges emerge from the very nature of biotechnology and reprogenetic research and development. Unlike earlier big science projects (for example, space exploration and the Manhattan Project), new biotechnologic developments do not rely on large-scale, centralized societal structures and public funding, but on decentralized, punctate, often privately financed systems. Indeed, the entire field of reproductive medicine remains scantly regulated in the United States. The decentralized nature of biotechnology in general and reprogenetic technology in particular allows for great potential benefit—for example, speed—but also an increased opportunity for abuse—for example, unwarranted secrecy. Stem cell technology places control of the biologic processes of aging and disease as well as germ line genetics into the invisible hand of the market and the fleshy hands of individuals, making public policy formation much more complex than for older technologies that required systematic societal involvement.

Recognizing these challenges, and relying on a consideration of justice as "fairness of access" that pays attention to the social lottery,[3] five ethical principles are suggested as a framework for policy formation within a just society.

THE DOLLY EFFECT

As research proceeds, opportunity arises for prospective deliberation of normative and social issues attendant to hES cell research and development. Prudence would dictate that it is best to avoid the Dolly effect; that is, attempting to close the ethical-legal door only after the sheep has left the barn. Dolly's unanticipated debut left the public and the bulk of the scientific community bereft of a framework for considering ethical and policy issues of nuclear transfer technology and cloning. As the Ethics in Genomics Group asserts, "[a]ttention to the direction in which cloning research was headed before Dolly's creation would have better served society than the overreaction which ensued" (Cho et al. 1999, 2087).

The current state of stem cell technology presents an opportunity to avoid the hysterics of the Dolly effect and to engage in broad debate of essential ethical and social issues. Research on stem cells is of such critical importance that responsible citizens should be aware of the current state of the technology and its implications for human biology and health. The public can begin to understand and fully examine what is at stake if endeavors are made to explain the nature and potential medical application of this science and to illuminate key moral, religious, and social concerns. There is a clear need for thoughtful consideration of the impact of biotechnologic innovations including hES cells on the values, commitments, and institutions that nurture both individuals and communities. The fundamental nature of this research imparts a high degree of moral gravity and mandates that ethical evaluation be integral to public policy formation.

It also seems best to avoid a second aspect of the Dolly effect—the rhetoric of inevitability. Often technologic advances are characterized as "inevitable" by both scientists and the public: "[T]he use of reprogenetic technologies is inevitable. It will not be controlled by governments or societies or even the scientists who create it" (Silver 1997, 11). In this view, science is unstoppable and, as such, is not to be the object of ethical concern or stringent regulation. This sense of fatedness profoundly limits our thinking. It is crucial to acknowledge that the possible, however tempting, however frightening, is not the inevitable.

SCIENCE—PUBLIC OR PRIVATE?

Because laws in many countries, including the United States, preclude public funding for human embryo or fetal research, human cell research has steamed ahead in a handful of privately funded labs. The panic-drenched, reactive atmosphere of the Dolly effect raises questions about the wisdom of it remaining confined to private, commercial enterprises. The extraordinary medical potential of hES cells to treat or cure everything from Alzheimer's disease to paralysis imposes the responsibility to consider openly the societal reverberations of the basic research on and medical use of these cells and the proper form of public policy.

To this end, scientists are compelled to include ethical reflection and research integrity in the scientific agenda. But considerations of stem cell technology are too far-reaching to be left to scientists or to professional moral philosophers or theologians alone. Meaningful dialogue about the advent and application of hES cell technology between scientists and the public is essential. "Meaningful dialogue" means conversations that are mutually informative, honest, thoughtful, broadening, and potentially transformative. If such conversations about human stem cells force reexamination of metaphysical questions concerning the nature of human personhood, the extent of human control over life, and humanity's place in the natural world, among other issues, our time is well spent.

Since there was neither public debate nor citizen oversight of initial forays into hES cell research (White 1999; Trauer 1999), the imperative for public deliberation is deeply compelling. It is notable that the Geron Corporation Ethics Advisory Board (GEAB 1999) invited public discourse on the ethical issues emerging from hES cell research. However, research protocol review and ethics review within a private company such as Geron are necessarily private. It is difficult to imagine that all the cards are on the table when lucrative patent rights and hefty shareholder returns are at stake. Meaningful dialogue in the public arena simply cannot be done in a context of proprietary information and profit enhancement. A true debate over public policy demands that both information and deliberation in fact *be public*. It is critical to move hES cell activities and attendant concerns into the public spotlight where they can be broadly deliberated and the research and its application supervised. This is perhaps the strongest argument for government funding, which requires public discourse and access to information generated by hES cell research.

10   In addition, the for-profit mode of the market necessarily influences research direction and access to products. Huge profits are to be made if the transplantation and reprogenetic dreams for stem cells come true. As Lisa Sowle Cahill (2000) notes:

> The individual rights of investigators, investors and companies to sell biomedical tools enjoy a priority in our legal and political system that is unmatched by the right of other members of society to a decent minimum of health care, much less by practical means of structuring behavior patterns so that they contribute to the common good, and further a humane, holistic approach to health, illness, suffering, finitude, scarcity, and social interdependence. (134)

How these profit rights are to be balanced with concerns for individuals, human health, and a just and humane future is a prime challenge for public policy formation.

ETHICS AND PUBLIC POLICY

People of good will disagree about ethical boundaries, private beliefs, and public policies that ought to govern hES cell research, development, and application. That different moral commitments and belief systems cannot be bridged easily is a frequent challenge to policy development in a pluralistic society. What is required is serious civic conversation about points of consonance and dissonance, benefit and burden. The goal is to cultivate policy that adequately mirrors shared visions of human health and flourishing, promotes society's best interest, and vigorously pursues social justice.

In deliberating policy regarding human stem cells, three observations are important (Shapiro 1999). The first is the pervading uncertainty regarding which rival moral points of view ought to shape public policies. A necessary duality to civic conversation involves concern with what ought or ought not be done and concern for how to determine what ought or ought not be done. The second observation is that we cannot (indeed, ought not) escape the tension that characterizes the current situation in which the justifiability of many ethical claims remains dubious to significant segments of the community. Public policy should strive to be the least offensive to the most persons. The final observation is that the set of optimal ethical views—those that produce the most reputable, responsible and redeeming outcomes—are not likely to remain fixed in the fluctuating circumstances of the biotechnologic age. It is inescapable that the scorching pace of biotechnology in general and hES cell research in particular are destined to create new ethical concerns and misgivings and a penchant for societal control.

The spectacular debut of hES cells immediately rekindled the fiery debate concerning the use of human embryos and fetal tissue for research. Investigations that provide no benefit to the embryo or fetus raise serious questions about the relative importance of treating or curing disease and respecting developing human life. Even thicker ethical concerns are raised by the deliberate creation of research embryos solely for investigative purposes.

However, embryonic and fetal sourcing may become less necessary. First, hES cells are regenerative, and existing cell lines may be of sufficient quantity and quality to produce the required cells if random genetic mutations and cell senescence can be avoided. If such proves to be the case, future need for further isolation of cells from embryonic or fetal tissue may be limited. Second, and seemingly more promising, is the spate of reports of success in isolating and channeling adult stem (AS) cells into particular cell types, including murine blood cells and human bone.[4] Recent research in mice suggests that stem cells taken from the adult brain can be coaxed into a wide variety of tissues, including liver, heart, and muscle (Clarke et al. 2000). In humans, liver cells were derived from circulating bone marrow stem cells, giving rise to speculation that it may be possible to repopulate livers damaged by hepatitis, drugs, or alcohol with healthy cells derived from a patient's own marrow stem cells (Theise et al. 2000). The potential of AS to convert into myriad cell types may eliminate the ethical dilemma inherent in obtaining stem cells from embryos.

15   Even those adamantly opposed to research involving embryonic or fetal stem cells do not deny the unprecedented potential benefit of cell therapy and tissue regeneration. Hence, if the sourcing moves from embryo to adult, it seems reasonable to assume that ethical and policy questions will shift to the scientific and therapeutic potential of this technology. In anticipation of such a sourcing detente, I focus on the question of access to the benefits of stem cell technology.

FAIRNESS OF ACCESS

Public policy often seeks to regulate behavior based on socially desirable outcomes. A speed limit of ten mph intends the prevention of harm to school children by an imprudent driver. Both the National Institutes of Health (1999) and the National Bioethics Advisory Commission (1999) appealed to consequences to maintain that hES cell research should proceed. Nonetheless, careful consideration ought to be given not only to the intended but also, and perhaps primarily, to the unintended consequences, especially with regard to burdens placed. Circumvention of the argument from inevitability is also necessary as citizens consider precautions to ensure that neither going forward nor staying put harms ourselves or others in an effort to heal, protect, and benefit.

Because human stem cell work portends such revolutionary human benefit, we ought to worry that the benefit will be distributed unjustly and further privilege the monied and powerful at the expense of those on the socioeconomic margins.[5] The tattered backdrop of our current booming national economy includes 46 million uninsured Americans, who lack consistent access to the basics of health care and 40 million, including 1 in 5 children, living in poverty. Privatization of health care in the form of for-profit health maintenance organizations has widened the gap between the medically well-off and the medically indigent, leading to grossly inadequate care for those without the bases for access; that is, money and transportation. Given our country's growing economic divide and the fact that private companies are riding the leading edge of biotechnology, it seems likely that, left undisturbed, stem cell technology will be available to some but not to all. This portends further stratification of human health and well-being within the richest country in the world.

The problem of just distribution of medical resources is not new, but the unprecedented promise of stem cell technology raises the stakes. Respect for the dignity of the human person imposes a communal obligation to treat disease and maintain individual and societal well-being. Every human being is a person of worth to be treated always as an end and never solely as a means to someone else's or society's ends. Because health is a social good and necessary for human flourishing, policies and procedures ought to seek to make stem cell technology available in ways that are responsive and responsible to persons and to society as a whole. Against those who argue solely for *equality of opportunity* in access to the benefits of medical innovation, let me suggest an ethic centered on *fairness of access* to the conditions and commodities necessary for human health and well-being, including stem cell technology.

Although equality of opportunity is an important value, it focuses only on limitations imposed by legal and formal barriers of discrimination (Buchanan 1995). However, to sustain human health, attention must be paid not only to legal barriers of discrimination but also to the social lottery that leaves some unable to grasp the ring of opportunity. Fairness of access removes the socioeconomic blockade imposed by the social lottery to health care and levels the playing field. Opportunities for equality of well-being can be secured only through access to those opportunities.

Present public commitments ought to be modulated by their effect on those who are the weaker members of society, especially children and those left poor in money, health, and access by the spin of the social lottery wheel. Power ought to be brought to bear to protect and advance the interests of such vulnerable persons by constraining action to what tangibly benefits the marginalized.[6]

SHAPING THE FUTURE

Stem cell and nuclear transfer technologies stretch human power so that future circumstances are subject to present discretions, desires, and duties in unprecedented ways. Hence, justice is not only concerned with contemporary resource distribution but also enjoins responsibility for how future generations are to live. Transgenerational justice imposes present self-limitation in the interest of the life and health of future generations. In turn, public policy formulated for the sake of a just future mandates that consequences of our present actions, both public and private, be appropriate to the flourishing of future generations. The seventh-generation rule obtains: we should consider the consequences of what is done today on each of the next seven generations.[7] Moral wisdom comes through having regard for the interdependence of present and future interests.

Success would be the development of public policy consistent with principles of social justice, especially fairness of access, and responsibility for the future. In view of the unprecedented and uncharted scientific and medical benefits that may result from research on human pluripotent stem cells, basic policy components would include the following:

1. Primary public understanding of stem cell and nuclear transfer technologies and the promises and perils of each.
2. Opportunities for vigorous, honest public debate with all the cards on the table.
3. Public funding of research with attendant public review, oversight, and accountability.
4. Guaranteed fairness of present and future access to the benefits of stem cell technologies, with privilege given to vulnerable persons and communities.
5. Development of standards of excellence for stem cell technology that are consistent with the full scope and goals of health care, just access and future sustainability.

CONCLUSION

White-knuckled, we are crossing medical frontiers at break-neck speed. Stem cell technology holds the promise not only of increasing human health and life spans but also of changing power structures and fundamental notions of human person-hood, moral status, and mortality. It is important that we do not prematurely or unwittingly slam the door on scientific advances that can relieve human suffering and restore health. At the same time, it is imperative that, in this biotechnologic age, we expand our moral imaginations to account for and be accountable to marginalized persons and concern ourselves with the shaping of a just future. Power is to be exercised on behalf of the least of us today and for the seven generations to come. If we wisely engage in shaping the future, we will create a world few of us ever imagined.

Endnotes

1. The term "reprogenetics," coined by Lee Silver (1997, 8), under-scores the increasing convergence of reproductive and genetic tech-nologies. This convergence is particularly evident with regard to stem. cells as evidenced by the recent announcement by Celera Genomics and Geron Corporation of a ". . . collaboration for human pluripotent stem cell genomics" (PE Biosystems 2000). Coupling ge-netic, nuclear transfer and stem cell technologies will potentially provide powerful tools for preimplantation genetic profiling, hES cell alteration, and germ line therapy.

2. The phrase "biotech century" is taken from the title of a book by Jeremy Rifkin (1998).

3. "Social lottery" refers to the manner in which one's social starting place affects opportunities (Buchanan 1995). Here the term is used particularly with respect to class and socioeconomic standing.

4. Whereas embryonic stem cells are the current focal point, there is evidence that the more differentiated stem cells (AS cells) in the adult may be able to "switch fates." Bjornson and colleagues (1999) reported that mouse neural stem cells that give rise to three types of brain cells can also develop into blood cells when transplanted into mice whose bone marrow has been destroyed. Human mesenchymal stem cells were isolated from adult skeletal muscle and were capable of differentiating into multiple mesodermal phenotypes including skeletal myotubes, bone, and cartilage (Williams et al. 1999). In addi-tion, stem cells from adult mouse skeletal muscle have a "remark-able capacity" to differentiate into blood cells including T and B cells (Jackson et al. 1999). If human stem cells derived from adult donors are consistently able to be channeled into particular cell and tissue types, they may be a viable therapeutic alternative to hES cells.

5. A subsidiary concern beyond the scope of this discussion is the potential for an increase in risky behavior by those with access to "replacement parts."

6. The Geron Ethics Advisory Board (1999), to their credit, set forth the principle that all stem cell research "must be done in a context of concern for global justice." Whereas the board's broaching of the justice question is crucial and courageous, it is difficult to fathom that Geron's primary obligation to its stockholders would be trumped by concern for marginalized stakeholders. In addition, meeting the demands of global justice is a complex matter that demands redistribution of resources well beyond the scope of a single company or a single medical advancement. For example, an argument from global justice could claim redirection of biotechnologic resources to the provision of clean water and sufficient food. For a further discussion, see Cahill (1999).

7. This responsibility for seven generations was expressed by Canadian aboriginals in their testimony to the Canadian Royal Commission on New Reproductive Technologies in 2000. In my usage, seven is to be seen for its symbolic meaning of completeness and totality.

References

Bjornson, C. R. R., Reynolds, B. A., Magli, M. C., and Vescovi, A. L. 1999. Turning brain into blood: A hematopoietic fate adopted by adult neural stem cells in vivo. *Science* 283: 534–537.

Buchanan, A. 1995. Equal opportunity and genetic intervention. *Social Philosophy and Policy* 12: 105–135.

Cahill, L. S. 1999. The new biotech world order. *Hastings Center Report* 29: 45–48.

Cahill, L. S. 2000. Social ethics of embryo and stem cell research. *Women's Issues in Health* 10: 131–135.

Cho, M. K., Magnus, D., Caplan, A. L., McGee, D., and the Ethics of Genomics Group. 1999. Ethical considerations in synthesizing a minimal genome. *Science* 286: 2087.

Clarke, D. L., Johansson, C. B., Wilbertz, J., Veress, B., Nilsson, E., Karlström, H., Lendahl, U., and Frisén, J. 2000. Generalized potential of adult neural stem cells. *Science* 288: 1660–1663.

Geron Ethics Advisory Board. 1999. Research with human embryonic stem cells: Ethical considerations. *Hastings Center Report* 29: 31–36.

Jackson, K. A., Mi, T., and Goodell, M. A. 1999. Hematopoietic potential of stem cells isolated from murine skeletal muscle.

Proceedings of the National Academy of Science of the USA 96: 14482–14486.

National Bioethics Advisory Commission. 1999. *Ethical Issues in Human Stem Cell Research,* Rockville, MD: National Bioethics Advisory Commission.

Parens, E. 2000. Embryonic stem cells and the bigger reprogenetic picture. *Women's Issues in Health* 10: 116–119.

PE Biosystems. 2000. Press release. Celera Genomics and Geron Corporation announce collaboration for human pluripotent stem cell genomics. www.pecorporation.com/ June 12.

Rifkin, J. 1998. *The Biotech Century.* New York: Jeremy P. Tarcher/Putnam.

Shapiro, H. T. 1999. Reflections on the interface of bioethics, public policy, and science. *Kennedy Institute of Ethics Journal* 9: 210.

Silver, L. M. 1997. *Remaking Eden.* New York: Avon Books.

Theise, N. D., Nimmakayalu, M., Gardner, R., Illei, P. B., Morgan, G., Teperman, L., Henegarie, O., and Krause, D. S. 2000. Liver from bone marrow in humans. *Hepatology* 32: 11–16.

Trauer, C. A. 1999. Private ethics boards and public debate. *Hastings Center Report* 29: 43–45.

U.S. Department of Health and Human Services. 1999. *Draft National Institutes of Health Guidelines for Research Involving Human Pluripotent Stem Cells.* Rockville, MD: National Institutes of Health.

White, C. B. 1999. Foresight, insight, oversight. *Hastings Center Report* 29: 41–42.

Williams, J. T., Southerland, S. S., Souza, J., Calcutt, A. F., and Cartledge, R. G. 1999. Cells isolated from adult human skeletal muscle capable of differentiating into multiple mesodermal phenotypes. *American Surgeon* 65: 22–26.

Questions for Discussion

1. According to McLean, "the current genetic revolution and the steady march of biotechnology deeply affect lives, relationships, ideologies, and social structures." Is this assertion defensible? Interchange the word *biotechnology* with *bioethics*. How do the variables change?
2. What effect did the Dolly experiment have on medical research?
3. What are the ethical considerations concerning hES cell research and public policy?
4. What conclusion does McLean come to at the end of her essay?

Questions for Writing

1. Should stem cells be used in medical research? Assess the pros and cons in a persuasive essay.
2. Consider the ethics of exploiting humans of any kind: stem cell research, abortion, cloning, euthanasia, capital punishment, and so forth. Are all of these, as opponents charge, forms of killing? Write an informative essay in response to this topic.

Cloning Human Beings: An Assessment of the Ethical Issues Pro and Con

DAN W. BROCK

What moral right might protect at least some access to the use of human cloning? A commitment to individual liberty, such as defended by J. S. Mill, requires that individuals be left free to use human cloning if they so choose and if their doing so does not cause significant harms to others, but liberty is too broad in scope to be an uncontroversial moral right (Mill, 1859; Rhodes, 1995). Human cloning is a means of reproduction (in the most literal sense) and so the most plausible moral right at stake in its use is a right to reproductive freedom or procreative liberty (Robertson, 1994a; Brock, 1994), understood to include both the choice not to reproduce, for example, by means of contraception or abortion, and also the right to reproduce.

The right to reproductive freedom is properly understood to include the right to use various assisted reproductive technologies (ARTs), such as in vitro fertilization (IVF), oocyte donation, and so forth. The reproductive right relevant to human cloning is a negative right, that is, a right to use ARTs without interference by the government or others when made available by a willing provider. The choice of an assisted means of reproduction should be protected by reproductive freedom even when it is not the only means for individuals to reproduce, just as the choice among different means of preventing conception is protected by reproductive freedom. However, the case for permitting the use of a particular means of reproduction is strongest when it is necessary for particular individuals to be able to procreate at all, or to do so without great burdens or harms to themselves or others. In some cases human cloning could be the only means for individuals to procreate while retaining a biological tie to their child, but in other cases different means of procreating might also be possible.

It could be argued that human cloning is not covered by the right to reproductive freedom, because whereas current ARTs and practices covered by that right are remedies for inabilities to reproduce sexually, human cloning is an entirely new means of reproduction; indeed, its critics see it as more a means of manufacturing humans than of reproduction. Human cloning is a different means of reproduction than sexual reproduction, but it is a means that can serve individuals' interest in reproducing. If it is not protected by the moral right to reproductive freedom, I believe that must be, not because it is a new means of reproducing, but instead because it has other objectionable or harmful features; I shall evaluate these other ethical objections to it later.

WHAT INDIVIDUAL OR SOCIAL BENEFITS MIGHT HUMAN CLONING PRODUCE?

The literature on human cloning by nuclear transfer or by embryo splitting contains a few examples of circumstances in which individuals might have good reasons to want to use human cloning. However, human cloning seems not to be the unique answer to any great or pressing human need and its benefits appear to be limited at most. What are the principal possible benefits of human cloning that might give individuals good reasons to want to use it?

1. Human cloning would be a new means to relieve the infertil- 5
ity some persons now experience. Human cloning would allow women who have no ova or men who have no sperm to produce an offspring that is biologically related to them (Eisenberg, 1976; Robertson, 1994b, 1997; LaBar, 1984). Embryos might also be cloned, by either nuclear transfer or embryo splitting, in order to increase the number of embryos for implantation and improve the chances of successful conception (NABER, 1994). The benefits from human cloning to relieve infertility are greater the more persons there are who cannot overcome their infertility by any other means acceptable to them. I do not know of data on this point, but the numbers who would use cloning for this reason are probably not large.

The large number of children throughout the world possibly available for adoption represents an alternative solution to infertility only if we are prepared to discount as illegitimate the strong desire of many persons, fertile and infertile, for the experience of pregnancy and for having and raising a child biologically related to them. While not important to all infertile (or fertile) individuals, it is important to many and is respected and met through other forms of assisted reproduction that maintain a biological connection when that is possible; that desire does not become illegitimate simply because human cloning would be the best or only means of overcoming an individual's infertility.

2. *Human cloning would enable couples in which one party risks transmitting a serious hereditary disease to an offspring to reproduce without doing so* (Robertson, 1994b). By using donor sperm or egg donation, such hereditary risks can generally be avoided now without the use of human cloning. These procedures may be unacceptable to some couples, however, or at least considered less desirable than human cloning because they introduce a third party's genes into their reproduction instead of giving their offspring only the genes of one of them. Thus, in some cases human cloning could be a reasonable means of preventing genetically transmitted harms to offspring. Here too, we do not know how many persons would want to use human cloning instead of other means of avoiding the risk of genetic transmission of a disease or of accepting the risk of transmitting the disease, but the numbers again are probably not large.

3. *Human cloning to make a later twin would enable a person to obtain needed organs or tissues for transplantation* (Robertson, 1994b, 1997; Kahn, 1989; Harris, 1992). Human cloning would solve the problem of finding a transplant donor whose organ or tissue is an acceptable match and would eliminate, or drastically reduce, the risk of transplant rejection by the host. The availability of human cloning for this purpose would amount to a form of insurance to enable treatment of certain kinds of medical conditions. Of course, sometimes the medical need would be too urgent to permit waiting for the cloning, gestation, and development that is necessary before tissues or organs can be obtained for transplantation. In other cases, taking an organ also needed by the later twin, such as a heart or a liver, would be impermissible because it would violate the later twin's rights.

Such a practice can be criticized on the ground that it treats the later twin not as a person valued and loved for his or her own sake, as an end in itself in Kantian terms, but simply as a means for benefiting another. This criticism assumes, however, that only this one motive defines the reproduction and the relation of the person to his or her later twin. The well-known case, some years ago in California of the Alayas, who conceived in the hopes of obtaining a source for a bone marrow transplant for their teenage daughter suffering from leukemia, illustrates the mistake in this assumption. They argued that whether or not the child they conceived turned out to be a possible donor for their daughter, they would value and love the child for itself, and treat it as they would treat any other member of their family. That one reason they wanted it, as a possible means to saving their daughter's life, did not preclude their also loving and valuing it for its own sake; in Kantian terms, it was treated as a possible means to saving their daughter, but not *solely as a means*, which is what the Kantian view proscribes.

Indeed, when people have children, whether by sexual means   10 or with the aid of ARTs, their motives and reasons for doing so are typically many and complex, and include reasons less laudable than obtaining lifesaving medical treatment, such as having someone who needs them, enabling them to live on their own, qualifying for government benefit programs, and so forth. While these are not admirable motives for having children and may not bode well for the child's upbringing and future, public policy does not assess prospective parents' motives and reasons for procreating as a condition of their doing so.

4. *Human cloning would enable individuals to clone someone who had special meaning to them, such as a child who had died* (Robertson, 1994b). There is no denying that if human cloning were available, some individuals would want to use it for this purpose, but their desire usually would be based on a deep confusion. Cloning such a child would not replace the child the parents had loved and lost, but would only create a different child with the same genes. The child they loved and lost was a unique individual who had been shaped by his or her environment and choices, not just his or her genes, and more importantly who had experienced a particular relationship with them. Even if the later cloned child could not only have the same genes but also be subjected to the same environment, which of course is impossible, it would remain a different child than the one they had loved and lost because it would share a different history with them (Thomas, 1974). Cloning the lost child might help the parents accept and move on from their loss, but another already existing sibling or a new child that was not a clone might do this equally well; indeed, it might do so better since the appearance of the cloned later twin would be a constant reminder of the child they had lost. Nevertheless, if human cloning enabled some individuals to clone a person who had special meaning to them and doing

so gave them deep satisfaction, that would be a benefit to them even if their reasons for wanting to do so, and the satisfaction they in turn received, were based on a confusion.

MORAL ARGUMENTS AGAINST HUMAN CLONING

Would the Use of Human Cloning Violate Important Moral Rights?

Many of the immediate condemnations of any possible human cloning following Wilmut's cloning of Dolly claimed that it would violate moral or human rights, but it was usually not specified precisely, or often even at all, what rights would be violated (WHO, 1997). I shall consider two possible candidates for such a right: a right to have a unique identity and a right to ignorance about one's future or to an open future. Claims that cloning denies individuals a unique identity are common, but I shall argue that even if there is a right to a unique identity, it could not be violated by human cloning. The right to ignorance or to an open future has only been explicitly defended, to my knowledge, by two commentators, and in the context of human cloning, only by Hans Jonas; it supports a more promising, but in my view ultimately unsuccessful, argument that human cloning would violate an important moral or human right.

Is there a moral or human right to a unique identity, and if so would it be violated by human cloning? For human cloning to violate a right to a unique identity, the relevant sense of identity would have to be genetic identity, that is, a right to a unique unrepeated genome. This would be violated by human cloning, but is there any such right? It might be thought that cases of identical twins show there is no such right because no one claims that the moral or human rights of the twins have been violated. However, this consideration is not conclusive (Kass, 1985; NABER, 1994). Only human actions can violate others' rights; outcomes that would constitute a rights violation if deliberately caused by human action are not a rights violation if a result of natural causes. If Arthur deliberately strikes Barry on the head so hard as to cause his death, he violates Barry's right not to be killed; if lightning strikes Cheryl, causing her death, her right not to be killed has not been violated. Thus, the case of twins does not show that there could not be a right to a unique genetic identity.

I turn now to whether human cloning would violate what Hans Jonas called a right to ignorance, or what Joel Feinberg called a right to an open future (Jonas, 1974; Feinberg, 1980). Jonas argued that human cloning in which there is a substantial time gap between the beginning of the lives of the earlier and later twin is fundamentally different from the simultaneous beginning of the lives of homozygous twins that occur in nature. Although contemporaneous twins begin their lives with the same genetic inheritance, they do so at the same time, and so in ignorance of what the other who shares the same genome will by his or her choices make of his or her life.

A later twin created by human cloning, Jonas argues, knows,   15
or at least believes she knows, too much about herself. For there is already in the world another person, her earlier twin, who from the same genetic starting point has made the life choices that are still in the later twin's future. It will seem that her life has already been lived and played out by another, that her fate is already determined; she will lose the sense of human possibility in freely and spontaneously creating her own future and authentic self. It is tyrannical, Jonas claims, for the earlier twin to try to determine another's fate in this way.

Jonas's objection can be interpreted so as not to assume either a false genetic determinism, or a belief in it. A later twin might grant that he is not determined to follow in his earlier twin's footsteps, but nevertheless the earlier twin's life might always haunt him, standing as an undue influence on his life, and shaping it in ways to which others' lives are not vulnerable. But the force of the objection still seems to rest on the false assumption that having the same genome as his earlier twin unduly restricts his freedom to create a different life and self than the earlier twin's. Moreover, a family environment also importantly shapes children's development, but there is no force to the claim of a younger sibling that the existence of an older sibling raised in that same family is an undue influence on the younger sibling's freedom to make his own life for himself in that environment. Indeed, the younger twin or sibling might gain the benefit of being able to learn from the older twin's or sibling's mistakes.

A closely related argument can be derived from what Joel Feinberg has called a child's right to an open future. This requires that others raising a child not so close off the future possibilities that the child would otherwise have as to eliminate a reasonable range of opportunities for the child autonomously to construct his or her own life. One way this right might be violated is to create a later twin who will believe her future has already been set for her by the choices made and the life lived by her earlier twin.

The central difficulty in these appeals to a right either to ignorance or to an open future is that the right is not violated
merely because the later twin is likely to *believe* that his future is
already determined, when that belief is clearly false and supported only by the crudest genetic determinism. If we know the
later twin will falsely believe that his open future has been taken
from him as a result of being cloned, even though in reality it has
not, then we know that cloning will cause the twin psychological
distress, but not that it will violate his right. Jonas's right to ignorance, and Feinberg's right of a child to an open future, are not
not violated by human cloning, though they do point to psychological harms that a later twin may be likely to experience and
that I will take up later.

Neither a moral or human right to a unique identity, nor one
to ignorance and an open future, would be violated by human
cloning. There may be other moral or human rights that human
cloning would violate, but I do not know what they might be. I
turn now to consideration of the harms that human cloning
might produce.

What Individual or Social Harms
Might Human Cloning Produce?

20   There are many possible individual or social harms that have
been posited by one or another commentator and I shall only try
to cover the more plausible and significant of them.

*1. Human cloning would produce psychological distress and
harm in the later twin.* No doubt knowing the path in life taken by
one's earlier twin might often have several bad psychological effects (Callahan, 1993; LaBar, 1984; Macklin, 1994; McCormick,
1993; Studdard, 1978; Rainer, 1978; Verhey, 1994). The later twin
might feel, even if mistakenly, that her fate has already been substantially laid out, and so have difficulty freely and spontaneously
taking responsibility for and making her own fate and life. The
later twin's experience or sense of autonomy and freedom might
be substantially diminished, even if in actual fact they are diminished much less than it seems to her. She might have a diminished sense of her own uniqueness and individuality, even if once
again these are in fact diminished little or not at all by having an
earlier twin with the same genome. If the later twin is the clone of
a particularly exemplary individual, perhaps with some special
capabilities and accomplishments, she might experience exces-
sive pressure to reach the very high standards of ability and ac-

complishment of the earlier twin (Rainer, 1978). These various psychological effects might take a heavy toll on the later twin and be serious burdens to her.

While psychological harms of these kinds from human cloning are certainly possible, and perhaps even likely in some cases, they remain at this point only speculative since we have no experience with human cloning and the creation of earlier and later twins. Nevertheless, if experience with human cloning confirmed that serious and unavoidable psychological harms typically occurred to the later twin, that would be a serious moral reason to avoid the practice. Intuitively at least, psychological burdens and harms seem more likely and more serious for a person who is only one of many identical later twins cloned from one original source, so that the clone might run into another identical twin around every street corner. This prospect could be a good reason to place sharp limits on the number of twins that could be cloned from any one source.

One argument has been used by several commentators to undermine the apparent significance of potential psychological harms to a later twin (Chadwick, 1982; Robertson, 1994b, 1997; Macklin, 1994). The point derives from a general problem, called the nonidentity problem, posed by the philosopher Derek Parfit, although not originally directed to human cloning (Parfit, 1984). Here is the argument. Even if all these psychological burdens from human cloning could not be avoided for any later twin, they are not harms to the twin, and so not reasons not to clone the twin. That is because the only way for the twin to avoid the harms is never to be cloned, and so never to exist at all. But these psychological burdens, hard though they might be, are not so bad as to make the twin's life, all things considered, not worth living. So the later twin is not harmed by being given a life even with these psychological burdens, since the alternative of never existing at all is arguably worse—he or she never has a worthwhile life—but certainly not better for the twin. And if the later twin is not harmed by having been created with these unavoidable burdens, then how could he or she be wronged by having been created with them? And if the later twin is not wronged, then why is any wrong being done by human cloning? This argument has considerable potential import, for if it is sound it will undermine the apparent moral importance of any bad consequence of human cloning to the later twin that is not so serious as to make the twin's life, all things considered, not worth living.

I defended elsewhere the position regarding the general case of genetically transmitted handicaps, that if one could have a *different* child without comparable burdens (for the case of cloning, by using a different method of reproduction which did not result in a later twin), there is as strong a moral reason to do so as there would be not to cause similar burdens to an already existing child (Brock, 1995). Choosing to create the later twin with serious psychological burdens instead of a different person who would be free of them, without weighty overriding reasons for choosing the former, would be morally irresponsible or wrong, even if doing so does not harm or wrong the later twin who could only exist with the burdens. These issues are too detailed and complex to pursue here and the nonidentity problem remains controversial and not fully resolved, but at the least, the argument for disregarding the psychological burdens to the later twin because he or she could not exist without them is controversial, and in my view mistaken. Such psychological harms, as I shall continue to call them, are speculative, but they should not be disregarded because of the nonidentity problem.

25 *2. Human cloning procedures would carry unacceptable risks to the clone.* There is no doubt that attempts to clone a human being at the present time would carry unacceptable risks to the clone. Further research on the procedure with animals, as well as research to establish its safety and effectiveness for humans, is clearly necessary before it would be ethical to use the procedure on humans. One risk to the clone is the failure to implant, grow, and develop successfully, but this would involve the embryo's death or destruction long before most people or the law consider it to be a person with moral or legal protections of its life.

Other risks to the clone are that the procedure in some way goes wrong, or unanticipated harms come to the clone; for example, Harold Varmus, director of the National Institutes of Health, raised the concern that a cell many years old from which a person is cloned could have accumulated genetic mutations during its years in another adult that could give the resulting clone a predisposition to cancer or other diseases of aging (Weiss, 1997). Risks to an ovum donor (if any), a nucleus donor, and a woman who receives the embryo for implantation would likely be ethically acceptable with the informed consent of the involved parties.

I believe it is too soon to say whether unavoidable risks to the clone would make human cloning forever unethical. At a minimum, further research is needed to better define the potential risks to humans. But we should not insist on a standard that requires risks to be lower than those we accept in sexual reproduction, or in other forms of ART.

3. Human cloning would lessen the worth of individuals and diminish respect for human life. Unelaborated claims to this effect were common in the media after the announcement of the cloning of Dolly. Ruth Macklin explored and criticized the claim that human cloning would diminish the value we place on, and our respect for, human life because it would lead to persons being viewed as replaceable (Macklin, 1994). As I have argued concerning a right to a unique identity, only on a confused and indefensible notion of human identity is a person's identity determined solely by his or her genes, and so no individual could be fully replaced by a later clone possessing the same genes. Ordinary people recognize this clearly. For example, parents of a child dying of a fatal disease would find it insensitive and ludicrous to be told they should not grieve for their coming loss because it is possible to replace him by cloning him; it is *their child who is dying* whom they love and value, and that child and his importance to them is not replaceable by a cloned later twin. Even if they would also come to love and value a later twin as much as they now love and value their child who is dying, that would be to love and value that *different child* for its own sake, not as a replacement for the child they lost. Our relations of love and friendship are with distinct, historically situated individuals with whom over time we have shared experiences and our lives, and whose loss to us can never be replaced.

CONCLUSION

Human cloning has until now received little serious and careful ethical attention because it was typically dismissed as science fiction, and it stirs deep, but difficult to articulate, uneasiness and even revulsion in many people. Any ethical assessment of human cloning at this point must be tentative and provisional. Fortunately, the science and technology of human cloning are not yet in hand, and so a public and professional debate is possible without the need for a hasty, precipitate policy response.

References

Brock, D. W. (1994). "Reproductive Freedom: Its Nature, Bases and Limits," in *Health Care Ethics: Critical Issues for Health Professionals,* eds. D. Thomasma and J. Monagle. Gaithersbrug, MD: Aspen Publishers.

Brock, D. W. (1995). "The Non-Identity Problem and Genetic Harm." *Bioethics* 9:269–275.

Callahan, D. (1993). "Perspective on Cloning: A Threat to Individual Uniqueness." *Los Angeles Times,* November 12, 1993:B7.

Chadwick, R. F. (1982). "Cloning." *Philosophy* 57:201–209.

Eisenberg, L. (1976). "The Outcome as Cause: Predestination and Human Cloning." *The Journal of Medicine and Philosophy* 1:318–331.

Feinberg, J. (1980). "The Child's Right to an Open Future," in *Whose Child? Children's Rights, Parental Authority, and State Power,* eds. W. Aiken and H. LaFollette. Totowa, NJ: Rowman and Littlefield.

Harris, J. (1992). *Wonderwoman and Superman: The Ethics of Biotechnology.* Oxford: Oxford University Press.

Jonas, H. (1974). *Philosophical Essays: From Ancient Creed to Technological Man.* Englewood Cliffs, NJ: Prentice-Hall.

Kahn, C. (1989). "Can We Achieve Immortality?" *Free Inquiry* 9:14–18.

Kass, L. (1985). *Toward a More Natural Science.* New York: The Free Press.

LaBar, M. (1984). "The Pros and Cons of Human Cloning." *Thought* 57:318–333.

Lederberg, J. (1966). "Experimental Genetics and Human Evolution." *The American Naturalist* 100:519–531.

Macklin, R. (1994). "Splitting Embryos on the Slippery Slope: Ethics and Public Policy." *Kennedy Institute of Ethics Journal* 4:209–226.

McCormick, R. (1993). "Should We Clone Humans?" *Christian Century* 110:1148–1149.

Mill, J. S. (1859). *On Liberty.* Indianapolis, IN: Bobbs-Merrill Publishing.

NABER (National Advisory Board on Ethics in Reproduction) (1994). "Report on Human Cloning Through Embryo Splitting: An Amber Light." *Kennedy Institute of Ethics Journal* 4:251–282.

Parfit, D. (1984). *Reasons and Persons.* Oxford: Oxford University Press.

Rainer, J. D. (1978). "Commentary." *Man and Medicine: The Journal of Values and Ethics in Health Care* 3:115–117.

Rhodes, R. (1995). "Clones, Harms, and Rights." *Cambridge Quarterly of Healthcare Ethics* 4:285–290.

Robertson, J. A. (1994a). *Children of Choice: Freedom and the New Reproductive Technologies.* Princeton, NJ: Princeton University Press.

Robertson, J. A. (1994b). "The Question of Human Cloning." *Hastings Center Report* 24:6–14.

Robertson, J. A. (1997). "A Ban on Cloning and Cloning Research is Unjustified." Testimony Presented to the National Bioethics Advisory Commission, March 1997.

Studdard, A. (1978). "The Lone Clone." *Man and Medicine: The Journal of Values and Ethics in Health Care* 3:109–114.

Thomas, L. (1974). "Notes of a Biology Watcher: On Cloning a Human Being." *New England Journal of Medicine* 291:1296–1297.

Verhey, A. D. (1994). "Cloning: Revisiting an Old Debate." *Kennedy Institute of Ethics Journal* 4:227–234.

Weiss, R. (1997). "Cloning Suddenly Has Government's Attention." *International Herald Tribune,* March 7, 1997.

WHO (World Health Organization Press Office). (March 11, 1997). "WHO Director General Condemns Human Cloning." World Health Organization, Geneva, Switzerland.

Questions for Discussion

1. According to Dan Brock, what are the moral arguments in support of human cloning?
2. What are the benefits of human cloning?
3. What are the moral arguments against cloning?
4. What are the harmful effects of cloning?

Questions for Writing

1. Brock lists a number of possible harmful effects associated with cloning. Do the harmful consequences outweigh the possible benefits of cloning? Analyze this issue an essay.
2. What are the ethical problems posed by human cloning? Respond to this question in an informative essay.

Student Essay

A Pretty Pill

TONI SANCHEZ

How do people know whether they are supposed to become teachers, lawyers, bankers, or even astronauts? Most people chose their professions for one of two reasons: either they are gifted at something, such as being able to play full length Mozart symphonies at age four, or they are influenced by someone. An example: some parents insist on making their children practice the piano everyday in order that they might become world famous in the future. Figuring out how your life can be productive for you is the first major step. However, the difficult, and more important, part is taking the initial steps to successfully obtain the desired career and still be able to see the bigger picture: That your life's work serves not only you but the greater good of humanity.

A person's passion for a career becomes a motivating force that fuels inquiry, creativity, and ingenuity in a respective field. Each field is completely unique from the others and has a corresponding aesthetic that is characteristic of each professional discipline. Science, for one, has branched out a long way from its foundational roots. Medicine, in particular, has responded to many of the health challenges throughout centuries through medical research and vaccines (Romasantra).

The beauty or aesthetics in medicine is something that both doctors and patients can easily see. From analgesics to antipyretics, many human and animal diseases have been treated, even cured, through the application of medicine. So many people have been saved from diseases such as cholera, scarlet fever, small pox, measles, and even hepatitis from early vaccinations. With the constant spread of disease and the rise in overpopulation, not having something to regulate disease would lead to an uncontrollable outbreak of sickness. Medical techniques, such as surgery and vaccinations, have done wonders for the world. Even though people were created with strong immune systems, an immune response needs to be built up and strengthened. Vaccinations offer low exposures to diseases that the human immune system can fight off in order to create a faster, more efficient response if a person is ever exposed to the same antigen again.

A characteristic of science that makes it a difficult barrier to cross is its basis on fact. When people look at medicine from a scientific perspective, they are looking for facts, for unyielding pieces of information that state in black or white whether something is true or false. An impression of truth will not matter to a scientist. If there is no evidence to prove a point, then the questioned field is to remain an inadequate source of information or a questionable work in progress. For example, a doctor sends test samples from a patient down to the laboratory for analysis. What the lab technician might "feel" about the results is of minimal importance to the doctor. The doctor is looking for truth or the facts when it comes down to something as serious as diagnosing a patient. There is very little room for error. If the results of the lab tests are not confirmed in a straightforward manner, more than likely the tests will be run again a second time and probably by a person who is not so caught up in a feeling or emotion concerning patients' results (Doyle).

5   Once the diagnosis is reached and a patient is given medicine (or has been operated on), the hypothesis is that the patient will get better after receiving the medical treatment. If this is not the case and the patient remains in the same physical state of health, what conclusion is then drawn? Would the doctor assume he was wrong about the person's original state and discontinue diagnosis? Hopefully for the patient's sake, the doctor would look at another alternative medical approach. Sometimes ending up at a dead end is the first step in the

right direction to solving a medical problem. Although the patient is not any better, what has been learned from the experience is important in eventually diagnosing the patient's problem, and the discovery of medical knowledge will assist future patients with similar cases.

However, scientific evidence supports the phenomenon that some terminal medical cases and their "Cinderella" outcomes exceed known medical research and treatment options. In cases like these, even some medical skeptics would contend that something miraculous occurs in these instances. Yet other physicians believe, in cases as such, that a higher power was at work in the healing medical process of these patient recoveries.

In the midst of medical procedures, facts, and diagnoses; the spirit of the medical field is one that excels beyond the temporal, withstanding possible death and hardship. By the end of the day, most physicians still hope to save a life in spite of the normal progression of human mortality.

Works Cited

Doyle, Amber. Personal interview. 25 Feb. 2003.
Romasanta, Tara. Telephone interview. 25 Feb. 2003.

Questions for Discussion

1. Discuss in detail your thoughts on the following statement: "Figuring out how your life can be productive for you is the first major step. However, the difficult, and more important, part is taking the initial steps to successfully obtain the desired career and still be able to see the bigger picture: That your life's work serves not only you but the greater good of humanity." Do you think that college students choose careers with the idea Sanchez articulates in mind? Explain.
2. How have science and the medical field advanced the quality of human life over the past two decades?
3. How might faith and reason work together in the medical profession?
4. What are the ethical concerns over religious beliefs and fact-based medicine?

Questions for Writing

1. Is it possible to combine medicine, faith, and healing in restoring the health of patients? Write an informative essay in response to this question.
2. Is Sanchez's essay logical and coherent? Are the facts balanced? Is it trustworthy? Write your assessment in an essay.

Questions for Making Connections Within the Chapter

1. What controversies over stem cell research and cloning have polarized the public, as McLean and Brock illustrate in their respective essays?
2. What place, if any, should faith and spirituality have in scientific research and the practice of medicine? Consider in your response the works of Sanchez and Brock.
3. What are the ethical considerations surrounding the value of human life as illustrated in Singer's and McLean's essays?
4. Exploitation of humans is a concern in the medical community. What kinds of exploitation do Barrett's essay and Singer's address?
5. Consider the issue of medical ethics in light of the articles presented in this chapter. Does the medical community have a responsibility to adhere to high ethical and moral standards in medical research and medical treatment of patients? Include in your answer several of the works from this chapter.

CHAPTER 6

Ethics, Plagiarism, and Computer Crimes

Ay, sir; to be honest,
as this world goes,
is to be one man picked out of ten thousand.

William Shakespeare, *Hamlet*

Plagiarism is a problem at a number of American universities and colleges. As the Internet and electronic databases have made research easier, some students have been tempted by the easy accessibility of technology literacy. But when students take information without acknowledging the source, they are not borrowing but stealing! The efforts of universities to teach accurate documentation and bibliography in the academy are being challenged by Web sites that encourage plagiarism. The mandate facing universities seems to be to teach not only documentation style and bibliography but also the ethics appropriate for surfing the Internet and sending e-mail, as well as citing sources. The number of students who create computer viruses and hack computer networking systems has also increased. In the end, each student must formulate his or her code of conduct in doing research and take responsibility for the outcome.

Sara Rimer documents in her article that Internet plagiarism has increased and shows that 38 percent of undergraduate students admitted to cheating at least once over the past year. In defense of their actions, some undergraduates claim that "they need to cheat because of the intense competition to get into graduate schools, and land the top jobs."

Verne G. Kopytoff looks at the number of students who have cheated and examines some of the sites, like Plagiarism.org, that offer instructors "Internet-based anti-plagiarism technology that teachers can use for a fee." This new technology can weed out many commercial term papers. While many supporters argue that the technology serves as a watchdog against academic cheating, some critics suggest that this approach "contradicts the spirit of the university."

In her article Karen Judson describes types of computer viruses and looks into why people create viruses. Judson also traces some of the infamous viruses from 1989 to 1998, when Microsoft built into their software anti-virus protection coding that prevents macro virus infections.

Like Judson, John Knittel and Michael Soto describe cyberspace crimes. The authors report that in 2001 the FBI apprehended hackers who had stolen over one million credit cards from Web sites of more than forty businesses. In a high-profile case, an MIT student "set up an electronic bulletin board for distributing pirated software." As a result of this case, the U.S. Congress passed the No Electronic Theft Act, prohibiting this type of unethical behavior.

College students account for a number of these computer crimes and most cases of electronic plagiarism. In an effort to combat this growing problem, Ann Lathrop and Kathleen Foss propose character education programs that promote integrity and honesty. The "six E's of character education" are explanation, exhortation, ethos, experience, and expectations of excellence.

These articles are designed to encourage you to give ethical consideration to the plethora of topics associated with computer crimes and plagiarism. By the end of this unit, you should have engaged in a number of wholesome dialogues about these issues.

A Campus Fad That's Being Copied
Internet Plagiarism Seems on the Rise
SARA RIMER

A study conducted on 23 college campuses has found that Internet plagiarism is rising among students.

Thirty-eight percent of the undergraduate students surveyed said that in the last year they had engaged in one or more instances of "cut-and-paste" plagiarism involving the Internet, paraphrasing or copying anywhere from a few sentences to a full paragraph from the Web without citing the source. Almost half the students said they considered such behavior trivial or not cheating at all.

Only 10 percent of students had acknowledged such cheating in a similar, but much smaller, survey three years ago.

This year's study, organized by Donald L. McCabe, a management professor at Rutgers University, surveyed more than 18,000 students, 2,600 faculty members and 650 teaching assistants at large public universities and small private colleges nationwide. No Ivy League schools were included.

"There are a lot of students who are growing up with the Internet who are convinced that anything you find on the Internet is public knowledge and doesn't need to be cited," Professor McCabe said.   5

The survey solicited students' comments about cheating, and one student wrote, "If professors cannot detect a paper from an Internet source, that is a flaw in the grader or professor."

Another student wrote: "One time I downloaded a program off the Internet for my class. I hated the class and it was mandatory so I didn't care about learning it, just passing it."

Forty percent of students acknowledged plagiarizing written sources in the last year. As with the Internet cheating, about half the students considered this sort of plagiarism trivial.

Twenty percent of the faculty members said they use their computers, such as the turnitin.com site, to help detect student plagiarism.

Twenty-two percent of undergraduates acknowledged cheating in a "serious" way in the past year—copying from another student on a test, using unauthorized notes or helping someone else to cheat on a test.   10

"When I work with high school students, what I hear is, 'Everyone cheats, it's not all that important,'" Professor McCabe said. "They say: 'It's just to get into college. When I get into college, I won't do it.' But then you survey college students, and you hear the same thing."

The undergraduates say they need to cheat because of the intense competition to get into graduate school, and land the top jobs, Professor McCabe said. "It never stops," he said.

One of the students from the survey wrote: "This isn't a college problem. It's a problem of the entire country!"

Professor McCabe said: "Students will say they're just mimicking what goes on in society with business leaders, politicians. I don't know whether they're making excuses for what they've already done, or whether they're saying, 'It's O.K. if I do this because of what's going on.' "

15   Many of the colleges involved in the survey have begun trying to fight cheating by educating both faculty members and students on academic integrity and revising school policies.

Princeton University was not involved in the survey, but it is among the schools that have been taking steps to make sure students know that it is wrong to use material from the Internet without citing the source.

"We need to pay more attention as students join our communities to explaining why this is such a core value—being honest in your academic work and why, if you cheat, that is a very big deal to us," said Kathleen Deignan, Princeton's dean of undergraduate students.

There has not been any noticeable increase in cheating at Princeton, Ms. Deignan said, with 18 to 25 cases reported a year. Administrators have noticed, however, that sometimes students and parents do not understand why it is wrong to "borrow" sections of text for a paper without providing attribution, Ms. Deignan added.

Princeton students are also concerned, and they have organized a campus assembly on integrity for Sept. 21.

20   "We live in a world where a lot of this is negotiable," Ms. Deignan said. "Academic institutions need to say, 'This is not negotiable.' "

CHEATING: WATER-BOTTLE TRICKS

Some of the comments submitted anonymously by college students who took part in a survey about cheating:

- If teachers taught better we wouldn't have to cheat.
- Maybe schools and parents should focus on learning instead of grades.
- You can't stop it. . . . Some people were just raised that way— "do whatever you have to do."
- In my freshman biology class, our professor would give us the answers to the test once we finished and turned in the test, so we could figure out what we missed before he got them out to us. One student turned in the test, went back to get his book bag and gave the sheet of paper to his friend who was still taking the test.
- Someone I know once soaked the label off a water bottle, printed up a fake label, copied notes onto the back of the fake

label, and pasted it back onto the water bottle. During the test, he had the water bottle on his desk. He'd take a drink, read the exposed line through the bottle and write down the answer.

Questions for Discussion

1. Rimer states that the number of students copying from the Internet without citing the source is increasing. Do students not recognize that copying from electronic sources is stealing from another person? Explain.
2. Discuss the validity of the following statement: "If professors cannot detect a paper from an Internet source, that is a flaw in the grader or professor."
3. What is "trivial" plagiarism? Are students missing the point of plagiarism and the issue of ethics? Explain.
4. What percentage of "students acknowledged plagiarizing written sources" within the year before Rimer wrote this article?

Questions for Writing

1. "Students will say they're just mimicking what goes on in society with business leaders, politicians." If people in high-profile positions behave unethically, does their behavior give others a license to make immoral decisions in their lives—for example, plagiarizing material for a research paper? Analyze this topic in an essay.
2. Write a persuasive essay convincing readers either that plagiarism is unacceptable or that it is acceptable.

Brilliant or Plagiarized? Colleges Use Sites to Expose Cheaters
VERNE G. KOPYTOFF

Dr. David Presti, a professor of neurobiology at the University of California at Berkeley, had always assumed that some of his students turned in term papers copied from the Internet. After all, there are dozens of Web sites where students who have no qualms about plagiarism can download ready-made term papers about topics like *Hamlet* and the Russian Revolution to use as their own.

Until recently, however, Dr. Presti had never caught a cheater because it would have required spending countless hours searching the Internet for evidence. But now, using Plagiarism.org, he can identify students who choose deceit over research.

Through Plagiarism.org, Dr. Presti found that 45 of 320 students from the last spring semester had plagiarized at least part of their essays from the Internet. "It's so easy to cheat now," Dr. Presti said. "But this increasing digitalization is also making it easier to find cheaters out."

A handful of companies, like Plagiarism.org, are offering Internet-based anti-plagiarism technology that teachers can use for a fee. The most complex sites compare student term papers with millions of Web pages and the archives of dozens of online sites that offer term papers free. While the anti-plagiarism sites do not have access to the databases of operations that sell term papers, they would be able to spot many commercial term papers because they can check databases that professors are starting to use to keep copies of term papers from past semesters.

5   If the service finds similarities, it notifies the teacher, who must then decide whether the similarities are coincidences, justified by proper footnotes or outright dishonesty.

Companies that sell anti-plagiarism services say dozens of schools are testing such services. Fees start at about $20 a year for a class of 30, with cheaper per-student or per-class rates for larger contracts. The fees are paid by universities or teachers.

Some students criticize the technology, saying it undermines honor codes based on trust between students and faculty.

Plagiarism.org was developed by John Barrie, a graduate student in biophysics at the University of California at Berkeley. He said he had developed the site to "level the playing field for honest students."

Papers sent to Plagiarism.org are checked by a computer, which looks for phrases matching those from other sources or are partly altered (www.plagiarism.org). The computer compares the term papers with the archives of free online cheating sites. The computer also does Web searches to look for similarities. It also compares essays with papers from previous semesters and other universities.

10   Within 24 hours, the company sends a report of its findings to the teacher by e-mail. Teachers are cautioned by the companies not to use that information as absolute proof of plagiarism. The reports merely point out phrases that should be examined more closely. Teachers must check for themselves whether flagged sentences are attributed.

Some cheaters may try to evade detection by stealing only a few paragraphs, changing words or inserting the plagiarized material into the middle of a term paper. But Matt Hunter, founder of the Essay Verification Engine, or EVE (www.canexus.com), an anti-plagiarism service based in Sackville, New Brunswick, said that software like his usually uncovered even subtle dishonesty.

"My software takes an essay, fragments it, and if a student has changed the words, it still finds the pieces," said Mr. Hunter, who is a college student.

This is not the first time that technology has been used to uncover cheating. A system that has been in use for years, the Glatt Plagiarism Screening Program, lets a teacher find out if a student is truly the author of a paper by posing a test: parts of the paper are deleted at random by the program, and the student is asked to replace the deleted material (www.plagiarism.com). If the student cannot do that, plagiarism is suspected.

Another program, called MOSS (www.cs.berkeley.edu/aiken/moss.html), which has been around since 1994 and is in widespread use, serves computer science classes. It automatically searches lines of computer code for similarities.

Currently, many schools do little to stop plagiarism, said Jeanne M. Wilson, president of the Center for Academic Integrity, whose member institutions include Duke University, the University of California at Los Angeles, the University of Maryland at College Park and Rutgers University. Ms. Wilson is also director of student judicial affairs for the University of California at Davis. Ms. Wilson said that some students had threatened lawsuits over the issue of plagiarism charges but that she knew of no lawsuits that had been filed.

"If you look at academic integrity problems at many campuses," Ms. Wilson said, "there aren't that many cases being examined, even though we think there is a good amount of cheating going on."

Anti-cheating technology is not embraced by everyone. At Stanford University, the student newspaper recently said that Plagiarism.org, which administrators are considering using, would violate the school's policy against using "unusual and unreasonable precautions" against cheating.

"The honor code is one of the most important tenets of the university," said Gil Lopez, the newspaper's editor in chief, in an interview. "Using technology to catch people contradicts the spirit of the university." Mr. Lopez said he also worried about the reliability of anti-plagiarism technology.

The anti-plagiarism companies agree that technology has limits. Warren Brantner, president of IntegriGuard, an anti-cheating service in Harrisburg, Pa., said that it was best to use anti-plagiarism Web sites with other measures, like assigning more unusual topics (www.integriguard.com).

20   Dr. Presti, the neurobiology professor at Berkeley, said that nearly 15 percent of his students had plagiarized even after he warned them about computerized scrutiny.

"They ranged from sloppy citations to, in one case, the entire paper was taken from several Web sites," Dr. Presti said.

"I went back and talked to the most serious violators, and they immediately admitted to it," Dr. Presti said. "When you show the color coding and where it came from, there's no denying it."

Questions for Discussion

1. Do you believe that the new anti-plagiarism sites that Kopytoff describes will strike fear in the hearts of students, deterring those who may be tempted to pass off another's work as their own? Explain.
2. "Some students criticize the technology, saying it undermines honor codes based on trust between students and faculty." Do you agree with these students? Explain.
3. Why did John Barrie develop his site? Do you think his goal is realistic?
4. How successful do you think the Glatt Plagiarism Screening Program can be in its long-term efforts to combat cheating?

Questions for Writing

1. Is it ethical to expose students by means of anti-plagiarism sites in order to combat plagiarism? Isn't this ironic? Make your case in a persuasive essay.
2. What are the long-term efforts of plagiarism—on students, universities, the professional world, and American culture? Analyze this question in an essay.

Viruses, Worms, and Other Sinister Programs

KAREN JUDSON

By September 1998 there were some twenty thousand known computer viruses.[1] The number was growing by about one thousand new viruses per month.[2]

A virus is code or a piece of software designed to alter the way a computer works without the user's knowledge or consent. Viruses may be benign or malicious. Benign viruses usually cause no damage. For example, some past viruses were simply intended to be funny. One was called the "Cookie Monster." It flashed the message "I want a cookie" on the screen, and users had to "feed" the word cookie to the monster to keep it under control.

Malicious viruses cause unintentional or deliberate damage. (Unintentional damage is caused by programming errors.) They may alter a program so that it does not work as it should, or they may completely erase the hard disk.

Viruses reproduce themselves. They can make themselves known immediately, or a trigger, such as a date, time, or command word, can activate them. (These delayed reaction codes are called *logic bombs*.) In some cases, the virus runs undetected, simply making the machine sluggish or causing unexpected results when programs are run.

TYPES OF VIRUSES

Viruses are classified according to the manner in which they infect computers: 5

Boot sector viruses are the most common. They attach themselves to the section of a floppy or hard disk that lets the user "boot up" to begin working with the computer. Boot sector viruses are most often spread by booting up the computer with an infected floppy disk in place. These viruses gain control as the computer is first turned on by moving from the boot sector of the floppy disk into the computer's memory. The virus can then infect the hard disk. At this point, any new disk placed in the floppy disk drive can also become infected.

File infectors replace or attach themselves to files with certain extensions (usually command or executable files with the extensions. COM and .EXE). Programs become infected when they are executed with the virus in memory. These viruses, if well written, operate without revealing their presence. Some reproduce until a certain date, such as Friday the 13th, then begin destroying files. Sometimes the only way to rid infected files of the virus is to delete them and reinstall the uninfected software.

Multipartite viruses are a combination of boot sector and file types. Because they infect both boot sectors and files, they are more easily spread. Variations of this type of virus, such as polymorphic and stealth viruses, are the most difficult to detect and delete. Polymorphic viruses keep changing in order to fool virus-scanner programs. Stealth viruses temporarily remove themselves from memory so that virus-scanners cannot find them.

Macro viruses, first discovered in 1995, infect documents created with Microsoft Word (version 6.0 and above) and Microsoft

Excel, a spreadsheet application. Macro viruses infect spreadsheets, documents, and templates, which can be opened by either Windows or Macintosh applications.

10   A Microsoft Word macro virus, dubbed the Melissa virus, was apparently first introduced by being uploaded to the Internet Newsgroup alt.sex from a stolen America Online account on March 26, 1999. It spread through Microsoft's Outlook Express (an e-mail program) via an e-mail attachment. Once the attachment was opened, the virus grabbed names from the computer user's address book and sent itself to each name on the list. Because the fast-spreading virus could quickly clog, then crash, even the large mail servers, companies who were warned quickly shut down all outgoing mail. Within a few days, patches that could disable the virus were made available by antivirus software companies.[3]

In a matter of days, David L. Smith, a New Jersey man, was arrested and charged with writing and sending out the virus, which had already infected more than one hundred thousand computers worldwide. Still, in just a couple of days, the virus clogged and in some cases incapacitated computer networks at about three hundred corporations.[4]

PATHS TO INFECTION

Any computer that is turned on can catch a virus, usually by:

- *Sharing infected diskettes.* Boot sector viruses often spread from infected floppy disks left in the drive while rebooting.
- *CD-ROMS.* Presently, the CDs themselves cannot become infected, but the files they contain may be infected.
- *Downloading infected files.* These files are downloaded from bulletin boards or the Web.
- *Opening an infected e-mail attachment.* (Macro viruses make this possible.) The infection is in the attachment, not in the e-mail message.
- *Linked computers that are not protected by antivirus software.* Viruses can spread from infected files located on file servers and attached to e-mail.

SOME INFAMOUS VIRUSES

From 1989 to 1993, 160 viruses credited to Bulgaria were in circulation. During that time, 10 percent of all viruses in the United States came from that country. Viruses were posted and exchanged on a Bulgarian bulletin board, the Virus Exchange BBS. Many were created by someone called "Dark Avenger," who named a malicious virus after himself in 1989.

The virus Dark Avenger was epidemic in the United States. It attached itself to MS-DOS- .COM and .EXE files, adding 1,800 bytes of code. Every sixteenth time the infected program ran, it overwrote a section of the hard disk. Then a message appeared: "Eddie Lives . . . somewhere in time." Another message was embedded in the code: "This program was written in the city of Sofia © 1988–89 Dark Avenger." Infected computers eventually crashed after having lost part of their operating system.

For some unknown reason, after 1993 the Bulgarian virus factory ceased production. That year the Dark Avenger created his last malicious virus—Commander_Bomber.[5] Some thought he and his colleagues had found more legitimate uses for their skills.

After the first macro virus, called Concept, was introduced in June 1995, it soon became the most common virus in the world. When an infected Microsoft Word document was opened, the virus copied itself into the global document template (the file NORMAL.DOT). Thereafter, whenever a document was saved with Save-File-As, the virus copied itself into the saved document. The first time an infected document was opened, a box appeared with the title "Microsoft Word" and the number "1." The number was apparently supposed to increase each time the virus duplicated itself, but due to bugs in the program it never counted above 1.[6] From 1998 on, versions of Microsoft Word and Excel contained built-in antivirus code to prevent macro virus infections.

OTHER SINISTER PROGRAMS

Some infectious computer programs are less deadly than viruses. For example, a worm, Robert Tappan Morris's toxin of choice, does not usually destroy data. It can reproduce itself and load up a computer's memory, however, causing it to crash.

Several other nuisance programs differ from viruses in that they do not reproduce themselves. The Trojan horse, for instance, is named for the fabled giant wooden horse in which Greek warriors were smuggled into Troy. True to its name, this program is disguised as innocent code, but it has a hidden purpose.

Members of the Inner Circle hackers' group used a Trojan horse concealed in a chess game to gain entry to a Canadian mainframe computer they had been trying to crack. They talked the system operator into playing the game with them. Then, while the chess program was running, it opened a powerful, unauthorized account in the host computer for the hackers to use later, undetected.[7]

20   The logic bomb, or time bomb, is similar to a Trojan horse, but it is programmed to go off at a particular time. Logic bombs are the favorite device of angry employees intent on getting even. They can plant such a program and set it to go off and do damage sometime after they leave the company.

TRAPDOORS CAN LET INTRUDERS IN

Trapdoors (also called "backdoors") allow others to penetrate a system, but they are not always created to cause damage. They are sometimes legitimate lines of code that are written into programs by programmers to provide an easy way in for maintenance. If the trapdoor is not closed after its purpose has been served, however, crackers can use it to gain unauthorized access.

VIRUS CONTROL

Antiviral software scans programs or disks for viruses. Most antiviral programs can also erase viruses. The better programs scan for thousands of known viruses, and technical support is available for users.

When a virus can be traced to its originator, that person faces prosecution for illegal computer activity. A case in point is Christopher Pile (a.k.a. "Black Baron"), a virus writer in Great Britain who was not only arrested but also went to prison under that country's 1990 Computer Misuse Act. Pile, a twenty-seven-year-old unemployed, self-taught programmer, wrote two viruses called Pathogen and Queeg. A computer crime specialist spent ten months tracing the code back to Pile. At his trial in 1995, a British company testified that it lost $1 million to damage caused by the viruses. Pile was convicted and sentenced to eighteen months in prison. The sentencing judge told Pile that "those who seek to wreak mindless havoc on one of the vital tools of our age cannot expect lenient treatment."[8]

AN APPLE A DAY . . .

Here are a few tips to guard against virus infection:

- Use reliable sources for programs. Shareware posted for the taking on bulletin boards can be infected, so computer users who trade programs should be careful. Pirated copies of software can also contain a virus. Purchased programs in shrink-wrap are most likely to be virusfree, but there have been exceptions.

- Write-protect all the disks used, so no one can transmit a virus to them.
- If the system in use has a hard or fixed disk, never boot from a diskette.
- Make backup copies frequently.
- Watch for changes in the way a system works. Do programs take longer than usual to load? Do disk access times seem excessively long for the task to be performed? Are there unusual error messages? Is less system memory available than usual? Have programs or files mysteriously disappeared? Has available disk space been suddenly reduced? The presence of any one of these "symptoms" can indicate the presence of a virus.
- Do not run programs received in e-mail or open e-mail attachments unless you know exactly what they are and where they came from.
- Use a reliable antivirus program regularly to scan for viruses. Update the program at least once every eighteen months.
- When a virus is detected, tell others who might have used the same disks, to prevent further spread of the infection.

VIRUS HOAXES

Virus hoaxes often circulate on the Internet. E-mail messages 25 may tell recipients, "Just wanted to warn you about a new virus. . . . Make sure you warn all your friends!" Most of these messages are untrue. At least one such message in 1998, however, was genuine. It warned some Internet users about a new computer virus called "RedTeam," which could spread via e-mail. The virus infected Windows executable files and the Windows kernel file. If it infected a computer running the Eudora e-mail program, it could use Eudora to send out an electronic mail message with an attached program. RedTeam was unusual because it could send e-mail with itself attached, and it could also circulate rumors about itself. The virus was not widely circulated, however, and it was easily contained simply by not opening the e-mail attachment that contained the code and by not forwarding the warning message to friends.[9]

E-mail messages circulated to warn others of "viruses" can take up Internet capacity and waste others' time. A better way to find out which viruses are a threat and which are hoaxes is to consult one of the several Web sites for that purpose.

Endnotes

1. Sarah Gordon interview with author, September 8, 1998.
2. Matt Richtel, "Virus Hunters: Stalking 'Disease' on the Net," *The New York Times.* September 15, 1998, <http://www.nytimes.com> (September 20, 1998).
3. Stan Miastkowski, "How to Protect Yourself Against Melissa," CNN Online, March 29, 1999, <http://www.cnn.com/TECH/computing/9903/29/melissa.02.idg/index.html> (April 6, 1999).
4. David Kocieniewski, "Man Is Charged in the Creation of E-Mail Virus," April 3, 1999, pp. A1, B6.
5. David S. Bennahum, "Heart of Darkness," *Wired*, November 1997, posted June 1998, <http://www.wired.com/wired> (July 13, 1998).
6. IBM Antivirus Web site, <http://www.av.ibm.com/BreakingNews/VirusAlert/Concept> (September 20, 1998).
7. Bill Landreth, *Out of the Inner Circle—A Hacker's Guide to Computer Security* (Bellevue, Wash.: Microsoft Press, 1985), pp. 95–97.
8. "Profile of a Virus Writer, *PC World,* March 1997, <http://www.pcworld.com/ software/utility/articles/mar97/1503p180w.html> (September 15, 1998).
9. IBM Antivirus Web site, <http://www.av.ibm.com/BreakingNews/VirusAlert/RedTeam> (September 20, 1998).

Questions for Discussion

1. Identify the various types of computer viruses.
2. How can a computer catch a virus?
3. What are some tips to safeguard your computer against virus infection?
4. What are virus hoaxes?

Questions for Writing

1. Karen Judson offers several suggestions for safeguarding your computer against viruses. According to Judson, "Use reliable sources for [purchasing your] programs. . . . Pirated copies of software can also contain a virus." Judson brings up an ethical issue: piracy. In an essay, analyze the problem of piracy and consider its consequences for artists; consumers; and the music, movie, and computer game industries.

2. What should be the legal consequences of committing computer crimes, such as hacking and creating viruses, virus hoaxes, worms, and so forth? Write your response in an informative essay.

Cybercrime Crackdown
JOHN KNITTEL AND MICHAEL SOTO

Until recently, hackers who broke the law received little more punishment than probation or a small fine that was a mere percentage of the *financial* damage they may have caused. However, as computers have become more and more important in our lives, the damage malicious hackers can do is often much greater and more costly. New laws have been passed to accompany the increase in cybercrimes. The result has been punishments that better fit the crimes hackers commit.

Many companies have been slow to upgrade computer security systems in response to the increase in cybercrime. Hackers are usually one step ahead of most computer security systems. And whether deliberate or accidental, computer break-ins have become so easy that little kids can—and have—done it.

EASY TARGETS

Over the last few years, Internet usage has grown at a phenomenal rate. As a result, major companies, as well as government agencies and communications systems, depend on computers and the Internet to become part of the global network. Unfortunately, many companies have been so eager to become a part of this network that they have set up their computer systems without taking proper security precautions. A company's employees often know little about the software on their computers. File-sharing, shared applications, and multiple computers downloading from a variety of Internet sources make accessing private files from outside the company extremely easy. Passwords and antivirus programs are no obstacle to a hacker. Furthermore, the new Internet businesses constantly need new software programs, which puts these businesses at risk because of the ongoing installation of new files.

In 2001, the FBI caught a highly organized ring of hackers who had stolen more than one million credit card numbers from the Web sites of over forty American businesses. The attacks, which came from Russia and the Ukraine, were incredibly simple. The hackers entered computers using a flaw in a Microsoft operating system, which allowed unauthorized users to disable security measures, access files, and even crash computers. People had known about the flaw since 1998. Microsoft had even issued public warnings and offered free, downloadable security "patches." Nonetheless, many companies didn't pay attention to the warnings. As a result, hundreds of thousands of dollars of damage occurred.

5   It can be very difficult to measure the damage a hacker does. A 2001 survey conducted by the Computer Security Institute (CSI) in conjunction with the San Francisco FBI's Computer Intrusion Squad, revealed that 85 percent of the large companies and government agencies that responded had been victims of computer break-ins during the previous year. Though 64 percent of the respondents suffered financial loss, only 35 percent knew the dollar amount. In fact, according to the FBI's National Computer Crimes Squad, between 85 and 97 percent of computer break-ins are not even detected. Despite this, it is estimated that, in 2000, $1.6 trillion in damage was caused by computer crime worldwide.

There are many ways malicious hackers can damage a company's computer system. The most popular is by stealing information, also known as industrial espionage. It is actually quite common for companies and even countries to hire hackers in order to steal important company or military secrets. Not only is this illegal, but it can lead to huge financial losses for corporations and put national security at risk.

HACKERS AND THE LAW

Cybercrime is such a new phenomenon that it has been tough not only to catch malicious hackers but also to decide how to punish them. Most laws regarding cybercrime are very new and still quite vague. With malicious hackers constantly accessing computers in new ways, it is often difficult for judges and juries—many of whom are not computer experts—to make informed decisions. Criminal defense attorney Jennifer Granick is well known for defending hackers accused of illegal activities. She recalls a preliminary hearing in which a witness talked about "cutting and pasting" text from one file to another. The judge responded: "You mean with scissors?" Defense attorneys like Granick worry that judges' lack of knowledge could lead them to give sentences that are overly severe. However, many judges are taking computer and technology courses to better understand these cases.

Another confusing problem the legal system faces is that so many offenders are minors. Historically, most federal crimes revolved around large sums of money, violence, or drugs. They didn't involve computers, and the criminals usually weren't juveniles.

The FBI knows that most hackers are kids who aren't particularly dangerous. More often than not they are well educated, upper-middle-class male teens with lots of time on their hands. Because of this, most juveniles convicted of computer crimes by federal courts receive light sentences. The most usual punishment is a probation period during which the hacker is prohibited from using a computer. However, with the rising incidence of computer crime, there has been a movement to increase sentences and to begin prosecuting underage malicious hackers as if they were adult criminals.

Meanwhile, new laws are being passed to tighten some of the 10 many loopholes that hackers slip through. One example is the No Electronic Theft Act. It was passed in 1997 after an MIT student, David M. LaMacchia, set up an electronic bulletin board for distributing pirated software. Because the year of the crime was 1994, by law, LaMacchia couldn't be prosecuted for copyright infringement because he did not profit from his acts. Now, however, with the passage of this act, anyone who gives away software illegally can be prosecuted, even if he or she does not profit from it.

In 1996, President Bill Clinton signed the U.S. Economic Espionage Act. The act made it a federal crime to take, download, or possess trade secret information without the owner's permission. This means that anytime a hacker breaks into a computer system and looks at any private company information, even by accident, he or she is breaking the law.

Since then, the federal government has continued to make its fight against cybercrime and cyberterrorism a major priority. In 1998, the Department of Justice and the FBI created the National Infrastructure Protection Center (NIPC), which is made up of government agencies and private companies that work together to crack down on cybercrime and to ensure cybersecurity. The Department of Justice has also been hiring many attorneys and specialists in computer crime. At the time of the writing of this [essay], President George W. Bush was planning to announce a massive, nationwide cybersecurity "strategy" as well. The "strategy" will likely offer incentives to companies that beef up their security systems.

Questions for Discussion

1. What did the 2001 survey by the Computer Security Institute (CSI) and the San Francisco FBI's Computer Intrusion Squad reveal?
2. What challenges are involved in persecuting hackers?
3. What is the No Electronic Theft Act? When was it passed?
4. How has the U.S. Economic Espionage Act aided in the crackdown on computer hackers?

Questions for Writing

1. According to Knittel and Soto, hackers are being dealt with using stricter laws, as computers have become more important in every aspect of our lives. What further legal actions would you recommend, in addition to those presented in this article? Respond in an informative essay.
2. Should the law deal with kids who become hackers any differently than it does adults? Why or why not? Examine both sides of the issue in a persuasive essay.

Integrity, Ethics, and Character Education

ANN LATHROP AND KATHLEEN FOSS

STUDENT DISCUSSIONS OF INTEGRITY AND ETHICAL BEHAVIOR

. . . Many students today view cheating simply as one way to enhance their grades. Preventive measures and penalties are not enough to counter such widely accepted beliefs. A renewed emphasis on integrity and ethical behavior at home and at school is necessary if students are to be persuaded to change their perception of cheating as "no big deal."

Now, much of the research being done on why students cheat has concluded that cheating *is* a problem of moral development—that many students have poorly developed value systems, making it difficult for them to consider issues beyond their desire for a certain grade when deciding whether or not to cheat.

Even though the mission statements of most institutions still include the development of students' ethical standards as an educational goal, many colleges and universities have taken a neutral position concerning traditional values in recent years, including taking a *laissez-faire* attitude toward students' moral development. (Kibler B1)

Classroom discussions about moral character can be developed around a variety of curriculum topics. Creative teachers will find ways to introduce the values of integrity into class work throughout the school year.

Questions that encourage students to express their feelings and opinions about honest and dishonest behaviors can lead to interesting discussions: "In what situation would you definitely *not* cheat?" or "When do you refuse to give test answers to a friend?" Some students might be willing to respond to the question, "Why *don't* you cheat when you know that most of your peers are cheating?" Two topics designed to challenge students to look seriously at their own behavior are suggested in the following pages. These topics are supported by two Copy-Me pages with discussion starters.

Topic 1: Does Cheating Harm Your Career?

Surveys and interviews that document extensive cheating by students raise concerns about the long-term effects on society of such widespread dishonesty. This topic can lead students to discuss how dishonesty in school could lead to dishonesty in college and eventually impact a person's career.

Students can develop their own scenarios. In small groups they might be willing to explore ways their own dishonesty could damage their ability to achieve career goals. Consider the following hypothetical situations:

- The architect who designed your home cheated his way through the mathematics class that provided the basis for determining building tolerances.
- The medical researcher who just announced a new drug fabricated test results in college and plagiarized research reports.

- The young lawyer who wrote your will bought a copy of the bar exam to study.

To what extent have these young professionals transferred their cheating from schools into their careers? Just how worried should we be?

> What all the evidence suggests—the use of ever more sophisticated technology and the instances of mass cheating—is a fundamental change of the human condition: The very perception of cheating as sin has begun to drop into the same moral gray zone as infidelity, tax evasion, recreational drug use and a host of other activities that once grimly stood at the gates of hell. Indeed, we live in a world in which our values are in flux, contorting, as it were, to adapt to the fragmented and hyper-speed atmosphere of modern life. (Dunn 31)

Do we want to live in a society where dishonesty is the normal behavior to be expected of each person? Is it important that we trust those with whom we are doing business? How do we know which people are honest and trustworthy?

Topic 2: Are These Valid Reasons to Cheat or Plagiarize?

This list is designed to spark a class discussion about which reasons, if any, would justify cheating or plagiarizing. Honest students can express their reasons for not cheating even when they face the same pressures other students use to excuse their cheating. The discussion can provide an opportunity to honor the ethical students and to reinforce their integrity and honesty.

The students who do cheat, and then justify their cheating to themselves, might begin to re-examine their personal values. Whether these discussions take place with an entire class, in small groups, or individually between a parent and child, thoughtful questioning can guide students toward critical self-evaluation.

Questions to ask students could include "Would any of these be a good reason to cheat or are they all just excuses?" or "Would any of these make it OK to cheat once in a while?" or "Can you think of other reasons that might make it OK to cheat?" A list of reasons why some students do not cheat, or why cheating can be self-defeating, might be generated by the discussion.

These same reasons can be used in discussions about cheating at faculty or parent meetings. Suggested questions to ask teachers include "Are any of these valid reasons? If so, what actions can or should we take to change the situations that might encourage cheating?" For parents: "Do you hear any of these excuses at home? Are any of them valid? Do they indicate school policies we should re-examine?"

These reasons for cheating come primarily from discussions 10 with students, colleagues, and friends, and ideas from the following authors: Alschular and Blimling; Anderman, Griesinger, and Westerfield; Stephen Davis; Maramark and Maline; and Schab.

COPY ME: DOES CHEATING HARM YOUR CAREER?

Many of today's young professionals cheated in high school and college. Will they transfer their successful cheating techniques into their new careers? How might this threaten society?

- The architect who designed your home cheated his way through the mathematics class that provided the basis for determining building tolerances. *Is your home safe?*
- The medical researcher who just announced a new drug fabricated her test results in college and plagiarized her research reports. *Did she perhaps "adjust" the data in the recent drug tests? Is the new drug safe?*
- Your lawyer paid for a copy of the bar exam to study. *Will the contract she wrote for you stand up in court?*
- The accountant who does your taxes hired someone to write his term papers and paid a "stand-in" to take several major tests. *Does he know enough to complete your tax forms correctly?*

1. What are some examples from other professions?
2. Can this type of cheating in professional preparation put all of us in danger?
3. Do we want to live in a society where dishonesty is the normal behavior to be expected of each person who provides a service to us?
4. Is it important that we trust those with whom we are doing business?
5. How do we know which people are honest and trustworthy?
6. How might cheating cause a problem in the career you have chosen?

COPY ME: ARE THESE VALID REASONS TO CHEAT OR PLAGIARIZE?

Individual Issues

- Lack of ethical training or personal philosophy, moral values
- Lack of time management skills; inability to meet deadlines
- Desire for better grades, scholarships, college admission, etc.
- Test anxiety
- Fear of failure

Family/Peer Pressure

- Unrealistic demands from parents
- Sibling rivalry
- Desire or pressure to help friends and peers

School-Related Issues

- There is no school policy that defines and penalizes cheating, or the policy is unclear.
- Teachers expect too much, especially when an older sibling was a strong student.
- Class or assignment is boring, isn't relevant, isn't important to the student's life.
- Large class sizes alienate students who feel they are "only a number."
- Advanced Placement students, at the top of their middle school classes with very little effort, must compete with students who are just as good or even better.
- The teachers don't seem to care about cheating.

"Poor Me" (I have no choice)

- Working to pay for a car or to save for college cuts into study time.
- Athletes must maintain their GPA to be eligible to play.
- Scholarship competition forces me to participate in lots of activities.

"Why Not Cheat?"

- Little risk of being caught or of serious punishment if caught
- Perceived disadvantage of not cheating
- Computers make it so easy!

Excuses

- I didn't realize that what I did was dishonest.
- We were collaborating—is this cheating?

THE SIX E'S OF CHARACTER EDUCATION: PRACTICAL WAYS TO BRING MORAL INSTRUCTION TO LIFE FOR YOUR STUDENTS (DR. KEVIN RYAN)

Politicians call for it. State education departments write memos about it. Parents and schools now agree on the need for it.

"It" is character education, and lately more and more educators are looking for ways to present and model the definition of it: to help each child know the good, love the good and do the good.

Like many human endeavors, it's easier to talk about character education than to actually do it. Because many secular teacher education programs dismiss the entire field of moral, ethical and character education, a great hole exists in teacher preparation. But there's hope.

Over the years I have developed six E's of character educa-   15
tion: example, explanation, exhortation, ethos (ethical environment), experience and expectations of excellence. The six concepts will help educators promote morality within each student and in the class and school environments.

Example

Example is probably the most obvious way to model character education. While I'm not suggesting that teachers be saints, they should take their moral lives seriously by modeling upright behavior. Students imitate their trusted teachers.

Another method of moral modeling is to teach the moral truths embedded in literature and history. Students need to know about George Washington and Benedict Arnold; Hester Prynne of *The Scarlet Letter* and Shakespeare's Richard III; Jonas Salk (who developed the polio vaccine) and Adolf Hitler. A child's education must include such examples of good and evil individuals.

One middle school social studies teacher emphasizes biographies in his curriculum. "When my students studied Harriet Tubman, I had them perform skits with Tubman as the central character," says the New Hampshire teacher, referring to the great abolitionist. "The skits taught them about courage and self-sacrifice. We then placed a poster of Tubman in the classroom so the students would remember her."

Explanation

We need to practice moral education by means of explanation—not simply stuffing students' heads with rules and regulations, but engaging them in great moral conversations about the human race. The very existence of this dialogue helps make us human.

20   A private school teacher, tired and discouraged by the hostility of her sophomore students, explained the meaning of friendship to them. "Many had never heard that values like compassion and trustworthiness are needed to be a true friend," says the Boston educator. She also had her students read essays on friendship by Cicero and C. S. Lewis. "My students began to understand what it means to be a friend," she says.

Forty years ago, as an undergraduate at the University of Toronto, I sat dazed listening to Marshall McLuhan, then an obscure literature teacher, rambling about the medium being the message. I see now that his point is relevant to schooling and the moral education of children. Our continual explanation of the rules is one of the most important messages of school.

Exhortation

A child discouraged by academic, athletic or artistic failure often needs something stronger than sweet reason to ward off self-pity. So do students who passively attend school, flirt with racist ideas and get denied entrance into a college of their choice. Sincere exhortation is needed.

When a fifth-grade class in upstate New York learned of its low scores on a statewide test, the teacher exhorted her students with pep talks. "I also led them in discussions about the qualities of a good student," she says. "My class felt that a good student achieved good grades. But I helped them understand that a good student is also someone who makes class contributions, does homework and assists other students."

Use exhortation sparingly and never stray far from explanation. But appeal to the best interests of the young and urge them to move in the proper direction when the need arises.

Ethos (or Ethical Environment)

A classroom is a small society with patterns and rituals, power rela-   25
tionships and standards for both academic performance and student behavior. Moral climate influences classroom environment.

Does the teacher respect the students? Do students respect
one another? Are the classroom rules fair and fairly exercised?
Does the teacher play favorites? Are ethical questions and issues
about "what ought to be" part of the classroom dialogue?

Disgusted by the bad language used by their students, members of a New Hampshire senior high faculty joined forces to
stamp out rudeness and obscenity use. At an in-service just before
the school year started, they discussed ways to promote a more
positive climate in their classrooms and around campus.

"When the students arrived on the first school day," recalls
their principal, "I announced that we were all going to work towards using a new kind of language, one free from obscenities
and rudeness. We got the students involved in changing their
crude environments into better ones."

There is little doubt that the ethical climate within a classroom promotes a steady and strong influence in the formation of
character and the student's sense of what's right and wrong.

Experience

Today's young people have smaller and less stable families than   30
kids two generations ago. A modern house or apartment offers
fewer tasks for children other than the laundry and dishes, the
trash and a few other light chores. Without the discipline of
work-related chores, students have difficulty building sturdy
self-concepts.

Today's young people also exist in the self-focused, pleasure-
dominated world of MTV, promiscuity, drugs, or simply "hanging
out." Only rare and fortunate teenagers have experiences that
help them break out of self interest mode and learn to contribute
to others.

Many schools respond by providing students both in- and
out-of-school opportunities to serve. Within such schools, students help other students; older children often help younger
ones learn academic or physical skills. Students also help teachers, librarians or other staff members with routine clerical
tasks.

Out-of-school programs represent a larger departure from the ordinary. They enable students to provide services to individuals in need, such as a blind shut-in or a mother with a mildly retarded child. Other students volunteer in understaffed agencies, such as retirement homes or day-care centers.

School staff members serve as troubleshooters between students and the individuals or agencies in need of assistance. Such service programs teach valuable humanitarian skills.

35 Through these activities, abstract concepts like justice and community become real as students see the faces of the lives they touch. Students begin to appreciate the need to couple moral thinking with moral action.

Expectations of Excellence

Children need standards and the skills to achieve them. They need to see themselves as students engaged in a continuing pursuit of excellence.

When the faculty of the Dexter School in Brookline, MA, discussed ways to boost high standards, it created the motto, "Our best today, better tomorrow." That brought home the concept in a focused way to the students of this private boys' school. The teachers there encourage their students and help them to set reasonable standards and work toward their goals.

These standards of excellence in school work and behavior will encourage students to develop qualities like perseverance and determination, and those virtues will affect every aspect of the children's lives as they mature.

Summary

Academic studies change rapidly; what we discuss in class today becomes passé tomorrow. But the values, moral influences and noteworthy characteristics we model and discuss will outlast academic facts and figures. We can leave our students a legacy that will remain constant throughout life: to know the good, love the good, and do the good.

References

Dunn, Ashley. "Welcome to the Evil House of Cheat." *Los Angeles Times Magazine* 7 Feb. 1999: 30t.

Kibler, William L. "Cheating." *Chronicle of Higher Education* 39.12 (1992): B1–2.

Ryan, Kevin. "The Six E's of Character Education: Practical Ways to Bring Moral Instruction to Life for Your Students." 10 Aug. 1999 <http://www.education.bu.edu/CharacterEd/6Es.html>.

Questions for Discussion

1. Does your cheating in school have any influence on you as a future career person? Answer the six questions Lathrop and Foss pose in this article under the heading "Does Cheating Harm Your Career?"
2. Are there "valid reasons to cheat or plagiarize"? How would you respond to each reason listed in this article?
3. What are "the six E's of character education"?
4. Should students who attend schools, colleges, and universities that have an honor code be given an opportunity to participate in the making of policy regarding cheating? Consider both sides of this debate in your response.

Questions for Writing

1. According to Lathrop and Foss: "Academic studies change rapidly; what we discuss in class today becomes passé tomorrow. But the values, moral influences and noteworthy characteristics we model and discuss will outlast academic facts and figures." Assess the validity of this statement in an essay.
2. What are the advantages and disadvantages for students who attend universities with honor codes? Write your response in an informative essay.

Questions for Making Connections Within the Chapter

1. How will improving the ethical standards addressed in Kopytoff's article potentially influence the issues discussed in Rimer's article? Is there hope for honesty in the educational system? Explain.
2. Examine the wave of computer crimes that seem more rampant than ever. How do Judson and Knittel and Soto deal with this topic in their respective articles?
3. Schools are exploring proactive methods to combat plagiarism, and the methods of intervention vary. Consider the measures that are presented in the articles of Lathrop and Foss and Kopytoff.
4. Consider the ethical concerns addressed by the authors in this chapter. What conclusions do you draw in terms of student responsibility, academic integrity, and technology?

MAKING CONNECTIONS ACROSS THE CHAPTERS

Questions for Making Connections Across the Chapters

1. Consider corporate scandals, false advertising, media frenzies, and ethics in response to Stark's article (Chapter 2), Grimm's article (Chapter 4), and Frohnen and Clarke's article (Chapter 4).
2. Exploitation of humans remains a problem in America, and we see it played out in every profession. Consider this topic as it relates to ethical issues presented in the essays by Rivers (Chapter 2), Brock (Chapter 5), and Zitrin and Langford (Chapter 3).
3. In her essay Masching (Chapter 4) acknowledges three keys of success in dealing with the public. Reconcile each key with the general topics in both Boatright's (Chapter 4) and Robinson's article (Chapter 2).
4. The differences between the essays by Hutchins (Chapter 1), Alexis (Chapter 3), and Sanchez (Chapter 5) are perhaps obvious. What do they have in common?
5. Discuss the relationships among the articles by Lathrop and Foss (Chapter 6), Judson (Chapter 3), and Byron (Chapter 1). Explain the crucial roles of each of the following on influencing student behavoir: school administrators and educators, technology, and the justice system and laws.

Questions for Further Application Across the Chapters

1. Some educators avoid concerning themselves with politics and educational policy; given this, how can you as an activist energize educators in your community to see the increasingly important role of lobbying law makers to allocate more funds for teacher salaries, school buildings, and so forth, as well as lobbying for the implementation of policies for effective

educational reform, such as school choice and vouchers? Design a plan to get teachers proactively involved in the process.

2. If you were called on as a business professional to speak to a group of college business majors on the topic of professional ethics in the business world, what advice would you give and what illustrations would you use in your presentation?

3. As a physician, you have an opportunity to clone a human being. If you took the opportunity, would you be making a medical miracle or violating the natural process of human life? You are to present a different speech to each one of the following groups: (1) the medical community and (2) a group of pastors, theologians, and others from the faith community. Compare and contrast your two approaches.

4. Devise a plan for lawmakers, physicians, drug companies, insurance companies, and patients to collaborate on a universal health care plan. What issues must be addressed before these respective groups will compromise?

5. If most professors lecture on what plagiarism is and is not, why do some students still plagiarize? In response to this question, you should consider polling other students in your class or on your campus to get a broader sampling. What conclusions do you draw concerning this topic?